Refreshing Rains
of the
Living Word

Refreshing Rains
of the
Living Word

Liturgical Resources
for Year C

Lavon Bayler

The Pilgrim Press
NEW YORK

Second printing, 1989

Library of Congress Cataloging-in-Publication Data

Bayler, Lavon, 1933–
    Refreshing rains of the living word: liturgical resources for
year C / Lavon Baylor.

    Includes index.
    ISBN 0-8298-0788-8
    1. Liturgies. 2. Hymns, English. I. Title.
BV198.B293   1988
264'.13—dc19   88-19477
                                                           CIP

The Pilgrim Press, 132 West 31 Street, New York, NY 10001

In loving memory
of
my father,
the Reverend Emil Burrichter,
and my uncles,
the Reverend Otto Stockmeier
and
the Reverend Dr. William C. Beckmann,
who encouraged,
inspired,
and welcomed
this woman
into
ministry

Contents

Introduction

"It never rains here in February" we were told as we rode through a downpour in southern India. The heavy rains were to continue for the next several days. In the thirty years she had spent in India, the missionary who spoke had never seen such a phenomenon during the winter dry season. For the squatters who had taken up residence on the dry riverbeds the rains brought disaster. But for those who worked small farms there was the instant prospect of a third crop and more abundant fodder for their animals. Wells that often gave out in the unbearable heat of May and June might continue to offer their life-sustaining refreshment.

The quest for water is a time-consuming preoccupation for many of our sisters and brothers around the world. For them, refreshing rains are not just a pleasing phenomenon of passing interest. They are a vital necessity, a life-and-death reality.

Some of us may feel far removed from such elemental dependence on rain. The nearest faucet is usually only a few feet away, and the supply of water is dependable. Unfortunately our profligate use and widespread pollution of this resource are threatening what we have so long taken for granted—the availability of the water of life.

What does all this have to do with a book of worship resources? Just as our bodies require water, our spirits also need the refreshment only God can give. We depend on the refreshing rains of the living word. For Christians, the Bible is a channel through which God's revelation comes to us. It is the document that introduces us to the living word in Jesus Christ and challenges us to become the body of Christ in our own day. *Refreshing Rains* is intended to be one facilitator of your contemporary encounter, not just with an ancient text, but with a living presence.

The ecumenical lectionary for each occasion of church year C has inspired the calls to worship, invocations, confessional services, collects, offertory resources, hymns, and benedictions in this book. Those who follow the pericopes will find here worship elements to reinforce the scriptural message. Some worship leaders will pick and choose resources to fit their particular emphasis. Others may rewrite prayers in their own unique idiom, or use them as springboards for creating pastoral prayers adapted to their situation. Because of our ever-changing calendar, and because of a number of special occasions covered by the lectionary that are usually not observed in our churches, this book provides many more resources than one can use in the regular worship schedule.

Worship planners who are more thematic in their approach to worship are directed to the Index of Themes and Key Words. If stewardship is the main emphasis of an upcoming sermon, for example, the user of this book will find in this index occasions in the church year, such as Pentecost 11, when the scriptures lift up our responsibility to use well the resources God entrusts to us. The Topical Index of Hymns lists a dozen hymns with a stewardship emphasis.

All the scriptures used in church year C appear in yet another index. Luke is the primary Gospel for this year. Suppose you intend to use the story of the good Samaritan for a men's breakfast. In the Index of Scripture Readings you can locate the occasion in the church year (Pentecost 8) that focuses on Luke 10:25–37. Prayers for that Sunday will reflect the themes of this and other readings for the day. The collect usually weaves together the major emphases of all the scriptures around the Gospel narrative.

Refreshing Rains of the Living Word: Liturgical Resources for Year C is intended as a resource for clergy who, week after week, face the challenge of preparing worship services that are vital and fresh. The book is also for laity who are readying themselves to participate fully in the encounter with God that worship is meant to facilitate. Worship, the central act of the community of faith, is more likely to inspire and empower our discipleship if we have prepared ourselves for the experience. I suggest—in addition to reading and studying the scriptures—the use of the weekly resources in this book in private personal devotions and in meetings of church groups. Liturgy is the "work of the people," the whole people of God, and this work is not limited to Sunday morning. Encourage worshipers to use the prayers printed in their Sunday bulletins in their daily devotions.

Instructions for credits required when copying materials for worship use are included on the copyright page at the beginning of this book.

One of my most helpful critics when I wrote *Fresh Winds of the Spirit* was Keith Karau, then pastor of First Congregational United Church of Christ in Geneseo, Illinois. He has since moved from that area to serve as senior pastor of Evangelical United Church of Christ in Highland, Illinois. Keith has prepared the worship elements for his congregations with great care and attention so that they include all people. His simple, direct, yet profound style of writing commends his efforts for wider distribution. He has graciously given me permission to include in this book some of his material for the Pentecost Season. He has much more to offer. Another writer who came to my attention is Merle Beckwith, a layman from Santa Barbara, California, who contributed one of his hymns, "God's Wonders." Thanks to both of these men for all their efforts.

New hymn texts based on one or more of the scriptures for each worship occasion are grouped together in the Appendix of Related Hymns. They are an integral part of each set of worship resources. The introduction to that appendix gives more information about their use.

I am once more deeply indebted to Pat Kitner, a licensed minister of our UCC Association, who spent many "leisure" hours typing my early morning scrawls into manuscript form. Many thanks, Pat, for your affirmation and assistance! My secretary, Inge Bisanz, and a youthful friend, Lise Schlosser, also deserve credit for their finishing touches. Family, colleagues, and friends have been with me in this undertaking, allowing me the writing time that makes such ventures possible. A whole lifetime of encounter with people has influenced and shaped what I can offer here. In awe and gratitude I release the many words of this book, praying that they will be a channel for refreshing rains of the living word.

Liturgical Resources for Year C

The Advent Season

First Sunday of Advent

Old Testament: Jeremiah 33:14–16
Psalm 25:1–10
Epistle: 1 Thessalonians 3:9–13
Gospel: Luke 21:25–36

CALL TO WORSHIP
Look up, all people, for the realm of God is near;
gather with the saints to praise our Creator.
We rejoice in the promise of salvation
as we give thanks for God's steadfast love.
The gifts of God are for all generations
and for people in every walk of life.
In humble obedience we accept our blessings
and embrace God's call to responsibility.
Surely God is faithful to the covenant
and eager to instruct us in the ways of peace.
We will watch and pray, and be ready to act.
Let us hear what God has in store for us.

INVOCATION
In thanksgiving we lift up our souls to your righteousness, O God of all truth. We await your revelation, for we cannot make sense out of life apart from you. Keep us from being paralyzed by our fears. In the midst of our perplexity grant us signs of renewed vitality and the promise of better things you have in store for us when Christ comes to live among us. Amen.

CALL TO CONFESSION
Before the steadfast love and justice of God we sense that much is lacking in our faith. How we need to be in touch with the Giver of Life to have our trust renewed and our love empowered! Reach out now that the Eternal may enter into your present need to restore you to wholeness.

PRAYER OF CONFESSION
All-embracing God, we marvel at your attention to our individual needs. You know the cares that weigh us down and the snares that captivate us. Grant us strength to escape the evil around us and to turn away from the wrong that we originate or allow. We confess that we have missed the signs of your presence as the earth's foundations shake. Our vision is narrow and uninspired. Intervene to save us and all your children. Amen.

2

ASSURANCE OF FORGIVENESS

Look up, for your redemption is drawing near. The realm of God can be known in the midst of us. When we come with humble intention to live God's way, the Ruler of all life chooses to forget our sin. All the paths of the Lord are steadfast love and faithfulness for those who keep God's covenant and testimonies.

COLLECT

Make your ways known to us, O God; teach us your paths. We await your instruction and inspiration. Penetrate the clouds that dim our sight and loosen the shackles that paralyze our actions. We are ready to hear and respond. Amen.

OFFERTORY INVITATION

In thanksgiving render to God that portion of your substance that God requires. Give not only what you have set aside for an offering, but dedicate all you have and are to realization of eternal truth.

OFFERTORY PRAYER

With joy and thanksgiving we celebrate this opportunity to share. Your promises are more real to us, O God, when we participate in the outreach our gifts make possible. Lead us, we pray, to do what is right with these offerings and with the time and talents you entrust to us. Amen.

COMMISSION AND BLESSING

Scatter to your accustomed places with a new outlook;
God is ruling in our midst.
   Nothing we do escapes God's notice,
   and no act of ours can separate us from God's love.
Take the promises of God to a needy world;
share good news with friends and co-workers.
   God turns us from all that destroys
   and builds us up to face and overcome evil.
God will direct your paths during the week ahead
and provide all that you need to face its choices.
   We will be watchful and prayerful,
   lest we miss the work of God all around us.
Amen.   **Amen.**

(See hymn No. 1.)

Second Sunday of Advent

Old Testament: Malachi 3:1–4
  Psalm 126
Epistle: Philippians 1:3–11
Gospel: Luke 3:1–6

CALL TO WORSHIP

Arise, people of God, to receive the Lord's messenger;
be reminded of our covenant with the living God.
  God has done great things for us;
  we are partners in the gospel of Jesus Christ.
The messenger of God reminds us of promises made
and of good work not yet completed.
  We are refined in the fires of God's love
  and purified to carry forward God's intent.
God will lead us in all times and places;
God is with us here to bless and confront.
  We dedicate this hour of worship to God's glory,
  opening ourselves to true encounter with the Eternal.

INVOCATION

You have gathered us, O God, from the many places of our habitation. We are answering your call to the mountaintop, that the valleys may seem less threatening. Break through our concerns and pretenses, that we may be free to laugh and sing and lift up prayers of joy. Amen.

CALL TO CONFESSION

John the Baptist preached a baptism of repentance for the forgiveness of sins. Our gathering reminds us that we have been baptized, set apart from the world, given a new spirit. Let us confess how we have clung to the old ways rather than let God make new people of us.

PRAYER OF CONFESSION

You have been patient with us, loving God, for we have blended in with our surroundings and denied your claims on us. We revel in the things we have made for ourselves, forgetting that you have supplied the resources and granted us the ability to create. We have failed to embrace your way of love and have become prisoners of our own self-seeking ways. Forgive us, O God, that we may partake of your grace and manifest the fruits of righteousness. Amen.

ASSURANCE OF FORGIVENESS

God restores the joy of those who weep. Our Creator gives us seeds to sow and grants an abundant harvest. In God's mercy we are forgiven, made pure and blameless for the day of Christ. The crooked are made straight and the rough ways made smooth, that all flesh may see the salvation of God.

COLLECT

How glad we are, O God, for the great things you have done for us. We listen now for your word of promise and for the instruction we need. Unite us in remembrance with all your saints. Link us with one another in gospel partnership, that love may abound more and more and our wisdom increase. Make us instruments of your saving grace. Amen.

OFFERTORY INVITATION

How shall we present right offerings to God? What does God expect of those who are blessed and forgiven, purified in the refiner's fire? May our gifts confirm our partnership in the gospel and our gratitude for God's abundant mercy.

OFFERTORY PRAYER

Receive the gifts of our hands as an outpouring of thanksgiving, O God, for you have begun a good work in us, and we are grateful. We are awed by the thought of partnership with the Almighty. Help us, O God, to respond by doing our part. Amen.

COMMISSION AND BLESSING

Our God, who has done great things for us,
sends us out as partners in the work of salvation.
We are being saved day by day
as we look forward to the coming of Jesus Christ.
May we abound more and more in love,
with all knowledge and discernment.
God is bringing forth in us
the fruits of righteousness.
Go forth in the name of God's messenger
to live out your baptism in servanthood.
May the gospel be confirmed in us
as we seek the excellence to which God calls us.
Amen.   Amen.

(See hymn No. 2.)

Third Sunday of Advent

Old Testament: Zephaniah 3:14–20
Canticle: Isaiah 12:2–6
Epistle: Philippians 4:4–13
Gospel: Luke 3:7–18

CALL TO WORSHIP

Sing aloud to God, our strength and our song;
rejoice and exult with all your heart.
God is in our midst, renewing us;
we will be glad and sing praises.
We have come together in faith
to draw water from the wells of salvation.
As we have received the water of baptism
we seek once more to be cleansed and made whole.
Come to be baptized with the Holy Spirit and fire;
for God is ready to change your life.
God is restoring us before one another;
We are witnesses to God's transforming power.

INVOCATION

We call on your name, Sovereign God of the universe. May your deeds be
known among all the nations, and especially within us. We see little we
can do to change the world, but we want to be open to possibilities for
inner transformation and more caring and compassionate outreach. Move
us toward authentic trust and love, we pray. Amen.

CALL TO CONFESSION

How can we stand before God when we know all is not right among us?
How can we claim the promises of God when we do not keep our part of
the covenant? We are invited to pour out our prayers of confession,
seeking God's mercy.

PRAYER OF CONFESSION

O God, we are anxious and ashamed. Too often we are shaped by our
fears, not by faith. We have said and done things unworthy of our calling.
Our thoughts have been so dominated by the past and the future that we
have failed to live fully in the present. Our lives are filled with discontent,
worry, and self-protective pursuits. We have not trusted you or let you set
us on fire with good news. Forgive us. Change us. Inspire our caring and
doing so we may bear fruit as your forgiven and forgiving children. Amen.

ASSURANCE OF FORGIVENESS

God is in our midst; we shall fear evil no more. God has lived among us in

Jesus Christ; we can do all things through Christ, who strengthens us. Let us then bear fruits that befit repentance. As forgiven sinners may we share what we have received from God's hand as generously as it was given to us.

COLLECT

God of our weakness and our strength, move our hearts to praise you, to trust and rejoice in your saving grace. God of our hungers and our contentment, lead us toward the generosity you intend and away from undue concern about self and possessions. God of peace, be with us to calm the wars within and resolve the differences among us. May our lives embody good news in all we say and do. Amen.

OFFERTORY INVITATION

"Let everyone who has two coats share with a person who has none; and let everyone who has food do likewise." Thus we will know the joy of sharing and appreciate more fully what God has entrusted to us.

OFFERTORY PRAYER

We praise you with our offerings, gracious God, and honor you with our gifts. Keep us from accepting more than our share of the world's resources or from thinking we have achieved all our successes by our own efforts. Take control of our lives in ways that will draw us nearer to you, yet increase our sense of responsibility toward your other children. Amen.

COMMISSION AND BLESSING

Carry your songs of praise into the world;
let others know the glad anticipation of Advent.
God goes with us, continuing to renew and bless;
filling our lives with joy and expectation.
We remember the promises and healing of our baptism
and celebrate the flames of the Spirit.
We are learning how to be abased and how to abound
that we may be content in all circumstances.
God is transforming us day by day,
working within and among us to heal the world.
The God of peace is with us;
we can do all things in Christ, who strengthens us.
Amen.   Amen.

(See hymns No. 3 and No. 4.)

Fourth Sunday of Advent

Old Testament: Micah 5:2–4
Psalm 80:1–7
Epistle: Hebrews 10:5–10
Gospel: Luke 1:39–55

CALL TO WORSHIP

Let us magnify the name of our God together
and ponder the wonder of God's majesty.
Our Creator knows our names
and chooses us to be carriers of good news.
Rejoice that God restores our strength
and equips us for tasks to which we are called.
God has done great things for us;
Holy is God's name, now and forever.
God values us even when others ridicule and scorn;
God turns even our mistakes into blessings.
From generation to generation, God is faithful;
we leap for joy when we feel God near us.

INVOCATION

Let your face shine on us, O God, to bring the salvation for which we long. Hear our prayers when we call on you, and do not turn away from our cries. Keep us from empty petitions and arrogant pretensions. Cure us from insincerity and selfishness. Meet us here that we may experience new life as we respond to your call. Amen.

CALL TO CONFESSION

God is angry with dishonest prayer and deceitful purposes. The proud and the mighty have failed to discern the Ultimate Power, who has no need or tolerance for our manipulations. Let us see ourselves as we are. Come to God in brokenness, hungering for a right relationship with the Eternal.

PRAYER OF CONFESSION

God of the humble and the poor, we recognize the poverty of our prayers and the faithlessness of our feeble petitions. We have doubted your reality and addressed you without expecting a response. We have observed rituals in your sanctuary while our thoughts pursued other gods. Come to save us, O God; grant us your mercy, for we long for the new day you have promised. Amen.

ASSURANCE OF FORGIVENESS

Something within us leaps for joy at the presence of forgiving love. God has done mighty things for us, satisfying our hunger and lifting us above the scorn and ridicule of those who do not understand our quest for meaning beyond this world's shallow conceits. The good news is meant for you: receive the baptism of the Holy Spirit.

COLLECT

Feed your flock, O Shepherd. Save us by your strength as we enjoy the sunshine of your love. Fill us with such gratitude that our first impulse is to praise you and do your will. Speak now to our deepest impulses, not just to our reasoning minds, as we anticipate Christ's advent. Amen.

OFFERTORY INVITATION

God does not desire from us sacrifices and offerings apart from our giving of self. In Jesus Christ we have witnessed the perfect offering that sanctifies us and inspires our renewed dedication and service. Bring your all to this time of giving.

OFFERTORY PRAYER

In the name of Jesus Christ we have come to do your will, gracious God. Our spirits rejoice in your saving mercy. Receive our offerings as a practical expression of our gratitude. May all who are given stewardship over these gifts use them to your glory. In Jesus' name. Amen.

COMMISSION AND BLESSING

Let your words and deeds this week
make God known to all in need.
The good news of saving grace
will be on our lips and in our lives.
God has restored our strength
and equipped us for the tests ahead.
We will sing to the glory of God
and proclaim the great things God has done.
The blessing of God will give you security,
even in the face of criticism and error.
The faithfulness of God is our strength,
and God's presence will be our joy every day.
Amen.   Amen.

(See hymn No. 5.)

The Christmas Season

Christmas Eve/Day

Old Testament: Isaiah 9:2–7
Psalm 96
Epistle: Titus 2:11–14
Gospel: Luke 2:1–20

CALL TO WORSHIP

Sing a new song to God, all the earth;
declare the glory of God's saving work.
We who have walked in gloom see a great light.
Into all the shadowy places of life, light comes.
Praise God, who created heaven and earth
as a sanctuary of beauty and strength.
We rejoice, for a child is born, an heir is given,
to bring peace, righteousness, and justice.
Tremble before God, who judges people fairly,
whose truth is proclaimed in unexpected places.
Glory to God in the highest!
We see in a manger good news of great joy!

INVOCATION

Call us once more, mighty God, into the story of Christmas. May it be for
us not a narrative of the long ago, but an experience of the here and now.
May hope be born anew in the midst of life's shadows, that our souls may
magnify your name and our spirits rejoice in the salvation Jesus brings.
Amen.

CALL TO CONFESSION

The purity of God's light in Christ Jesus reveals once more how deeply
the gloom of irreligion and worldly passions has fallen over our lives. Our
daily routines and the expectations of others have dimmed our vision and
our commitment. Let us cast off the burden of dull existence, that the
excitement of God's intervention in our history may penetrate our defenses and bring new life.

PRAYER OF CONFESSION

Holy God, we confess our resistance to the mystery and beauty of the
Christmas story. It is easier for us to hear a sentimental tale than to
experience a Savior's coming. Yet we are strangely moved to confess all
that is wrong within us and around us, hoping for the freshness of a faith

newly re-born. Help us, O God, to claim our places as your chosen people, zealous for good deeds. Amen.

ASSURANCE OF FORGIVENESS

The grace of God has appeared for the salvation of all. We are freed to accept God's truth in new ways and to experience the good news of great joy with fresh enthusiasm. Let us glorify and praise God for all we have heard and seen.

COLLECT

We rejoice before you, gracious God, as Jesus is born anew into our little worlds, stretching our perceptions toward the truth that is universal. Help us to sense day by day the coming of your salvation. Alert us to the songs of angels, that we may respond as did the shepherds, sharing good news of great joy. Amen.

OFFERTORY INVITATION

We who have divided the spoils of the earth as our own are presented in this season with a gift beyond price, one we can receive or reject but never control. In Jesus, God grants us a Savior and the only way of life that ultimately works. In these moments we have an opportunity to express our gratitude through gifts that will bring good news to others in need.

OFFERTORY PRAYER

With joy and thanksgiving, we present our offerings, rejoicing in the opportunity to share. We would glorify and praise you with our gifts, even as we seek to lend a helping hand to our sisters and brothers. May your light shine on them and penetrate all the shadows that diminish life for any of your children. Amen.

COMMISSION AND BLESSING

Go forth with singing, for you have a song to share.
You have been moved by an old story to new life.
   We have been re-born in our commitments
   and strengthened in our resolve to live godly lives.
Be filled with hope, and with zeal for good deeds.
Praise God for all you have heard and seen.
   We will not fear before good news of great joy,
   but will embrace the signs and wonders God reveals.
The good news of peace with justice
is for you and for all humankind. Rejoice!
   To us a child is born who makes everything different.
   To us a Savior has come who makes all things new.
Amen.   Amen.

(See hymn No. 6.)

Christmas Day
(Additional Lections, First Set)

Old Testament: Isaiah 62:6–7, 10–12
Psalm 97
Epistle: Titus 3:4–7
Gospel: Luke 2:8–20

CALL TO WORSHIP
Glory to God in the highest,
and on earth peace among all people.
   Let the earth rejoice;
   let the coastlands be glad.
The heavens proclaim God's righteousness,
and all people behold God's glory.
   God's mercy has appeared in a Savior
   whose rule is not subject to human authorities.
Bow down before the babe of Bethlehem,
for in the lowly and commonplace, God appears.
   God re-creates us to be a holy people:
   delivered, redeemed, and justified, by God's grace.

INVOCATION
God of goodness and lovingkindness, appear to us now and renew us by
your Holy Spirit. Awaken us to respond with praise to all that you reveal.
May we ponder your truth and be led to fuller commitment and service.
Amen.

CALL TO CONFESSION
How often have we heard the story of Christmas and been unmoved by it?
How often have we received the mercy of God and then refused to extend
pardon to those who wrong us? How often have angels sung, and we have
neither heard nor responded? Let us confess to God all that separates us
from fullness of life.

PRAYER OF CONFESSION
Where we have been adversaries rather than followers of your will, O
God, forgive us. When we have rolled stones in the way of others rather
than cleared a path for them, we beg your pardon. For the times when we
have torn down rather than built up, good Lord, deliver us. Show us the
idols we have worshiped and turn us away from them. Have mercy on us.
Penetrate our defenses. Help us hear and heed your message of justice
and peace. In the name of One who came humbly, bearing your peace.
Amen.

ASSURANCE OF FORGIVENESS

By the mercy and lovingkindness of God we are forgiven. What no deed of ours could have accomplished has been done for us. The Holy Spirit is waiting to renew us, to fill us with blessings beyond our imagination. Keep all the evidence of Jesus' arrival in your hearts, pondering what you have seen and heard. You are freed from your old ways to respond more fully to God's love in Christ.

COLLECT

O God, by whom all of life is changed for the better, move us now, through the words of long ago, to hear your Word today. Open our hearts and lives to make room not just for the babe of Bethlehem, but for the Savior of the world. Reign within us and fill us with your joy. Amen.

OFFERTORY INVITATION

If light has dawned on us, we will want to share it. If there is good news to tell, we cannot help but proclaim it. Offerings are important, for what we give here extends the ministry of Christ. These tokens are but a symbol of the larger offerings of self that Christians give gladly in response to the Christ-event. May this act of giving bless all who receive and all who give.

OFFERTORY PRAYER

May these offerings exalt you, O God, and make visible the good news of Christmas. Take away the fear that prompts us to hoard your blessings, and thus to find the joy of them diminished. Increase our capacity to share, and thus to participate in your ministry of redemption and righteousness. In the name of the One you gave at Christmas, who in turn gave life for us, even Jesus Christ, whom we would love and serve. Amen.

COMMISSION AND BLESSING

Go and tell what the angels have revealed
and all that your own eyes have seen.
**We have seen Jesus and are moved to praise;
eternity has touched us, and we give God the glory.**
Go out to prepare a way for God's people.
Build up the highways and clear them of stones.
**We will share good news with the world:
behold, our salvation has come.**
God reigns; let the earth rejoice;
let people of every land be glad!
**Glory to God in the highest
and on earth peace among all people.**
Amen.   Amen.

(See hymn No. 7.)

Christmas Day
(Additional Lections, Second Set)

Old Testament: Isaiah 52:7–10
Psalm 98
Epistle: Hebrews 1:1–12
Gospel: John 1:1–14

CALL TO WORSHIP
God has spoken to us by a Child,
by whose word the power of the universe is upheld.
We have known the Word-made-flesh in Jesus
and have come to worship at the manger.
The True Light that enlightens everyone is coming,
but many in the world have not seen it.
Jesus is that light, sent to help us see;
we long to become children of light.
The glory of God is made known in a child's face,
and the deepest night is overcome.
Let all God's angels worship the Child,
and let us find ourselves in Jesus' Presence.

INVOCATION
You reign, O God, over all that you have made. You have redeemed and
comforted your people. Number us among those who have responded to
the good tidings your messengers bring. Create peace in our midst and
empower us to proclaim your peace. May our worship be filled with the
glad sounds of people eager to sing your praise. Amen.

CALL TO CONFESSION
The Word comes into our human scene, only to be rejected. We have
heard the Word again and again without being changed. How shall we
know we are children of God unless we confess our reluctance to respond,
and seek to change our ways? We are invited to confess our sin that seeks
to hold God at a distance.

PRAYER OF CONFESSION
God of steadfast love and faithfulness, judge us with equity, and let the
whole world know your righteousness. Purify us from our sin by the Child
whom you have sent among us. Turn us from lawlessness and deceit, from
the shadows of day and the deepest night. We long to believe your Word
and live as your children. May all the ends of the earth see your salvation.
Amen.

ASSURANCE OF FORGIVENESS

Sing a new song to God, who has done marvelous things. God is victorious over sin, and embraces us with a love that will not let us go. God judges us with equity and righteousness and frees us from the burden of past sin. God anoints us with the oil of gladness so we are free to break forth in joyful noises. Sing praise to God with trumpet and lyre. Join with the seas and the hills to glorify the Ruler of all.

COLLECT

Let us hear once more your good tidings of peace in a world that often rejects the Word and turns away from your revelation. May the coming of your Child prompt a new song within us and bring depths of joy to this community of faith. We await your Word of grace and truth. Amen.

OFFERTORY INVITATION

How shall we make fitting response to the One who brings God's truth among us? How will we express the joy that comes with steadfast love and faithfulness? Surely our first impulse is to offer to God the work of our hands. Out of the abundant mercies of God we return a portion for the special work God calls the church to do—and we dedicate all the rest, that our daily lives may reflect good news for all people. Come, let us give.

OFFERTORY PRAYER

May our offerings sing a new song of praise, as we marvel at your care for us, gracious God. Bless them, that they may bear witness to the light and show forth your grace and truth. We dedicate them in thanksgiving for your glorious gift of Jesus Christ. Amen.

COMMISSION AND BLESSING

Speak to all the world of the Child
by whose Word the universe is held together.
   We have worshiped at the manger
   and are eager to share the Word-made-flesh.
Carry forth the light you have seen,
that all the world's darkness may be exposed.
   We recognize ourselves as children of light,
   for the light of the world has helped us to see.
God reigns! Let all the earth rejoice!
The glory of God is revealed, and we are changed!
   With all God's angels we worship the Child
   and commit ourselves anew to Jesus' way.
Amen.   Amen.

(See hymn No. 8.)

Christmas 1

Old Testament: 1 Samuel 2:18–20, 26
Psalm 111
Epistle: Colossians 3:12–17
Gospel: Luke 2:41–52

CALL TO WORSHIP
Give thanks to God with your whole heart
in the company of this gathered congregation.
Great are the works of God,
studied by all who have pleasure in them.
The wonderful works of God are remembered
from generation to generation.
God is gracious and merciful,
full of honor, righteousness, and majesty.
The covenant of God is faithful and just,
and all God's precepts are trustworthy.
The fear of God is the beginning of wisdom,
and all who are in awe before God have good understanding.

INVOCATION
Gracious God, who has chosen us for abundant life, teach us to be compassionate and forgiving people. May we be kind and patient in all our dealings, putting aside false pride to serve in meekness and humility. We approach you in the name of Jesus Christ, giving thanks that you have called us to be bearers of your covenant. Amen.

CALL TO CONFESSION
We have come together out of our need to be in God's house. On our own we have found it hard to be faithful or to continue to grow. Let us confess before God our waywardness and our disobedience.

PRAYER OF CONFESSION
O God, we have wandered far from the promises of our covenant with you. We have taken for granted the blessings we enjoy from your hand. We seldom stop to ponder who you are or to bow down in awe before your holiness. We resist your will and ignore your activity in our midst. Only when life is difficult do we think of ultimate realities. Then you seem far away and unreal. Forgive us, we pray, for trying to play God and for substituting lesser loyalties for faithfulness to you. Show us how to grow in relation to you and to other people. Amen.

ASSURANCE OF FORGIVENESS
God is gracious and merciful and keeps covenant with us, even when we

go our own way. God sends redemption for all people. It is ours to receive. Let us give thanks for God's saving action on our behalf and accept the forgiveness we are offered.

COLLECT

May we grow in thanksgiving and praise as you speak to us once more. Call to mind your wonderful works and the heritage of faith and trust that is ours. Encounter us now in all your glory, that the word of Christ may dwell in us richly, that we may begin to understand and have the wisdom to follow where you would lead. Amen.

OFFERTORY INVITATION

In awe and gratitude let us return to God a portion of all that is entrusted to us. In compassion and concern let us share with those who have received less of God's bounty. Out of our own need to be generous if we are to become whole, we bring our gifts and offer ourselves once more to the will and purposes of our Creator.

OFFERTORY PRAYER

Bless these offerings, O God, to our growth and for the intentions you design. May all we give honor the name of Jesus and make us more faithful followers. Amen.

COMMISSION AND BLESSING

You are loved, forgiven, and blessed;
share with all compassion, kindness, and patience.
**In lowliness of heart and meekness of spirit
we offer to all the forgiveness we have received.**
Let your work and your leisure honor God
in faithfulness and uprightness.
**Great are the works of God; holy is God's name;
in awe we seek to understand and be transformed.**
Remember and share God's covenant
to which you are called and in which you stand.
**God grant us increased wisdom and favor
and call forth from us the best we can give.**
Amen.   Amen.

(See hymn No. 9.)

January 1
(New Year)

Old Testament: Isaiah 49:1–10
Psalm 90:1–12
Epistle: Ephesians 3:1–10
Gospel: Luke 14:16–24

CALL TO WORSHIP
Come to the banquet God provides;
begin the new year aware of God's faithfulness.
God has named our names
and entered into covenant with us.
Come to the springs of living water,
that your hunger and thirst may be satisfied.
God has called us as ministers and servants,
even though we are the least of all God's saints.
God gives you to the nations as a light
through which salvation is proclaimed.
We will extend God's invitation to others,
that they may know the unsearchable riches of Christ.

INVOCATION
Great God, our strength and our salvation, answer us when we call and
guide our feet in your way. Grant wisdom in the midst of our toil and
trouble, and grace when we are overwhelmed by life's problems. Confront us here with Mystery far beyond our understanding, and expand
our vision to include the new possibilities you set before us. Amen.

CALL TO CONFESSION
We who have taken God for granted and regarded discipleship far too
lightly are invited to seek forgiveness and renew our commitment. In the
presence of Mystery know yourself as you are and sense anew all God
intends for you to be. Let us confess our sin.

PRAYER OF CONFESSION
O God, our host and our dwelling place, forgive the ways we have ignored
you and turned away from your invitation. We have made excuses when
you called us and failed to extend your welcome to the poor and dis-
possessed. We have spent our strength for nothing and vanity. Turn your
anger away from us as we admit the ways we have failed you. Reveal to us
those sins we have not recognized that we may be freed from their power.
In Jesus' name. Amen.

ASSURANCE OF FORGIVENESS

God, who has chosen us, is faithful and offers strength to overcome our weakness. With pity and grace the Spirit enfolds us, that we may know salvation through Christ. God calls us into the church to empower us to communicate to the world the compelling wisdom of the One who gives us life.

COLLECT

Sovereign God, who has called us from the womb of our mothers and named our names, grant purpose to our days and significance to our labors. Let us hear again of your saving grace and empowering covenant. Send your light, that we may be lights; your revelation, that we may understand and serve. Include us in your banquet invitation, and inspire us to extend your invitation to all whom you want to include in your church. Amen.

OFFERTORY INVITATION

As stewards, by God's grace, we offer ourselves as we bring our offerings. God has promised to bless and multiply our efforts to serve the world in Christ's name. May we be as generous as God has been toward us.

OFFERTORY PRAYER

Thank you, God, for all the opportunities you have given us to feast at the table of your bounty. You have granted us more than we need and far more than we deserve. Turn us away from excuses that limit our sharing and from selfishness that grasps for ourselves what you intend for all your children. May the refreshment of your grace reach far beyond the horizons of our caring, that all people may enjoy the banquet of life. Amen.

COMMISSION AND BLESSING

Go forth as sharp swords and polished arrows
to serve the One who sends you into the world.
    God has given us our names
    and called us to be as Christ to our neighbors.
As we have been sustained by God's love,
we are eager to give it practical expression.
    God strengthens us for ministry,
    even though we are the least of the saints.
God is our light and salvation
and grants strength for all we undertake.
    God sends us out to be lights to the world,
    nourishing all who hunger and thirst.
Amen.   **Amen.**

(See hymn No. 10.)

January 1
(Celebration of Jesus and Mary)

Old Testament: Numbers 6:22–27
                    Psalm 67
Epistle: Galatians 4:4–7
                    Philippians 2:9–13 (alt.)
Gospel: Luke 2:15–21

CALL TO WORSHIP
May God be gracious to us and bless us,
and make God's face to shine upon us,
    Let all the people praise you, O God;
    let all the people praise you!
May God's way be known upon earth,
God's saving power among all nations.
    Let all the people praise you, O God;
    let all the people praise you!
Let the nations be glad and sing for joy,
for God judges and guides with equity.
    The earth has yielded its increase;
    let all the ends of the earth praise God!
Amen.   **Amen.**

INVOCATION
We glorify and praise you, O God, for all we have heard and seen. For the Child you sent to claim us all as your children, we give thanks. For the Spirit that lifts us all from servitude to servanthood, we rejoice. May we, in your presence, work out our own salvation with fear and trembling, as we bow down before Christ in humility and obedience. Amen.

CALL TO CONFESSION
What mercies of God have we failed to acknowledge, and what good news have we neglected to share? Our sin is not alone in the evil we do, but also in the good we neglect. Let us seek God's face, that we may know the grace that makes for right relationships with one another and with the Eternal One.

PRAYER OF CONFESSION
O God, whom we have obeyed only when it is convenient to do so, hear our cries and lift up your countenance to bless us. We have neglected your law and turned away from your love. We worship the Babe of Bethlehem but deny the adult Jesus of Nazareth. Our doubts and fears

mire us in questions without answers and in pondering without praise. Free us to see promise in a manger and blessing on every hand. You are at work within and among us. Help us to cooperate with your purposes, through Christ. Amen.

ASSURANCE OF FORGIVENESS

God's saving power is, even now, being poured out upon us. God sent Jesus to redeem us and lead us all to recognize ourselves as God's children. We are heirs with Christ of all God's bounty. God has blessed us; let us sing for joy as we praise God.

COLLECT

Open our ears and our eyes, that we may discover much to ponder day by day. Adopt us into your own family, that we may know we belong to you and one another. Speak through ancient words to evoke contemporary praise. Pour out on us your peace and joy. Amen.

OFFERTORY INVITATION

As the shepherds gave themselves as carriers of good news, we come to this time of giving, bringing the gifts God has entrusted to us. As heirs of God's grace, we pass on to others the inheritance we have received from God's hand.

OFFERTORY PRAYER

You have blessed us, O God, with abundance of provisions and possibilities. Give wings to the gifts we bring, that they may soar into places of need and uplift people bowed down, discouraged, and afraid. Work through our fear and trembling, and theirs, to bring assurance, faith, and praise. Amen.

COMMISSION AND BLESSING

The Lord bless you and keep you;
may God's face shine on you and be gracious to you.
We receive God's blessing and assurance
and pour out our praise and thanksgiving.
May God's countenance be lifted up to bless you
and grant you eternal peace.
We open ourselves to dwell in God's peace
and to show that peace to the world.
God sends you out to share good news
of all that you have seen and heard.
Let all your people praise you, O God,
let all your people praise you!
Amen.   **Amen.**

(See hymns No. 11 and No. 12.)

Christmas 2

Old Testament: Jeremiah 31:7–14
Psalm 147:12–20
Epistle: Ephesians 1:3–6, 15–18
Gospel: John 1:1–18

CALL TO WORSHIP

God gathers us and leads us;
may we respond and follow.
Along straight paths, by refreshing streams,
our God ministers to our needs.
The weeping find consolation
and the suffering find healing and renewal.
Our mourning is turned to joy and gladness,
and our souls feast on God's abundant goodness.
God comforts us like a shepherd
in the midst of overwhelming circumstances.
We will sing and be radiant
in the great company of God's people.

INVOCATION

We praise you, God of all nations, ruler of all creation. Your goodness reaches far beyond our experience, and your grace in Christ moves us to hope beyond our highest dreams. Meet us here to overcome the limitations we too easily accept and the deep night that paralyzes our souls. Let your light shine among us, that we may be empowered to bear witness to your good news in Christ. Amen.

CALL TO CONFESSION

God calls to all who languish in discouragement and guilt, to all who have given up and ceased to hope. God does not give up on us even when we turn away and fail to respond to the care and leadership God provides. Let us confess all that separates us from the resources of God's love.

PRAYER OF CONFESSION

O God of light, we have welcomed the shadows of night to hide us from your truth and obscure the way you want us to live. We have accepted abundance from your hand without giving thanks and have destroyed your bounty rather that shared it. We have denied our identity as your children and our kinship with all to whom you have given life. Forgive us, O God, and grant light for our paths. Direct us in the way you want us to go. Amen.

ASSURANCE OF FORGIVENESS

The light shines into the dark night of our souls. Christ, the true Light, brings God's word to us and grants us power to become children of God. We have received grace upon grace from the One who makes God known to us. In Christ, God pours out on us an abundance of spiritual blessings. Receive God's forgiveness and walk in the light.

COLLECT

May the words of scripture put us in touch with the Word-made-flesh in Jesus Christ. Open our lives to receive the wisdom and revelation Christ offers us. So refresh us with grace and truth that we might find comfort and consolation in our sorrow and new hope and purpose in each day's tasks. Lead us on straight paths, we pray, and keep us from stumbling. Amen.

OFFERTORY INVITATION

Be radiant over the goodness of God, and find satisfaction in the abundance with which you are blessed. Do not cease to give thanks as you bear witness to the Light. May others be empowered by all that you share.

OFFERTORY PRAYER

We come as your children, eager to offer the gifts you have entrusted to us in Christ's service. Receive us as partners with all your saints in reaching out to the blind and lame, those who are hungry and thirsty, and all who are bowed down with sorrow. May our offerings witness to the One through whom the Eternal becomes present and transforming reality. Amen.

COMMISSION AND BLESSING

Carry the light of Jesus Christ into the world,
that others may know the Word dwelling with them.
> **God has given us grace upon grace**
> **and empowered us to become children of God.**
All the spiritual blessings we know in our time together
are given to strengthen us in our daily activities.
> **We will share the good news of God's love**
> **by which all are destined to live as God's children.**
Sing aloud and be radiant over God's goodness,
and your life will be like a watered garden.
> **We rejoice that God leads us day by day,**
> **offering healing and comfort to the world through us.**
Amen.   **Amen.**

(See hymn No. 13.)

The Epiphany Season

Epiphany

Old Testament: Isaiah 60:1–6
Psalm 72:1–14
Epistle: Ephesians 3:1–12
Gospel: Matthew 2:1–12

CALL TO WORSHIP

The mystery of Christ is for all nations,
and God's revelation, for the whole human race.
We come to the light of the gospel,
eager to partake of its promises in Jesus Christ.
The stewardship of God's grace is given to us,
revealed to us by prophets and apostles.
We are all members of one body, the church,
through which God's wisdom is made known.
By God's power, we are called to be ministers,
to express our faith with bold confidence.
We are the least of all the saints,
yet God chooses us to preach the good news.

INVOCATION

God of justice and righteousness, open us to new insights and equip us to
deal fairly with the people we meet and the circumstances we face.
Minister to us in our weakness with your strengthening power. Surround
us with the unsearchable riches of Christ, that we may become a new
creation. Use us to defend the poor and deliver the needy from oppression, that all may rise up to sing your praise. Amen.

CALL TO CONFESSION

Come, all who have missed or ignored God's revelation; the stars still
shine. Come, all who have dwelled in the shadows; nations shall come to
the brightness of your rising. Confess now all that separates you from
God's intention for you and all that divides you from your sisters and
brothers. Come, to know the wholeness God intends for you in Christ
Jesus.

PRAYER OF CONFESSION

Forgive us, gracious God, for our senses have been dulled to the radiance
of your light and the justice of your ways. Our concerns are narrow and
local even when you try to introduce us to a world of differences. You
grant stars to lead us, and we develop smoke screens to hide their light.
You pour out treasures for our use, and we hoard them rather than share

them to your glory. Free us from the oppression of selfishness and the tyranny of greed. Attune us to your revelation, that we may partake of your promises in Jesus Christ. Amen.

ASSURANCE OF FORGIVENESS

Arise, shine, for your light has come. The glory of God has risen upon you and will be seen through you. Be radiant in your praise and service. Rejoice in the gift of God's grace. Witness with confidence to your faith in Jesus Christ.

COLLECT

May the star of wonder guide our journey through the scriptures, that we, too, may find the Child of Bethlehem and bow down to worship. We would shout our praise in acts of justice and kindness as much as in words. Equip us for good deeds that will water the earth, and nourish within and among us the continuing gospel story. Attune us to the great joy of serving Christ. Amen.

OFFERTORY INVITATION

The wealth of many nations has come to us, and we have considered it our due. The needs of the world beckon us to share, and we have turned instead to accumulating more things than we can use. The unsearchable riches of Christ are at our disposal, but we let them go untapped. May our offerings today reflect a new attitude of joy in giving.

OFFERTORY PRAYER

Liberate us, O God, to give as we are able and to rejoice in the opportunity of sharing. We bring our gifts as an act of awe and wonder, knowing that you multiply our efforts. Take us, the very least of your saints, and use us, along with our gifts, to make Christ known. Amen.

COMMISSION AND BLESSING

The mystery of Christ we have encountered here
is to be shared, in awe and wonder, with the world.
The promises of Christ send us to all people
with the light and peace of the gospel.
By God's grace we are empowered to minister,
to deliver the poor and needy from oppression.
The church unites us in one body
through which we are nourished to help others.
May the radiance of your faith shine as a beacon,
inspiring all you meet to look up to the stars.
As we have responded to God in worship
so now we respond with joy to challenges to serve.
Amen.   Amen.

(See hymns No. 14, No. 15, and No. 16.)

Epiphany 1
(Baptism of Jesus)

Old Testament: Isaiah 61:1–4
Psalm 29
Epistle: Acts 8:14–17
Gospel: Luke 3:15–17, 21–22

CALL TO WORSHIP
Worship God, whose glory fills the universe,
whose majesty is over all the earth.
The voice of God shakes the wilderness
and flashes forth flames of fire.
God builds up the ancient ruins
and raises up the former devastations
God gives strength to people who respond,
and blesses them with joy and peace.
The Spirit of God calls and empowers us
to bring good tidings and proclaim liberty.
God anoints us to bind up the brokenhearted
and open the prisons of those who are bound.

INVOCATION
Send your Spirit among us, O God, and into each one. Confirm our baptism with the fire of your love. Direct our ministry in the footsteps of Jesus, that we may experience liberation, and extend the blessings of freedom to those who are bound. Lift up and inspire our work and worship. Amen.

CALL TO CONFESSION
Before the strength and glory of the living God our witness appears weak and uninspired. Before God's power and majesty we can only bow in acknowledgment of our sin and unfaithfulness. Let us seek forgiveness from the Triune God.

PRAYER OF CONFESSION
O God, who created us whole, we come in our brokenness to remember that we have been baptized. You have reclaimed us by water and the Holy Spirit's fire, but we have wandered far from the inspiration you provide. We have lived as if there were no standards but our own self-interest. We have sought power by our own manipulations rather than accepted the strength you alone can provide. Refashion us in your image and empower us once more to follow Jesus as true disciples. Amen.

ASSURANCE OF FORGIVENESS

God gives us strength and blesses us with peace. God's favor grants comfort and gladness in our mourning, hope and power in the midst of devastation, and ability to serve even when our own resources have been depleted. Praise God for opening our hearts to receive the gifts of heaven!

COLLECT

Fulfill the scriptures in our midst, amazing God. Send your Spirit to open our ears, enlighten our eyes, and loosen our tongues in praise and thanksgiving. We ascribe to you glory and strength, revealed ever more clearly as the Holy Spirit baptizes us with fire. May the dove that descended on Jesus also bring to us your blessing and peace. Amen.

OFFERTORY INVITATION

All we possess comes from God's hand. All that we share has been provided to us. We cannot give except as God has blessed us. Our offerings are first of all a response to God's generosity. Let us glorify God through our gifts.

OFFERTORY PRAYER

We worship you with our offerings, O God, even as we seek through them to bring good news, comfort, and healing to the afflicted, brokenhearted, and oppressed. May all the ministries and outreach of this church honor you and use well the resources you entrust to us. Amen.

COMMISSION AND BLESSING

Ascribe to God glory and strength;
worship God not only in prayer, but also in deeds.
  Our eyes are open to the majesty of God;
  we will seek by our actions to make God known.
God grants the mantle of praise to our faint spirits
and liberates us from bondage to ourselves.
  We will use the freedom God provides
  to open the prisons in which others are bound.
God baptizes and empowers you
by water and the Holy Spirit.
  Equipped by God's blessing
  we dare to serve in Christ's name.
Amen.   **Amen.**

(See hymn No. 17.)

Epiphany 2

Old Testament: Isaiah 62:1–5
Psalm 36:5–10
Epistle: 1 Corinthians 12:1–11
Gospel: John 2:1–11

CALL TO WORSHIP

God, whose steadfast love fills the universe,
rejoices in our presence here.
How precious is your steadfast love, O God!
People take refuge in the shadow of your wings.
God breaks through the silences of our lives
and calls us by a new name.
With you, O God, is the fountain of life;
in your light do we see light.
God blesses us with varieties of spiritual gifts
and inspires us to use them well.
Your righteousness is like the mountains, O God,
and your faithfulness extends to the heavens.
Amen. **Amen.**

INVOCATION

Faithful and loving God, we come to the abundance of your house to
drink again from the river of your delights. You inspire our gathering and
equip us for living. You pour out your Spirit upon us for the common
good. Meet us now, that we may hear what you want us to hear and know
what you want us to do. In Jesus' name. Amen.

CALL TO CONFESSION

Come, all who feel forsaken and desolate. Come, all who sense your own
need and the world's desperate state. Come, all who feel powerless before
the evil within and without. Come, to make confession and find forgiveness and true freedom.

PRAYER OF CONFESSION

O God, how do you have time for us when we have given so little time to
you? We have tried to live by our own designs rather than to seek your
purposes. We have become mired in our mistakes and then imagined that
you do not care. We have suffered the agonies of loss and have blamed you
rather than sought the comfort and help you alone can give. We have
turned away from the judgment we deserve in order to justify ourselves.
Where can we find the integrity for which we yearn and the healing we so

desperately need? Help us, God, to face our own need and to accept your guidance. Amen.

ASSURANCE OF FORGIVENESS
God vindicates and liberates. The Ruler of the universe offers salvation as a burning torch that brightens and transforms all within reach. God recognizes and evokes the beauty within you. God calls you by name and rejoices in you. The glory of God shines through you. Praise God!

COLLECT
Transforming God, whose presence in Jesus blessed the wedding feast in Cana of Galilee, and whose gifts are available to all who will accept them, inspire us now as you speak once more through the scriptures. Grant us the courage to answer when you call our names. Amen.

OFFERTORY INVITATION
We have good news to share with all who feel forsaken and desolate. We have gifts to share with those whose resources are depleted. In those times and places where we cannot give ourselves, we offer our treasure, that others may carry forward and extend our ministry. Let us give in gratitude to God and in response to our neighbors' need.

OFFERTORY PRAYER
Accept our gifts, O God, because we need to give. Use our gifts to the greatest good they can accomplish here in our midst and far beyond our individual reach. We present them in thanksgiving for all you have given us and in gratitude for the privilege of sharing in your work. Amen.

COMMISSION AND BLESSING
Go, tell the world of God's steadfast love.
Share the abundance you have received.
We cannot keep silent, and we will not rest
until the light we have seen is shared.
You have experienced cleansing and salvation;
carry to others this experience of healing.
The new vitality we feel equips us
to use the gifts God entrusts to us.
The good wine is yet to be tasted;
do not be afraid to claim God's miracles.
There are varieties of working,
but one God inspires our unique witness and service.
Amen.   Amen.

(See hymns No. 18 and No. 19.)

Epiphany 3

Old Testament: Nehemiah 8:1–4a, 5–6, 8–10
                 Psalm 19:7–14
Epistle: 1 Corinthians 12:12–30
Gospel: Luke 4:14–21

CALL TO WORSHIP

The Creator of the universe bids us come to worship;
let us come in awe, reverence, and eager anticipation.
We gather in unity with other Christians,
for in Christ we are one body.
We are together to learn, to care for one another,
and to gain strength for our common ministry.
We need one another to discern God's will,
and we depend on one another to carry it out.
The Spirit of God is upon us, teaching and empowering.
The joy of God is our strength, today and always.
We open ourselves to the word of life
as we lift up hands and hearts to the source of help.

INVOCATION

How shall we come before you, O God, when we have closed our ears to
your law and dismissed your ways as out of date? Yet we long for clear
direction and would be attentive to the word you want us to hear. Let the
words of our mouths and the meditations of our hearts be acceptable in
your sight, O God, our Rock and our Redeemer. Amen.

CALL TO CONFESSION

Only when we are together once more do we realize how fragmented our
lives have been. As God gathers us we recognize how far we have
wandered from the truth God reveals. The errors we have not discerned
in our daily routines are brought to light and our presumptuous sins are
revealed. Let us confess them before God and one another.

PRAYER OF CONFESSION

Sovereign God, we are not worthy to come before you, for we have
neglected your word and resisted your law. We make and break our own
standards to suit our momentary whims. We deny the bonds of mutual
concern and caring that link us with your whole human family. Help us to
hear both your warnings and your good news, that we may find release
from all that holds us in bondage. Free us to respond to your love. Amen.

ASSURANCE OF FORGIVENESS

The law of God is perfect, reviving the soul;
the testimony of God is sure, making wise the simple;
the precepts of God are right, rejoicing the heart;
the commandment of God is pure, enlightening the eyes;
go your way, eat the fat and drink the sweet wine,
   and send portions to those for whom nothing is prepared.
Do not be grieved, for the joy of God is your strength.

COLLECT

Grant that we may hear with understanding and be moved to compassion. Knit us together, that our varied talents may be fully engaged in your service. Send your Spirit upon us, that we, like Jesus, may preach the good news of liberation. Amen.

OFFERTORY INVITATION

Our worship is complete when we bring all the resources at our disposal to receive God's blessing and fulfill God's purposes. In joyous gratitude we bring more than money: we bring ourselves as an offering to God.

OFFERTORY PRAYER

For the abundance with which you have enriched our lives we give thanks, gracious God. For your truth, more precious than gold, and for our individual gifts, granted for the common good, we are most grateful. Receive now the offerings we return to you, that they may declare good news and fulfill your purposes. Amen.

COMMISSION AND BLESSING

You are the body of Christ
and individually members of it.
   We drink of one Spirit
   and are united in a common ministry.
Care for one another,
that there may be no discord in the body.
   If one member suffers, all suffer together;
   If one member is honored, all rejoice together.
God anoints us to preach good news to the poor
and proclaim release to the captives.
   God sends us out to help the blind see
   and to free the oppressed from their bondage.
Amen.   Amen.

(See hymns No. 20 and No. 21.)

Epiphany 4

Old Testament: Jeremiah 1:4–10
Psalm 71:1–6
Epistle: 1 Corinthians 13:1–13
Gospel: Luke 4:21–30

CALL TO WORSHIP
Jesus Christ, the Great Physician, invites us
into the healing presence of God, our refuge.
God knew us before we were born,
and summoned us to service in our youth.
God, our Rock and Fortress, rescues us
from injustice, cruelty, and wickedness.
God touches our lips and puts words in our mouths.
God commands us to speak and removes our fears.
God, our hope and trust, meets us where we are
and leads us to times of witness and praise.
God's revelation comes in unexpected places
to meet our needs and empower our service.

INVOCATION
God of love and mercy, incline your ears to us and rescue us from all that
weighs down and diminishes us. Enter into dialogue with us, so we may
hear what you command. Put your words in our mouths and your praise
in our daily lives. Add to our understanding and equip us for action, we
pray. Amen.

CALL TO CONFESSION
We who take for granted the abundance and freedom we enjoy are
summoned to recognize the sovereignty and generosity of God. We who
are blind to the mystery of God's presence among us and insistent on our
own way are brought face to face with Love and here recognize our sin.
Let us seek the forgiveness of God.

PRAYER OF CONFESSION
O God, we have been noisy gongs and clanging cymbals, impressed with
our own knowledge and misled by childish reasoning. We have mistaken
our hazy insights for your truth and have resented others for whom your
love is life-changing. Forgive not only our arrogance, gracious God, but
also our timidity. Equip us for an authentic witness to your love. Amen.

ASSURANCE OF FORGIVENESS
Our God says to us, "Do not be afraid, for I am with you to deliver you."

God rescues us from wickedness, injustice, and cruelty. With God's help, we can leave childish ways behind. Because we are understood by God we can grow in understanding. So faith, hope, and love abide in you, and love is the greatest of all God's gifts.

COLLECT

Grant, O God, that we may know the fulfillment of the scriptures we hear. Touch us with your word revealed in Jesus of Nazareth, that we may sense your presence here and now. May love be real to us in patience, kindness, and faithful endurance. Fill us with the conviction of your purposes for us, so we may speak to others the message you entrust to us. Amen.

OFFERTORY INVITATION

In this imperfect world God entrusts love to us and bids us share it in practical and helpful ways. Our offerings are one response we make to the love of God, poured out in Jesus Christ. We pass on that love in word and deed as we commit our gifts to God's purposes.

OFFERTORY PRAYER

In hope and trust we dedicate ourselves and our offerings to your service, O God. Deliver us from our fears and make us bold to express your love in word and deed. May others know your outstretched hand and arms of support because we have shared what you entrust to us. Amen.

COMMISSION AND BLESSING

God touches our mouths and bids us speak.
God sends us forth to build and to plant.
We put our trust in God day by day
and commit ourselves to lives of praise.
Be patient and kind, full of trust and hope,
for God is eager to show love through you.
Our faith is nothing without love,
and our good deeds are empty without God.
God is our rock and our fortress,
the source and fulfillment of our lives.
Now faith, hope, love abide, these three,
but the greatest of these is love.
Amen.   Amen.

(See hymns No. 22 and No. 23.)

Epiphany 5

Old Testament: Isaiah 6:1–8 (9–13)
Psalm 138
Epistle: 1 Corinthians 15:1–11
Gospel: Luke 5:1–11

CALL TO WORSHIP

Holy, holy is the Lord of hosts;
the whole earth is full of God's glory.
We give you thanks, O God, with all our hearts
for your steadfast love and faithfulness.
Your name, O God, is exalted over all things,
and your word goes forth to the ends of the earth.
When we call to you, O God, you answer,
and preserve our lives in the midst of trouble.
You stretch out your hand to deliver us,
and fulfill your purposes through us.
We will sing of the ways of God,
for great is the glory of God forever.
Amen.   Amen.

INVOCATION

Come to us, O God, when we are discouraged and afraid. Fill us with the vision of your majesty and the reality of your care. Touch our feelings as well as our understanding, that we may walk by faith as well as by knowledge and trust in you even when the way before us is not clear. Amen.

CALL TO CONFESSION

The voice of God shakes the foundations on which we build our lives. Before the majesty of God we tremble in the knowledge of our own deceits and inadequacy. It is an awesome thing to stand in the presence of God. We can only kneel to confess our guilt and our need.

PRAYER OF CONFESSION

Depart from us, O God, for we are sinful people. Our lips are unclean and the communities in which we dwell are full of evil. We despair that this desolate wasteland is beyond hope and our confused ways cannot be straightened. Who can save us from ourselves? Do not leave us, O God, but answer us and help us. Amen.

ASSURANCE OF FORGIVENESS

Christ died for our sins in accordance with the scriptures. Our guilt is taken away. Our sins are forgiven. Know the purifying touch of burning coals on your lips and in your lives.

COLLECT

Grant light to our eyes and strength to our souls as you touch us once more with your word of truth. Appear to us here as the risen Christ came to the disciples, that our lives may be made whole and our work for you become productive. In Jesus' name. Amen.

OFFERTORY INVITATION

We hear the voice of God saying, "Whom shall I send, and who will go for us?" May each of us reply, "Here am I! Send me." When we offer our time and talents, God commissions us and grants us strength for the tasks we undertake. When we offer our treasure, God uses it in places where we cannot go and in causes beyond our reach. Let us give as God has blessed us.

OFFERTORY PRAYER

May our offerings provide places where the voice of Jesus may be heard. May they empower those who let down the nets at Christ's command to bring others into discipleship. Send us and our gifts on your mission, O God, and equip us by your grace to make a difference as apostles of your good news. Amen.

COMMISSION AND BLESSING

Go to all the people to announce good news:
the purposes of God are being fulfilled.
    Christ appears to the least of the apostles
    and promises to walk life's road with us.
By the grace of God we have our lives to share,
and the grace of God is not given in vain.
    We go forth in faith at Christ's command
    to try what appears impossible.
The love of God empowers us,
and serving God increases our trust.
    We will serve with songs of thanksgiving,
    for the steadfast love of God endures forever.
Amen.   Amen.

(See hymns No. 24, No. 25, and No. 26.)

Epiphany 6

Old Testament: Jeremiah 17:5–10
Psalm 1
Epistle: 1 Corinthians 15:12–20
Gospel: Luke 6:17–26

CALL TO WORSHIP

Gather with the crowds who seek to touch Jesus;
come to hear and be healed.
We are poor and hungry,
in need of food for our souls.
Cursed are those who put their trust in human beings
and make flesh their arm.
Blessed are those who put their trust in God
and find their hope in Christ Jesus.
Christ has been raised from the dead,
the first fruits of those who have fallen asleep.
Our faith is not in vain and our hope is sure;
we rejoice and leap for joy at the good news.

INVOCATION

Great Planter and Provider, we rejoice at the streams of living water you
send within our reach. Help us to grow deep roots that partake of your
truth and thick branches that reach out in loving support to all in need of
our embrace. In this hour we seek, with enthusiasm, the energy you
provide as we sense your presence, blessing us. Amen.

CALL TO CONFESSION

We gather to discover together the good grain within and among us and to
rid ourselves of the chaff. We seek the cleansing winds of the Spirit, that
what is unnecessary and evil may be removed from us. Let us confess our
sin, that God's loving presence may be real to us.

PRAYER OF CONFESSION

O God, our hearts are deceitful, and our ears are tuned to the counsel of
this world. Our lips join the chorus of scoffers, and our deeds betray the
impurity of our motives. We seek personal gain more than the reign of
your love, and individual fulfillment more than the building of community. Heal us, O God, of the diseases that distort our perception and
trouble our spirits. Free us to drink the pure water you provide. Amen.

ASSURANCE OF FORGIVENESS

By the power of God, Jesus reached out to heal the afflicted and cleanse troubled spirits. When we want that transformation within and among us more than we want to cling to the past, we will know the blessing of forgiveness. Jesus Christ has been raised from the dead and offers to lift us from the death of sin. Claim the victory over sin that comes to those who hope in Christ.

COLLECT

Lead us, O God, to the streams of living water that will keep us fresh and green with new growth and vitality. So nourish us amid the droughts of our lives, that we may bear good fruit. Bless all who hunger for your truth and all whose hope remains steadfast. We trust you, O God, in life and death, to provide the healing we need most and the blessing to see beyond present circumstances the joy of your presence. Amen.

OFFERTORY INVITATION

From our poverty and from our wealth we rejoice in the opportunity to give to others what we have received. We give, not to be thanked, but that all of us may come to trust in God and delight in the way of life God sets before us. Let us give thanks to God with our offerings.

OFFERTORY PRAYER

May these gifts of response to your love enable many to touch Jesus and be healed. May all who suffer for the sake of Christ be empowered to continue their witness. May your church manage well the resources entrusted to us, that faith and hope may abound. We rejoice in the resurrection and its power to transform us. Amen.

COMMISSION AND BLESSING

We have known the touch of Jesus Christ
in our listening, our songs, and our prayers.
**We have felt Christ's presence
in the company of people who love one another.**
The God who searches our minds and tries our hearts
has met us here to bless and make whole.
**We leap for joy in our resurrection faith
as we experience the hope made real in Christ.**
We are empowered to endure in all circumstances,
so we face the new week with confidence.
**In all times and places God blesses us.
We go now to be channels of God's blessing.**
Amen.   Amen.

(See hymn No. 27.)

Epiphany 7

Old Testament: Genesis 45:3–11, 15
Psalm 37:1–11
Epistle: 1 Corinthians 15:35–38, 42–50
Gospel: Luke 6:27–38

CALL TO WORSHIP
Come near to the One in whom we can trust;
God will give us the desires of our hearts.
God has provided for us day by day
and preserves us in the midst of life's calamities.
Dwell together in the security God offers
and fret not about the world's standards.
We would be still before the majesty of God
and wait patiently for the Spirit's leading.
Open yourselves, that God may equip you to love,
to forgive, and to give.
We seek to respond to the God who loves us
by loving as we wish to be loved.

INVOCATION
Loving God, lead us to take such delight in you that our thoughts and desires become attuned to your will. Teach us the ways of trust and commitment, so we can face with confidence all times of trouble and distress. Reveal to us here your purposes and design, so often hidden from us in our preoccupation with immediate concerns. Open us to care as you have cared for us. Through Christ. Amen.

CALL TO CONFESSION
God invites us to recognize within ourselves and in our church those attitudes that diminish us and mute our witness. God welcomes all who are envious of wrongdoers, and fret over their prosperity, all who are distressed and angry with themselves over their mistakes, and all who become self-righteous because of the good they have done. Let us recognize and admit the evil within us, so we may be freed from it.

PRAYER OF CONFESSION
Forgive us, God, for betraying others, for making comparisons that trigger envy and revenge, for harboring attitudes that destroy rather than build up. We confess our tendency to excuse ourselves for behavior we condemn in others. We have been satisfied with less than our best and with good appearances rather than true substance. Be merciful to us, O God, and transform our ways. Amen.

ASSURANCE OF FORGIVENESS

God is kind, even to the ungrateful and the selfish. Receive God's forgiveness, that you may leave behind the image of dust, with its hatred, judgment, and revenge. God seeks to implant in us the image of heaven, empowering us to love our enemies, bless those who curse us, and pray for those who abuse us. Because God loves us we are enabled to treat others as we wish to be treated.

COLLECT

God of mercy, penetrate all our defenses, so we may receive a fresh understanding of your boundless love and be equipped to share it. Help us to discern the abundant prosperity in which we live and to appreciate the spiritual inheritance that is ours. Inspire us to give without expectation of reward and to seek the best for those who lack the capacity to reciprocate. Open all our senses to your message of new life. Amen.

OFFERTORY INVITATION

Give, and it will be given to you; good measure, pressed down, shaken together, running over, will be put into your lap. For the measure you give will be the measure you get back. Rejoice in this opportunity to share the goodness of God.

OFFERTORY PRAYER

With these offerings we would extend your love, O God, to those who have not experienced its healing power. May hatred be overcome and enemies turned from their evil intent. May the joy we know as we give flow out to those who benefit from our gifts. Amen.

COMMISSION AND BLESSING

Love your enemies and do good;
lend, expecting nothing in return.
  Sharing God's love provides its own reward,
  and praying for others is a blessing to us.
Be merciful, even as God is merciful;
treat others as you wish to be treated.
  Giving what others need fills us with joy,
  and forgiving them helps us to know God.
Wait patiently for the blessings God offers,
and take delight in the One who is trustworthy.
  We commit ourselves to the God who acts
  to bring out the best in each one of us.
Amen.   **Amen.**

(See hymns No. 28 and No. 29.)

Epiphany 8

Old Testament: Isaiah 55:10–13
Psalm 92:1–4, 12–15
Epistle: 1 Corinthians 15:51–58
Gospel: Luke 6:39–49

CALL TO WORSHIP

It is good to give thanks to God,
to sing praises in the name of the Most High.
**We declare God's steadfast love in the morning
and the faithfulness of God through the night.**
The presence of God makes us glad,
and the work of God's hands calls forth our joy.
**We flourish in the courts of our God
and bear fruit as God blesses us.**
The goodness of God dwells in both youth and aged,
and God's mercy flows through all who receive it.
**We open our hearts to the love of God
and seek to be taught by Jesus Christ.**

INVOCATION

Send the refreshing rains of love to water the seeds you have planted within us, O God, that we may accomplish all you intend. May the abundance you entrust to us overflow in words of praise and deeds of kindness. Amen.

CALL TO CONFESSION

Before the majesty of God we sense the logs that block our vision, the poor foundations that threaten to crumble before life's storms, the thorns and brambles that choke out the abundant goodness of God within us. Come to seek the help God alone can give to cleanse our hearts and heal our relationships.

PRAYER OF CONFESSION

Merciful God, we are dead in our sins, cut off from the source of life, unable to receive the treasure you offer us. We claim to follow Christ but instead go our own way. We call on you for insight and blessing but fail to do that for which you empower us. We dry up inside, ignoring the healing waters of your love that bring new life and growth. Save us, God, for we cannot save ourselves. Amen.

ASSURANCE OF FORGIVENESS

The love of God is steadfast and faithful, and God's forgiveness triumphs over our self-preoccupation. Instead of the thorn shall come up the cypress; instead of the brier shall come up the myrtle. God nourishes the best within us to bring new growth and vitality. Praise God, who delivers us from death to life.

COLLECT

Grant us signs of your continuing work among us, O God of faithful ancestors. As we hear the witness of those who have gone before may their experience become our own. Make us living memorials of your care, that all whose lives we touch may sense the abundant treasure of your love. Help us build on solid foundations a faith that cannot be shaken. Amen.

OFFERTORY INVITATION

The good person out of the good treasure of the heart produces good, and the evil person out of evil treasure produces evil, for each one gives from the abundance of the heart. May our giving be a generous outpouring of gratitude for the love we want to share with others.

OFFERTORY PRAYER

May these gifts carry your word to the hearts and homes of every member of our church and community, flowing through us into all the world. Grant that they may accomplish your purposes and prosper the work you call us to do. Use our gifts and our lives as you will. Amen.

COMMISSION AND BLESSING

Go out in joy and be led forth in peace,
for God has granted victory over death.
The hills shall break into singing
and the trees of the field shall clap their hands.
Dig deep to lay firm foundations for faithfulness,
for God will build with you day by day.
God is the rock on which our faith is built;
we will praise God both morning and night.
Be steadfast, immovable, abounding in God's work,
that your labor may not be in vain.
We will walk with one another as forgiven sinners,
eager to do what we have heard.
Amen.   **Amen.**

(See hymns No. 30 and No. 31.)

Last Sunday After Epiphany

Old Testament: Exodus 34:29–35
Psalm 99
Epistle: 2 Corinthians 3:12—4:2
Gospel: Luke 9:28–36

CALL TO WORSHIP

God reigns; let the people tremble!
God rules over all creation; let the earth quake!
We praise your great and terrible name!
We worship at your footstool, O holy God!
God spoke to our ancestors from the clouds
and led them by pillars of fire at night.
When we cry to you, O God, you answer
and forgive our inattention and wrongdoing.
God fills our lives with hope and anticipation
and changes them in the likeness of Christ.
We extol your name, O God of all people,
for with you there is perfect freedom.
Amen. **Amen.**

INVOCATION

When we gather in your name we feel your presence in new ways, mighty Ruler. All the worlds are subject to your authority, and we can only quake before your majesty. As we recognize your power and authority we are moved to speak and our faces shine with your glory. Our consciences are stirred by new perceptions of reality and we long to stay in the dazzling splendor of this high and holy moment. Keep us in your covenant, Sovereign God. Amen.

CALL TO CONFESSION

Who can stand before God or dare to worship at God's holy mountain? Only those who keep God's statutes and testimonies and recognize their wrongdoing for what it is. With fear and trembling we confess our sin and seek forgiveness. Let us pray.

PRAYER OF CONFESSION

We confess, glorious God, that our minds have been hardened in narrow ways of thinking and self-satisfied means of responding to people and circumstances. We like systems that favor our advantages, and welcome freedom for ourselves more than for those whom we oppress. We have tampered with your word to make it serve our own ends. Forgive us, O God, and expand the horizons of our understanding and caring. Amen.

ASSURANCE OF FORGIVENESS

God answers our prayers and is forgiving toward us. In Christ the veil is lifted from our minds and we are changed in the likeness of our Creator. By God's mercy we are entrusted with a ministry to one another and to our world. Embrace God's truth and do not lose heart.

COLLECT

Shine upon us, Transforming Light, to illumine the shadowed areas of our lives. Let us hear your word with an awe that moves us to listen with our whole being. Change us from one degree of glory to another, that we may respond to your truth not just on the mountaintop, but also in the valleys where you call us to serve. Amen.

OFFERTORY INVITATION

What shall we offer to God to break the silence of our past witness, and extend good news to those who have not experienced it? May these moments bring a new dedication of life, as well as consecration of these tokens of thanksgiving we share. May our offerings enable high mystical moments and practical, everyday assistance, for we are all in need of both. To that end we bring our tithes and sacrificial gifts.

OFFERTORY PRAYER

May these offerings awaken those who give and those who receive to your glorious presence, mighty God. Turn us from our desire to have you serve us to a joyous willingness to serve wherever you send us. So fill us with your Spirit that we may know the freedom you alone provide. Extend these gifts beyond our reach to touch and change lives by your truth. Amen.

COMMISSION AND BLESSING

God reigns, not alone in this place,
but wherever we go this week.
There is nowhere we can go
that is beyond the reach of God's care.
Renounce disgraceful and underhanded ways,
for God is not served by cunning and deceit.
We seek to live the truth of God
and commend ourselves to everyone's conscience.
The holiness of God shines upon you
and empowers your witness and service.
We will meet God in prayer
and walk with God in places of human need.
Amen.   **Amen.**

(See hymn No. 32.)

The Lenten Season

Ash Wednesday

Old Testament: Joel 2:1–2, 12–17a
Psalm 51:1–12
Epistle: 2 Corinthians 5:20b—6:10
Gospel: Matthew 6:1–6, 16–21

CALL TO WORSHIP

Call a solemn assembly; gather the people.
Let all inhabitants of the land tremble before God.
God knows all the secrets of our hearts
and is aware of all our ways.
The day of God is coming; it is near,
a day of clouds and shadows and gloom.
God's judgments are blameless and sure,
and God's grace is sufficient for all our needs.
Rend your hearts and not your garments;
come to God with fasting, weeping, and mourning.
We will worship God in purity and genuine love,
seeking to be faithful to the best we know.

INVOCATION

Meet us, O God, in the special observances of this lenten season.
Discipline us, and put a new and right spirit within us. Bless our
corporate worship and our private devotions, that this may be a time of
self-examination and growth. Amen.

CALL TO CONFESSION

God desires truth in our inward being. When we face ourselves we know
the truth is not in us. We justify words and deeds that distort and harm.
Before the judgment of God we stand condemned. Yet God is merciful
and forgiving. God does not give up on us, even when we give up on
ourselves. Let us seek the forgiveness of God.

PRAYER OF CONFESSION

Merciful God, we cannot escape from our transgressions. We have sinned
against you and have done what is evil in your sight. We have tried to
cover up our wrongdoing and have exaggerated our role in accomplishing
good things. We seek to lay up treasures on earth, while neglecting
permanent values and selfless commitment to causes greater than ourselves. Forgive us, we pray, and set us on a new course. Amen.

ASSURANCE OF FORGIVENESS

In steadfast love God is merciful and gracious, sparing us from the punishment we deserve and lifting us above the consequences of our sin. God washes away all the stains of our past to create in us clean hearts and a right spirit. We are reconciled to God! Let us rejoice in our salvation!

COLLECT

In this solemn assembly we are eager, O God, to open up a place for your truth deep within each one of us and in our corporate body. Continue to cleanse us and help us to live by your Spirit working among us. Grant that we may endure through disappointment, loss, and sorrow. Make us rich in quiet piety, generosity, and genuine love. May times of fasting put us in touch with lasting values. Amen.

OFFERTORY INVITATION

From the treasures of earth we are invited to share our offerings, that others may know the saving power of God. We give, not that people may praise our generosity, but to accomplish those tasks to which God calls us. Let us give as we have been blessed.

OFFERTORY PRAYER

Accept the gift of our hearts as we share the treasure your love has bestowed on us. Use us and our offerings to extend the riches of your grace to people who see no meaning or purpose in life. We would be carriers of your forbearance, kindness, and love wherever you send us. Amen.

COMMISSION AND BLESSING

Carry God's reconciling love to a needy world,
for God's grace rests on you and will remain with you.
**As servants of God, we rejoice with others and stand
with them to help them endure.**
God empowers your witness and your work;
be slow to anger, abounding in steadfast love.
**Like a blanket spread over the mountains,
we go out a great and powerful people.**
The riches of heaven are ours to share;
by God's mercy we can give more than we possess.
**We do not accept the grace of God in vain,
but go out to accomplish that to which God calls us.**
Amen.   **Amen.**

(See hymn No. 33.)

Lent 1

Old Testament: Deuteronomy 26:1–11
Psalm 91:9–16
Epistle: Romans 10:8b–13
Gospel: Luke 4:1–13

CALL TO WORSHIP

God is our refuge and habitation,
present in times of trouble and responsive when we call.
God has given us an inheritance
and led us from times and places of oppression.
The Most High delivers those who love God
and protects those who know God's name.
God's word is on our lips and in our hearts
as we come together for worship and renewal.
You shall worship the Sovereign One, your God,
and God only shall you serve.
We know we do not live by bread alone,
so we open ourselves to the Spirit's leading.

INVOCATION

Sovereign God, source of life and all the gifts that add meaning to our days, we rejoice in your goodness and give thanks for your saving activity among us. You have heard our cries and provided the help we need. You guide our decision-making when we seek your aid. Make us conscious of your presence in this time and place, that we may be for one another channels of your righteousness and deliverance. Amen.

CALL TO CONFESSION

We who have wandered far from God instead of following in the paths where God directs us often find ourselves in difficult places. We have made harmful decisions and avoided difficult choices. We are not all that God has created us to be. God is with us to draw us back into a vital relationship in which we can realize more of the possibilities within us and in our shared life as a faith community. Let us confess our need.

PRAYER OF CONFESSION

God of our ancestors, we confess our attempts to play God as we manage things for our advantage. We rely on our own wit and wisdom instead of seeking spiritual depths. We imagine that our hungers can be satisfied by bread alone. Forgive us, God, for the chasms we create, cutting us off from sisters and brothers and from you. Save us from ourselves, we pray. Amen.

ASSURANCE OF FORGIVENESS

God hears our cries and reaches out to rescue us. If we confess that Jesus is Lord and believe that God raised Jesus from the dead, we will be saved. When we trust God we live this salvation story and know that God bears us up, lest we stumble and fall on life's rocky places.

COLLECT

God of lonely journeys and difficult decisions, we seek the guidance of your word. You challenge us and send us forth. You welcome us and provide us refuge. Amid temptations you point out the better way, and in our troubles you show forth the path of salvation. Speak to us now, that we may hear and respond. Amen.

OFFERTORY INVITATION

You shall take the first fruits of all God entrusts to you, all the results of your labors, and return a goodly portion to the altar of God. It is a true measure of our worship and commitment. Through our gifts and the investment of time and talents we praise the God who makes all things possible.

OFFERTORY PRAYER

For all the riches you bestow, for all the good you supply, for the guidance you offer day by day, we give thanks, gracious God. All that we give we owe to you, and life itself is a gift from your hand. We dedicate our lives with our offerings, to your honor and glory. Amen.

COMMISSION AND BLESSING

Go where God sends you,
and follow in the paths where Christ leads.
God guards us all along life's way
and keeps us from evil.
God delivers those who love their Creator
and is a present help in all times of trouble.
God rescues us and honors us when we call;
God satisfies us with salvation and long life.
Rejoice in the goodness of God,
and share your joy with all whom you meet.
May our words truly reflect our faith
and our actions match our convictions.
Amen. Amen.

(See hymn No. 34.)

Lent 2

Old Testament: Genesis 15:1–12
            Psalm 127
Epistle: Philippians 3:17—4:1
Gospel: Luke 13:31–35

CALL TO WORSHIP

Come away from the gods of your own creation
to worship the living God.
We leave our anxious toil and worries
to find rest in our Creator's presence.
Turn from preoccupation with earthly things
to ponder truths that are eternal.
Before all the wonders of creation that we can see
we come to ponder realities that are unseen.
Fear not, for God is your shield;
your reward shall be very great.
God gathers us together in covenant,
as a hen gathers her brood under her wings.

INVOCATION

Eternal One, who grants us rest and raises us to a new day, we give
thanks for your watchful care. As you gather us here, we open ourselves
to the vision you would set before us. Help us to build with you the kind
of community that welcomes your prophets and responds in love to all
your children. Amen.

CALL TO CONFESSION

How shall we stand before the One who numbers the stars and calls us
each by name? How shall we keep covenant with One whose words we
have not heeded and whose will we have denied? Let us confess the sin
that cuts us off from God and one another.

PRAYER OF CONFESSION

Sovereign God, you have granted us life and brought us to this day, ~~but~~ *yet*
we deny you~~and kill your prophets~~. We live as the enemies of the cross
because the goodness of the One who bore its pain exposes our evil. We
toil anxiously day by day as if everything depended on us, without
acknowledging all your gifts that make possible all that we do. Forgive,
we pray, our faithlessness, rebellion, and lack of gratitude. Amen.

ASSURANCE OF FORGIVENESS

God casts out the demons within us and makes us whole. Our commonwealth is in heaven, where Christ claims us and dwells with us. The relationships of eternity are already ours to receive. Believe God, and it will be reckoned to you as righteousness.

COLLECT

Come with your Word, O God, through words written long ago, that we may live by faith, not fear. We listen as your covenant people, eager to know what you would have us do. Change us to be like Christ and set our minds on things that are above. Amen.

OFFERTORY INVITATION

This is a time for rededication of our lives to the purposes of God. Let us move away from complaints and from longing for what we do not have, to give thanks for all that has been entrusted to us. In our offerings we return a portion of God's gifts to accomplish the work to which God calls our church.

OFFERTORY PRAYER

As our spiritual ancestors brought sacrifices to your altar, O God, we bring our costly treasure for your blessing. Use all our resources to gather earth's children under your wings, where we may dwell in safety and security, in mutual love and growing commitment. Amen.

COMMISSION AND BLESSING

In God's name return to your everyday world,
knowing that it is also the realm of God.
   We will not dwell on our anxieties and worries,
   for God is our shield and our reward.
Go forth a believing and serving people,
for God calls forth your righteousness.
   The gifts of God fill us with happiness,
   and imitation of Christ fills us with joy.
Therefore, as beloved sisters and brothers,
stand firm in the faith and in love for one another.
   We have received the blessing of our God
   and will be faithful in God's service.
Amen.   Amen.

(See hymn No. 35.)

Lent 3

Old Testament: Exodus 3:1–15
Psalm 103:1–13
Epistle: 1 Corinthians 10:1–13
Gospel: Luke 13:1–9
Luke 13:10–17 (alt.)

CALL TO WORSHIP
Bless the Lord, O my soul;
and all that is within me, bless God's holy name!
Bless the Lord, O my soul,
and forget not all God's benefits.
As the heavens are high above the earth,
so great is God's steadfast love to all who fear God.
God satisfies us with good as long as we live,
so our youth is renewed like the eagle's.
Turn aside and see a great sight;
attune your ears to the voice of God.
The place where we are standing is holy ground.
In awe, we seek the One who heals the penitent.

INVOCATION
Place your hands on us, gracious Redeemer, for we need your healing touch. Loose us from our bondage to fear and temptation. Silence our grumbling and complaining. Turn us away from criticism of others whose good works do not conform to our design. Free us all to worship in God's holy name. Amen.

CALL TO CONFESSION
Come to the bush that burns but is not consumed. Approach the holy ground where God, who is unseen, is made known. In awe and reverence come before the God from whom we cannot hide. Here all our sins are exposed. Here and now God forgives us as we confess and let go of our sins.

PRAYER OF CONFESSION
Faithful and loving God, we have tried to live without you amid the idols we have created. We have closed our minds and hearts to your presence and your invitation. Our advantages have oppressed unknown multitudes of our sisters and brothers who receive only token leftovers from our hands. Our immorality is killing us, and them. O God, is there any way out of the prisons we have built around ourselves? Amen.

ASSURANCE OF FORGIVENESS

God does not always chide, nor remain angry forever. God does not deal with us according to our sins or repay us according to our iniquities. Bless the Lord, who forgives all our iniquity, heals all our diseases, and redeems our lives from the pit. God is merciful and gracious, removing our transgressions from us and pitying all who fear God. The God of steadfast love leads us from our bondage into freedom from our sin. Praise God!

COLLECT

God of our ancestors, confront us now as you confronted them. We would not hide our faces from your truth or turn aside from your call. Renew our baptism so we may know surely whose we are. Straighten our misshapen lives and distorted spirits, that we may rejoice together in the glorious things Christ can accomplish through us. Amen.

OFFERTORY INVITATION

God has given us a good inheritance in a land flowing with milk and honey, and we cannot forget all the benefits we have received from God's hand. God's investment in us bears good fruit when we respond to the physical and spiritual needs in our world with our time and efforts and with gifts that extend beyond our personal reach. Let us give with joy!

OFFERTORY PRAYER

Faithful God, grant food and drink to all your children as we share from your bounty. Nourish the spirits of all who give and all who receive, and extend to us the healing we most need. In your name we dare to face oppressors with your truth, on behalf of your afflicted people. Accept and sustain these offerings, we pray. Amen.

COMMISSION AND BLESSING

Our spirits can stand straight
even though our bodies are bent and infirm.
We can walk from this holy ground
with our faith reaffirmed and our spirits made whole.
Bless the Lord, O my soul,
and all that is within me, bless God's holy name.
Bless the Lord, O my soul,
and forget not all God's benefits.
Let all who stand take heed lest they fall.
Be open to God's new revelation day by day.
God is faithful and will not let us be tempted
beyond our strength, but helps us to endure.
Amen.   **Amen.**

(See hymns No. 36 and No. 37.)

Lent 4

Old Testament: Joshua 5:9–12
Psalm 34:1–8
Epistle: 2 Corinthians 5:16–21
Gospel: Luke 15:1–3, 11–32

CALL TO WORSHIP

Bless God at all times;
may praise of God be always in your mouth.
Our souls make their boast in God;
the afflicted hear and are glad.
O magnify our God with me,
and let us exalt God's name together.
We sought our God, who answered us
and delivered us from all our fears.
Look to God and be radiant,
so your faces shall never be ashamed.
O taste and see that God is good!
Happy is the one who takes refuge in God.

INVOCATION

In poverty and in plenty we look to you, O God, the source of all good things. You have accepted us even when we cannot accept ourselves and have loved us when we are most unlovable. Help us in this hour to let go of all that separates us from you. Amen.

CALL TO CONFESSION

God was in Christ, reconciling the world to God's self. Therefore we come, in the name of Jesus Christ, to claim that healing within and among us. The One who received sinners and ate with them invites us to feast on God's forgiving love. Let us confess our sin.

PRAYER OF CONFESSION

O God, we have journeyed to far places and lived as if you were not accompanying us. We have wasted the inheritance you entrusted to us and used other people as if they were things. Then we complain to you as if our dilemmas were your fault rather than our own. O God, we are not worthy to be your children. Forgive us, and grant us just a small place in your love, which we do not deserve. Amen.

ASSURANCE OF FORGIVENESS

God rolls away our reproach. In Christ we are a new creation, and God does not count our trespasses against us. God gives us the very best and celebrates our return. The new life God grants us enables us to reach out to those we have wronged and those who wrong us. We are reconciled to God and one another. Live, then, as ambassadors for Christ.

COLLECT

Great God, our Refuge and Provider, grant us now the ears to hear your message, the eyes to see others from your point of view, and the lips to speak your message of reconciling love. Meet us in our jealousy, false pride, and anger, that we may rejoice with you in welcoming sinners to places of honor among us. Amen.

OFFERTORY INVITATION

As stewards of all God has entrusted to our care we bring our offerings with a deep concern that they accomplish God's will in our day. We hold one another accountable in our mutual service, and struggle together to discern more clearly the mission to which God calls us. Let us rededicate ourselves with our tithes and offerings.

OFFERTORY PRAYER

How grateful we are, O God, that you have claimed us and provided for us, even when we have been unfaithful. In thanksgiving for your compassion, and in recognition of needs among your children that you call us to address, we bring our best in these offerings. Make us useful in your service. Amen.

COMMISSION AND BLESSING

You are precious to God who loves and forgives you.
Go out to proclaim this good news to the world.
In Christ we are a new creation;
the old has passed away; behold, the new has come.
We are ambassadors for Christ,
God making God's appeal through us.
All who repent are welcomed home,
and all who serve faithfully are blessed.
Look to God and be radiant,
so your faces shall never be ashamed.
O taste and see that God is good!
Happy are all who take refuge in God.
Amen.   **Amen.**

(See hymns No. 38 and No. 39.)

Lent 5

Old Testament: Isaiah 43:16–21
Psalm 126
Epistle: Philippians 3:8–14
Gospel: John 12:1–8

CALL TO WORSHIP

Come to sit at the feet of Jesus,
to worship and hear God's message for you.
We count everything else as loss
because knowing Jesus is worth so much more.
God has done great things for us,
and is doing a new thing among us now.
We come, not because we are righteous,
but because our faith compels us to stand with Christ.
The power of Christ's resurrection
is ours to proclaim and to share.
Forgetting what lies behind, we press toward the goal
of the upward call of God in Jesus Christ.

INVOCATION

We are glad as we gather to recognize your presence. You are with us in
our tears and in our shouts of joy. You uphold us in times of sowing and
times of reaping. You stand by us when we complain and withhold, and
when we are thankful and generous. Move us now to be more like Christ,
in whose name we worship. Amen.

CALL TO CONFESSION

At the feet of Jesus we see the contrast between the Christ and ourselves.
We are not worthy to represent Jesus Christ to one another or to the
world. Therefore, we bring once more our prayers of confession, asking
God to remove from us all deceit and unfaithfulness.

PRAYER OF CONFESSION

O God, we have hidden impure motives behind pious words and covered
up selfish actions with good works that draw attention to ourselves rather
than to the gospel. We have ignored your law as if it did not apply to us, or
tried to keep its letter without being changed by the grace and power of
its Author. Forgive us, we pray, and save us from this way of death. Amen.

ASSURANCE OF FORGIVENESS

Remember not your former ways, that God's new way may find a place
within you and among us all. God forgives and makes new. God sends

water to refresh us and food for our spirits. Come home to God with shouts of joy, for the harvest of salvation is ours.

COLLECT

Awaken us, O God, to your promises and equip us to receive the vitality you offer. May faith in Christ Jesus empower our discipleship and inspire our generosity. Fill us with the joy of serving you, and set a vision before us to which we can aspire. Amen.

OFFERTORY INVITATION

What costly treasures do we have that are good enough to offer to Jesus Christ? How sacrificial are our offerings of thanksgiving? Let us bring our gifts, not out of habit or as reluctant duty, but as joyous opportunity to share in the work to which Christ summons the church and every member.

OFFERTORY PRAYER

May nothing be worth more to us, O God, than the opportunity to know Jesus Christ, to share in Christ's suffering, and to know the transforming power of the resurrection. Bless these offerings, that our church programs may bear fruit and your mission may be accomplished, here and everywhere in the world. Amen.

COMMISSION AND BLESSING

In Christ, you are a new creation;
the old has passed away; the new has come.
  In newness of life we re-enter our everyday world,
  seeing it through new eyes, seeking the upward call.
Christ sends us to the least and the lost,
that tears may be turned to rejoicing.
  God's way is being revealed to us day by day.
  We seek to walk in it with our sisters and brothers.
Declare the praise of God before all people;
press on toward the perfection of Christ.
  God has done great things for us;
  we are glad for the opportunity to serve.
Amen.   Amen.

(See hymn No. 40.)

Lent 6
(Palm Sunday)

Old Testament: Isaiah 50:4–9a
Psalm 118:19–29
Epistle: Philippians 2:5–11
Gospel: Luke 19:28–40

CALL TO WORSHIP
This is the day which God has made;
let us rejoice and be glad in it.
Blessed be the one who enters in the name of God!
we bless you from the house of God.
The Sovereign One is God,
who has caused light to shine upon us.
You are our Maker; we will give thanks to you.
You are our Sustainer; we will extol you.
O give thanks to God, for God is good;
Our Creator's steadfast love endures forever.
Open to us the gates of righteousness,
that we may enter and give thanks to God.

INVOCATION
Open our minds to the mind of Christ. Loosen our tongues to share what Christ is teaching us. Empty us of false pride and arrogant pretension, so we can join the humble servant on a donkey in our ministry among the earth's multitudes. We are ready to hear you, saving God, and to respond to your steadfast love. Amen.

CALL TO CONFESSION
Empty yourselves, before the living God, of all your doubts and rebellion, your limitations and fears. Come, not as adversaries, but as petitioners, in the assurance that God is ready to hear and forgive. Let us confess our sin.

PRAYER OF CONFESSION
O holy Parent, we acknowledge our dependence on you, even as we confess our efforts to dismiss you and live without you. We take life into our own hands and close our ears to the prompting of your Spirit. We hasten to still the voices of religious fanatics and withdraw from their celebration. We shrink from the ridicule and shame that awaits us when we embrace the mind of Christ. We prefer religion without a cross and salvation without sacrifice. O, God, forgive, and grant courage to face our own Calvaries. Amen.

ASSURANCE OF FORGIVENESS

Jesus Christ is our salvation. The stone that the builders rejected has become head of the corner. Our pretension and rebellion are forgiven, and we are freed to sing our halleluias. God does not keep us from hard times, but helps us through them. Praise be to God!

COLLECT

Do not be silent, but cry out to us with your Word that transcends all words. May our response to your humble servant on a donkey be genuine and steady. Waken our ears to hear your message and equip our feet to carry it into the world. We await your light, even as we rejoice and give thanks for your answer to our prayer. Amen.

OFFERTORY INVITATION

What will we offer to carry the message of Jesus Christ into the Jerusalems of our day? Will we offer transportation, the witness of our voices, the clothes off our backs? Will we invest our tithes, and follow them with personal involvement? Our offerings are a measure of our commitment.

OFFERTORY PRAYER

As we empty our pockets for the programs and causes our church supports, we seek the courage to empty ourselves of power and position, that we may be humble servants of Jesus Christ. We do not seek to be martyrs, but we want to be faithful. We do not want to be shamed, but we dare to witness to the truth of God. Bless us and our gifts to your glory. Amen.

COMMISSION AND BLESSING

The light of God has shone into our lives,
giving us cause for praise and rejoicing.
> **The truth of God has come to us in Jesus Christ,**
> **equipping us to sustain the weary with our words.**
The humility of Jesus reveals true greatness,
challenging us to embrace the mind of Christ.
> **The sacrifice of Christ moves us to awe and gratitude,**
> **summoning us to give ourselves for others.**
The gates of righteousness are open to us,
that we may enter and give thanks to God.
> **The gift of God is to answer our prayers**
> **and to grant us salvation day by day.**
Amen.   **Amen.**

(See hymn No. 41.)

Lent 6
(Passion Sunday)

Old Testament: Isaiah 50:4–9a
Psalm 31:9–16
Epistle: Philippians 2:5–11
Gospel: Luke 22:14—23:56

CALL TO WORSHIP
Why are you asleep? Rise and pray,
that you may not enter into temptation.
Wake us to your purposes this day, O God,
for we did not realize that we were asleep.
Let the greatest among you become as the youngest,
and the leader as one who serves.
We seek to be faithful to the new covenant
in the name of Jesus, who lived as a servant.
Pray that your faith may not fail,
that you may strengthen your sisters and brothers.
Make us ready to follow where Christ leads,
even if it means mocking, prison, and death.

INVOCATION
Lead us through the denial and desertion of Holy Week with the mind of
Christ. Keep our eyes on the far horizons more than on our immediate
suffering. Focus our thoughts on our neighbors' need more than on our
own pain or ambition. Keep us faithful, even when we are tempted to fall
away. To this end bless our worship and equip us for the trials we must
face. Amen.

CALL TO CONFESSION
We who have lashed out with swords in both word and deed are summoned to the side of the One who said, "No more of this!" We who have
denied our discipleship are called to account by the penetrating eyes of
One who knows us better than we know ourselves. We who have been
ready to crucify goodness for the sake of gain must ourselves stand
judged. Let us repent and change before it is too late.

PRAYER OF CONFESSION
Be gracious to us, O God, for we are in distress. Our sorrow over Christ's
suffering is heightened by our failure to stand with him. By our way of life
we have scorned Jesus' example. By trying to make him what he was not
we crucify him anew. Forgive us, O God, and save us from our guilt.
Amen.

ASSURANCE OF FORGIVENESS

Trust in God! Your times are in God's hands. The Merciful One delivers you, in steadfast love, from your own worst self. God grants you the mind of Christ to discern the good in others and to see the glory of God. In Christ your faith will not fail you, but will sustain you in every trial. You are forgiven. Look up, and live!

COLLECT

Take us by the hand as a Parent, God, to lead us through Jesus' last days as participants, not just as spectators. As we share the sorrow and distress Jesus knew grant us also the humility and courage to face our own times of suffering. Keep us faithful to the role of servant leader and responsive to your purposes. Grant us strength to forgive as we have been forgiven. Amen.

OFFERTORY INVITATION

In the name of one who lived without home or possessions and was buried in a borrowed tomb, we dare to bring not just leftovers, but gifts we thought we needed for ourselves. Jesus' example of giving changed the world. Those who respond generously find themselves changed. May we put our lives on the line for Christ, along with our offerings.

OFFERTORY PRAYER

We give up our complaints and our tendency to dwell on our suffering and losses, even as we give of our treasure. May the joy of sharing move us beyond grief and pain. We dedicate our offerings to spreading good news of your love for all people. Through Jesus Christ. Amen.

COMMISSION AND BLESSING

Go from this place a praying, serving people.
God has given you tongues to share good news.
God wakens us to new possibilities
and equips us for faithfulness in adversity.
Remember Jesus when you are at table together,
and when you walk through troubled places.
We do not want to fail Jesus in our witness
or to put off any who might become followers.
God's love in Christ is for all people, including you.
God will not fail or forsake you.
In confidence we claim the grace of God
and trust God to lead us through all trials.
Amen.   Amen.

(See hymn No. 42.)

Monday of Holy Week

Old Testament: Isaiah 42:1–9
Psalm 36:5–10
Epistle: Hebrews 9:11–15
Gospel: John 12:1–11

CALL TO WORSHIP

Behold God's servant, the high priest of all things;
God has chosen Jesus to lead our service.
Christ opens our eyes to new possibilities
and calls forth the best we can offer.
The Spirit of God brings forth justice
and equips us to keep covenant with the Eternal.
The Creator grants courage through Jesus Christ,
who purifies and strengthens our discipleship.
How precious is the steadfast love of God.
People take refuge under the shadow of God's wings.
We feast on the abundance that God provides
and drink from the fountain of life.

INVOCATION

Loving God, whose watchful care sustains us wherever we are, we come
to this place where you are especially known. Keep us upright, that we
may hold all you are ready to give us. Make possible our sharing, so
Christ may be honored by our generosity. Enliven our worship, so we
may be lights to all who sit in gloom. Amen.

CALL TO CONFESSION

Our responses to the living God follow our own timetable. We try to use
God for our own ends. We seek to hoard the riches of God for our private
use. We cannot untangle ourselves from the web of our own deceits. Let
us confess our sin before God, seeking pardon and new directions.

PRAYER OF CONFESSION

O God, we have taken life into our own hands, seeking to chart our own
course and distrusting any who choose another path. We have heard the
cries of your people for justice and have turned a deaf ear to their claims.
We close our eyes so we cannot see the painful conditions our brothers
and sisters are enduring. Turn us, mighty God, from our self-concern and
from our graven images as we contemplate Jesus' preparation for death—
for us. Amen.

ASSURANCE OF FORGIVENESS

God has called you in righteousness and has taken you by the hand and kept you. Salvation comes to the pure in heart by the mercy of God. Take refuge in the steadfast love of God and receive the courage to venture forth in affirmation of all God's children.

COLLECT

Set before us the challenge and opportunity to minister for our dying Savior by reaching out to others in Jesus' name. Grant that we may be your servants in our hearing and in our doing. Make us instruments of justice and love as we seek to live within the new covenant you are proclaiming in our midst. Amen.

OFFERTORY INVITATION

The wisdom of the wise and the cleverness of the clever say to us, "Save yourself. Keep for yourself all you have earned." But the foolishness of God is wiser than human wisdom, and the generosity of God prompts the sacrifice and fulfillment of living for others and for causes beyond ourselves. Thus we give our best with joy.

OFFERTORY PRAYER

For the gift of breath and the re-creating energy of your Spirit we give thanks, gracious God. For letting your light shine through us to open eyes that were blind and to bring release to prisoners, we are grateful. For blessing us with abundance that we can share to honor our Savior, we sing your praises. Keep us from trembling before the judgment of this world, but attune us to your own, that we may make a faithful response. Amen.

COMMISSION AND BLESSING

By the sacrifice of Christ we are being purified
from dead works to serve the living God.
> **We have been strengthened in our servanthood**
> **and empowered for our ministry.**
Christ's witness for freedom and justice
must be multiplied in our time and place.
> **We cannot rest as long as neighbors are oppressed,**
> **nor keep silent when change is resisted.**
Even when we have nothing else to give
we can pour out love for the least and the greatest.
> **We will not be discouraged before opposition,**
> **for God is with us in covenant and in Spirit.**
Amen.   Amen.

(See hymn No. 43.)

Tuesday of Holy Week

Old Testament: Isaiah 49:1–7
Psalm 71:1–12
Epistle: 1 Corinthians 1:18–31
Gospel: John 12:20–36

CALL TO WORSHIP
God is our refuge and our rock,
a strong fortress, and our salvation.
God delivers us and rescues us;
the Spirit inclines an ear to us and saves us.
God rescues us from the hands of the wicked
and from the grasp of the unjust and the cruel.
We have leaned on God from our birth,
since the Creator took us from our mothers' wombs
We are servants of God and lights to the nations.
God is the source of our life in Christ Jesus.
Our mouths are filled with praise
and the glory of God is ever on our lips.

INVOCATION
Gather us to yourself, Almighty One, our Strength, for we want to hear all you are ready to teach us. Grant purpose to our labors and empower our service. We trust you to stay with us, even when our strength is spent. Deliver us and help us. Amen.

CALL TO CONFESSION
Living by the standards and wisdom of the world, we have wandered far from the will of God, who calls us back with the word, "You are my servant . . . that my salvation may reach to the end of the earth." Let us confess our unfaithfulness to the Holy One, who has chosen us for a responsible ministry.

PRAYER OF CONFESSION
Holy God, we spend our strength for nothing and for vanity. We live for limited goals and focus our energies on self-serving pursuits. We are stumbling blocks to others on their faith journeys, for we deny by our actions the faith we proclaim. Forgive us, gracious God, for our inconsistencies and untruthfulness are intolerable for us and others. Amen.

ASSURANCE OF FORGIVENESS
Those who die to self will bear much fruit. As we give up our self-centered ways our usefulness to God grows. As we minister to others in

Christ's name the results of our efforts will be their own reward. We are forgiven to serve God in this hour.

COLLECT

God of all times and places, we wish to see Jesus. Draw us to yourself, as words written long ago speak to us now. Send your light, that we may walk in it, and your truth, that we may live it. Grant eternal wisdom transcending the competing voices of our time, that your salvation may reach to the ends of the earth. Amen.

OFFERTORY INVITATION

We bring our offerings to praise God for the gift of life and for the new life we experience as disciples of Jesus Christ. Let us be generous on behalf of others as God has been gracious to us.

OFFERTORY PRAYER

Caring God, we invest in the foolishness of the cross because we sense its life-changing power. Bless our gifts to bear fruit within this congregation, in our community, and to the ends of the earth. We dedicate ourselves with our offerings, that all of us may become children of light. Amen.

COMMISSION AND BLESSING

God, our Refuge and Rock, send us forth
to live courageously as Jesus' disciples.
We go out as listeners and caregivers,
for God has freed us to serve with joy.
God, the source of our life in Jesus Christ,
has redeemed and sanctified us.
No evil will keep us from faithful service
and no dark threats turn us from the Light.
God overcomes our weakness and makes us strong;
may our spirits rejoice in God's saving grace.
Our mouths will continue to praise God,
and our daily lives will glorify our Creator.
Amen.   Amen.

(See hymn No. 44.)

Wednesday of Holy Week

Old Testament: Isaiah 50:4–9a
Psalm 70
Epistle: Hebrews 12:1–3
Gospel: John 13:21–30

CALL TO WORSHIP

Surrounded by a great cloud of witnesses
we approach the Sovereign God in awe and wonder.
Make haste, O God, to help us;
may all who seek you rejoice and be glad.
God delivers us from those who would harm us
and saves us from shame and dishonor.
May those who love your salvation, O God,
proclaim to all they meet: "God is great!"
God teaches us and opens our ears;
God gives the word that frees our tongues to speak.
May this time of worship lead us to Jesus,
the Pioneer and Perfecter of our faith.
Amen.   Amen.

INVOCATION

Meet us in our weariness, O God, awakening us to all the possibilities you
set before us. Prepare us once more for the race of life, and grant us the
joy of selfless discipleship. Help us to hear all that you would teach us in
this hour. Amen.

CALL TO CONFESSION

Before we can truly listen to God we need to let the Spirit break through
all our defenses—the excuses we have made for ourselves, the sins that
have become so comfortable we cannot give them up, the broken relationships we are too proud to mend, the pretensions we wish to protect.
Bring them all to God, in silent confession. . . .

PRAYER OF CONFESSION

Gracious God, we are poor and needy, weighed down with sin we cannot
wash away. We have joined the betrayers, participated in denials, and
condoned the crucifiers of Jesus Christ. We have broken faith with those
who love us and failed to love those who most need our care. We
recognize our guilt and plead for your forgiveness. Help us, God. Amen.

ASSURANCE OF FORGIVENESS

God comes to us in our darkest night, when our spirits are troubled and we know not where to turn. God delivers us and helps us. In saving love God grants perspective to knit the pieces of our lives back together and make us whole. Praise God for our salvation. Let us say again and again, God is great!

COLLECT
Sustain us by your Word, Almighty One, that we may not grow weary and lose heart. Help us to stand with Jesus as other disciples fall away. Keep us faithful when we are tempted to take the easy way. Surround us with that cloud of witnesses who will keep us in touch with the Eternal. We sense the joy you have in store for us. We listen to hear and risk all to respond. Amen.

OFFERTORY INVITATION
Let us stand together as disciples of Jesus, who give, from the abundance of God's blessing, all they have—time, talents, treasure, and life itself. God is not satisfied with tokens of respect, for God seeks our complete commitment. May our offerings bear witness to our response.

OFFERTORY PRAYER
We are glad, O God, for the opportunity to give. Through our offerings we praise your salvation and commit ourselves anew to faithful service. We rejoice in your love and are grateful for the help you offer us day by day. For the sake of all who need your good news we dedicate these gifts. Amen.

COMMISSION AND BLESSING
Go out to join the cloud of witnesses
who testify to the goodness of God in Christ Jesus.
   We have heard the good news
   and want to share it with others.
Do not be afraid of those who are put off by commitment,
and heap oppression and ridicule on the just.
   We would dare to be faithful
   and risk the consequences, as Christ did.
Look to Jesus, the Pioneer and Perfecter of our faith,
who for the joy set before him endured the cross.
   In humble gratitude we make our response,
   praying that we will not grow weary or fainthearted.
Amen.   Amen.

(See hymn No. 45.)

Maundy Thursday

Old Testament: Jeremiah 31:31–34
Psalm 116:12–19
Epistle: Hebrews 10:16–25
Gospel: Luke 22:7–20

CALL TO WORSHIP

The God of the covenant draws us to the Eternal
with laws that are carved within us.
We are the people of God,
for our Creator's promises are true.
Offer up sacrifices of thanksgiving,
and call on God's name day by day.
From the least of us to the greatest,
we seek to know the One who knows us.
Draw near with hearts that are true
and hold fast to your confession of hope.
We will not neglect to meet together,
for God bids us to encourage one another.

INVOCATION

Draw us to yourself, covenanting God, for we want to grow in love and good works. Unite us in words and actions that transform and empower. Write your truth on our consciousness so we cannot escape it. Sit at table with us so we cannot doubt your presence. Fill us with hope that turns from limitations of the past to embrace future possibilities. In Jesus' name. Amen.

CALL TO CONFESSION

We cannot escape the consequences of disobeying God's law. Our evil cuts us off from God and one another, and the covenant becomes empty promises. Only God is faithful, and it is God who calls us to find forgiveness and renewal. Let us pray.

PRAYER OF CONFESSION

Loving God, whom we have ignored and disobeyed, we are amazed and awed that you continue to care for us. Our troubled spirits have chased after gods of our own making, and our self-centered ways have broken the community you intend for your children. Forgive us, we pray, and renew your covenant with us. Amen.

ASSURANCE OF FORGIVENESS

There is forgiveness with God, who promises: I will remember their sins and their misdeeds no more. God is faithful to covenant promises and offers us the new covenant in Christ Jesus. Christ welcomes us to the communion table to give thanks and to remember. Praise be to God!

COLLECT

Write your law within us, Holy One, as we listen to more than words. Speak your Word to our spirits, that Jesus Christ may become a living presence and your eternal realm a present reality for us. Build hope within and among us, that we may provide encouragement to one another. Move us powerfully at Christ's table to become faithful disciples who stir up one another to love and good works. Amen.

OFFERTORY INVITATION

What shall we render to God for all the Generous One's bounty to us? We will offer sacrifices of thanksgiving and call on God's name every day. We will keep covenant with our Creator and offer God's love not simply in money offerings, but in the gift of ourselves.

OFFERTORY PRAYER

Gracious God, may our offerings show that we have been stirred up to love and good works. Use them to prepare people to enter fully into the communion of Christ's table and service in your name. We welcome one another to the new and living way you set before us. Amen.

COMMISSION AND BLESSING

Christ sends us from this table into the world.
We are disciples on whom Jesus depends.
The mission of Jesus Christ is our own.
In covenant we live for the realm of God.
Approach all encounters with hearts that are true.
Meet all people in ways true to your faith.
We seek to encourage one another
and bring out the best in other people.
God is faithful and will bless all your efforts.
God takes you by the hand and will not fail you.
We receive all God's gifts with thanksgiving
and vow to be faithful to our covenant in Christ.
Amen.   **Amen.**

(See hymn No. 46.)

Good Friday

Old Testament: Isaiah 52:13—53:12
Psalm 22:1–18
Epistle: Hebrews 4:14–16; 5:7–9
Gospel: John 18—19 (or 19:17–30)

CALL TO WORSHIP
The day of trial and suffering has come;
we are tempted to flee from the test.
Be not far from us, O God, for trouble is near.
Stay with us, for no one else can help.
Stand with the despised and rejected One,
full of sorrows and acquainted with grief.
We trust you, gracious God, to deliver us,
to keep us safe, now as in the past.
Let us with confidence draw near the throne of grace
to receive mercy and help in time of need.
Through times of suffering keep us faithful;
stir our obedience and loyal witness.
Amen.   **Amen.**

INVOCATION
Meet us, loving God, at the place of the skull, when we had hoped for a
peaceful garden. Meet us in our defeats, when we had hoped for victory.
Meet us in our temptation, when we had hoped for clear and easy
decisions. Meet us here, O God, in this healing moment, for we need you
now. Amen.

CALL TO CONFESSION
See the One stricken for the transgressions of others, and weep. Come to
the One bruised for our iniquities, and wonder at so great a love. Feel the
oppression of sin, and come to confess it before the One by whose stripes
we are healed.

PRAYER OF CONFESSION
Good Shepherd, all we like sheep have gone astray; we have turned
everyone to our own way. Our mouths have spoken deceit, and our easy
acceptance of advantages has led to violence. We have fallen before
temptation and led others to stumble and fall. Before the law of love our
sins of omission are all too apparent. We have not cared for your earth and
your people with the energy we devote to our own self-interest. Our
indifference adds to the evil intent that nailed Jesus to the cross. Of all
this we repent, seeking the forgiveness we do not deserve. Save us, we
pray. Amen.

ASSURANCE OF FORGIVENESS

Jesus bore the sins of many and is the source of eternal salvation to all who hear and obey. God will deliver you and renew your strength. Trust in God, and you will not be disappointed. Hear the truth of God, and bear witness to its transforming power.

COLLECT

Lead us, loving God, through the confusion and pain of Jesus' last hours. Reveal your purposes once more through the silent witness before wrongful accusers and the nonviolent response to pretensions of power. Help us to see ourselves among the secret admirers, the jealous religious leaders, and the fearful crowds. Grant us strength, that in our own day we may avoid denial, betrayal, and desertion. Keep us from choosing easy avoidance of controversy or danger. Give us assurance that we are not forsaken, even when there is no one left to put in a good word for us. Speak to us now of triumphant faithfulness. Amen.

OFFERTORY INVITATION

Jesus chose to be an offering for sin, that we might be accounted righteous. How shall we give thanks for the One who bore our sins and makes intercession for transgressors? We can offer our talents and time for the sake of others, as we dedicate our tithes and offerings. Give generously, that you may experience the cost and joy of discipleship.

OFFERTORY PRAYER

Bless our offerings to bear witness to the truth in Jesus Christ. May they proclaim forgiveness and hope when shadows fall and evil seems to triumph. May our joy in giving lead others to faithful discipleship. Use us and all our gifts, that your will may be known among us. Amen.

COMMISSION AND BLESSING

Go out to stand near the cross with all who weep.
Lend your support to those weighed down by loss and pain.
   We will offer the water of life to those who thirst,
   the cup of salvation to those broken and bewildered.
When your discipleship is challenged, claim it.
Bear taunts and scorn with understanding and faith.
   We seek to bear faithful witness to truth
   in our words and in all our ways.
What you have not been told you will see,
and what you have not heard you will understand.
   God is not far away when trouble is near.
   We will trust in God, who delights in us and rescues us.
Amen.   Amen.

(See hymns No. 47 and No. 48.)

The Easter Season

Easter Sunday

Old Testament: Isaiah 65:17–25
                           Psalm 118:14–24
Epistle (or first reading): Acts 10:34–43
                           1 Corinthians 15:19–26
Gospel: John 20:1–18
                           Luke 24:1–12 (alt.)

CALL TO WORSHIP

Rejoice and be glad in God's new creation.
As in Adam all die, so in Christ all shall live.
Sounds of weeping are changed to joy
and cries of distress are turned to gladness.
God has anointed Jesus of Nazareth
with the Holy Spirit and with power.
God has raised Jesus from the dead,
the first fruits of those who have fallen asleep.
We are witnesses to all Jesus said and did,
as we share the good news of Easter.
God is our Strength and our Song,
and has become our Salvation.

INVOCATION

O God of pleasant vineyards and fulfilling days, come among us to establish your day of peace. May this place be as your holy mountain, where none shall hurt or destroy. Raise us up with Christ to share in your realm, where even death is destroyed. Your work, O God, is marvelous in our eyes. Live mightily in our hearts. Amen.

CALL TO CONFESSION

Come all who are perplexed and all who are full of wonder. God reigns, and in God all things are possible. Let us rid ourselves of the ways of death, that we may embrace new life in Christ. Let us confess all that hurts and destroys, that we may build anew as God directs. God is ready to hear and answer and roll away stones.

PRAYER OF CONFESSION

O God, whose love is impartial, we confess that we favor those who are most like us, and seek special advantages for ourselves. We are slow to believe the witness of some who have seen your truth, and discount the messages that contradict our expectations. We are afraid when you call for

boldness and daring and lifeless when you call for vital proclamation. *Ingird Uo*
Turn us around and save us from ourselves, we pray. Amen.

ASSURANCE OF FORGIVENESS

Before we call, God answers us; when we speak, God hears and responds.
God is our Strength and our Song, and has become our Salvation. We
shall not die, but shall live, recounting the deeds of God. Let us rise up as
people of faith who are prepared to invest the gifts of God, that all may
find life.

COLLECT

Open our ears, that we may hear more than ancient words and idle tales.
Grant that the good news of Easter may bear fruit in our lives, resurrect-
ing the perfection of your creation and putting down cynicism, despair,
and unfaithfulness. Anoint us with your healing power, enabling us to do
good in the name of Jesus Christ. Amen.

OFFERTORY INVITATION

God calls us to be planters and builders and to enjoy the work of our
hands. Reach deeply to dedicate the fruits of our labors, both what we
share through the church and what we keep for other ventures. May
everything we do with all our resources honor our crucified and risen
Savior.

OFFERTORY PRAYER

We dedicate this offering and all our resources to drying tears and sharing
good news of peace. Make us instruments of healing and channels of
forgiveness, so all your children may realize opportunities for new life.
We rejoice in the promise of salvation that we are privileged to share.
Amen.

COMMISSION AND BLESSING

Go forth believing what ears and eyes have revealed:
Jesus Christ is alive among us today.
We go home, wondering at what has happened
and seeking the reign of Christ in our midst.
Be alert as God calls you to witness and serve,
leaving behind old ways that deny God's peace.
We will call on God, who answers us,
and witness to all people that Christ saves us.
Your promise and work are acceptable to God:
live as people freed from doubt and fear.
God is our Strength and our Song,
as we recount the deeds of God day by day.
Amen.   Amen.

(See hymn No. 49 and No. 50.)

Easter Evening

Old Testament:	Daniel 12:1–3
	Psalm 150
Epistle:	1 Corinthians 5:6–8
	Acts 5:27–32 (alt. for OT or Epistle)
Gospel:	Luke 24:13–49

CALL TO WORSHIP *(using Psalm 150)*
Praise God! Praise God in the sanctuary;
praise God in the mighty firmament!
   Praise God for mighty deeds;
   praise God's exceeding greatness!
Praise God with trumpet sound;
praise God with lute and harp!
   Praise God with timbrel and dance;
   praise God with strings and pipe!
Praise God with sounding cymbals;
praise God with loud clashing cymbals!
   Let everything that breathes praise God!
   Praise God! Praise the risen Christ!

INVOCATION
We praise you, faithful God, for your promises in which we find new life in the face of incredible odds. May Christ walk once more through ghetto streets, dark prison cells, hospital corridors, barren deserts, and quiet country roads, meeting the poor, oppressed, suffering, hungry, thirsty, and confused of this world. We have been all of these, and we are surrounded by others who are also bewildered and hurting. Send your Spirit to make us whole and wholesome, celebrating the festival of life with the unleavened bread of sincerity and truth. Amen.

CALL TO CONFESSION
We whose lives have been leavened with malice and evil, even while we boast of our goodness, are called to meet God face to face, not in some future time, but in this very moment. We are called to repentance for our disobedience and our slowness of heart to believe that which has been lived out among us in Jesus Christ. Let us pray.

PRAYER OF CONFESSION
God of Easter, meet us in the darkness of our troubled times and in the bitterness of our hatreds to bring your dawn of joyous community. Keep us from walking through life without discerning Christ's presence beside us. We have lived as if no God watched over us, and made decisions

without acknowledging our eternal connections. We have obeyed human demands and ignored your commands. Forgive our foolish choices, our dull conformity to this world, and our lack of sensitivity and compassion. We want to wake up and live! Amen.

ASSURANCE OF FORGIVENESS
Do not be troubled or afraid. Jesus has come as Leader and Savior, bringing forgiveness of sins. You are delivered from your past to begin life anew, set free from the malice and evil in which you have lived. Walk with Christ, and see life through new eyes.

COLLECT
God of our ancestors, we claim your Word anew through the drama of Easter. Meet us where we are along life's road, and stay with us, even when we do not recognize your presence or heed your truth. Make us wise, and turn us toward righteous ways. Quicken our hearts to believe and to respond in love to you and to all your creation. Amen.

OFFERTORY INVITATION
Give, that hopes may find fulfillment. Share, that many may join the committed community of Christ's disciples. Contribute your time and effort with your treasure, that the bread of our common life may be leavened with sincerity and truth.

OFFERTORY PRAYER
All we have to give we offer in praise and thanksgiving for the amazing good news of resurrection. Our gifts evoke in us a new sense of appreciation for our heritage and faith in the risen Christ. May these equip us and others to serve you. Amen.

COMMISSION AND BLESSING
Praise God along the paths where you walk this week.
Praise God at table, enjoying life's bounties.
With talents and voices we offer our praise.
With time and energy we serve where we are.
Praise God for the Holy Spirit, who is ever near.
Praise God for sisters and brothers, who keep us alert.
With open minds we seek new understanding.
With open hearts we commit ourselves to new tasks.
God's promises are for you and for all you meet.
God's love shines on you and will sustain you.
We receive the promises and love of God
for moments of trouble and times of rejoicing.
Amen.   **Amen.**

(See hymns No. 51 and No. 52.)

Easter 2

Historic Message: Acts 5:27–32
Psalm 2
Epistle: Revelation 1:4b–8
Gospel: John 20:19–31

CALL TO WORSHIP

Grace to you and peace from the One who is
and who was and who is to come.
We gather in the name of Jesus Christ,
the faithful witness and firstborn of the dead.
God calls us to proclaim our faith,
to put our trust in reality as yet unseen.
In Christ we know the peace of God
and freedom from the fears that bind us.
Receive the Holy Spirit and recognize your call.
God meets and empowers you now.
We know God has expectations of us;
we want to hear and respond.

INVOCATION

Penetrate our closed minds, loving God, with the assurance of your
supportive presence and the challenge of discipleship. Quiet the fears
that keep us from living the truth and witnessing to it. Come to deliver
us, as individuals and nations, from the temptations of coercive power. Be
to us the beginning and ending of all things and our motivation and
direction in all the in-between times. Amen.

CALL TO CONFESSION

Christ is risen, but our lives do not reveal this good news. Christ has
showed us the ways of peace, but we still battle in our own way. Christ
has freed us from sin and bitterness, but we are often resentful and
unforgiving. The Holy Spirit calls us to repentance and transformation.

PRAYER OF CONFESSION

O God, we want the world to be different, but we resist changes in our
own lives. We want you to reign in our midst, but we want you to do it our
way. We want to live by faith, but we are ruled by our doubts. As fearful
as we are, we dare, right now, to open the closed doors of our minds and
hearts to let you in. Let us know we can take refuge in you and find the
new life Christ offers. Amen.

ASSURANCE OF FORGIVENESS

Jesus Christ frees us from our sin and removes from us the burden of our guilt. Through the gift of the Holy Spirit we are granted the power to forgive others and to reach across the barriers that divide us from one another. Jesus Christ lifts us above our fears to see the possibilities of life yet before us. Receive and use these gifts in the assurance of God's continuing help.

COLLECT

We are glad for your revelation amid our doubts and fears, loving God. Come to us now with the peace only you can give. Grant us the courage of faith and the freedom of those who have burst the bonds of earth. We would dare to obey you rather than bow to human demands. Help us to reach out in understanding and love to those whom some label enemies. Speak to us of abundant life in Jesus' name. Amen.

OFFERTORY INVITATION

Serve God with fear and trembling, lest God be angry with you. Offer the refuge of God's love to all in need by sharing what you have.

OFFERTORY PRAYER

May the world be filled with the teachings of Jesus, O God, as we seek through these gifts to obey you and extend your love. Grant that we may improve rather than destroy the good earth you have given us to possess. Amen.

COMMISSION AND BLESSING

You are children of God; live your heritage.
Take refuge in God; serve with fear and trembling.
   We are witnesses to all God has done in Christ,
   and we intend to obey God rather than human beings.
As God sent Jesus into the world,
so now Jesus sends you to witness and forgive.
   The Spirit is opening our eyes to the truth
   and teaching us to be faithful, believing people.
Grace to you and peace from the One who is
and who was and who is to come.
   God is the Alpha and the Omega, the Almighty One.
   We trust God in the future as we have in the past.
Amen.   Amen.

(See hymn No. 53.)

Easter 3

Historic Message: Acts 9:1–20
Psalm 30:4–12
Epistle: Revelation 5:11–14
Gospel: John 21:1–14 (or 15–19)

CALL TO WORSHIP

Let your speech be silenced and your ear be attentive.
Open your hearts to the presence and word of Christ.
Worthy is the Lamb who was slain,
to receive honor and glory forever and ever!
Hear, O people of God, and turn from your sorrow;
God loosens our sackcloth and girds us with gladness.
Weeping may tarry for the night,
but joy comes with the morning.
Sing praise to God, O you saints of God,
and give thanks to God's holy name.
Let our souls praise you and not be silent.
O God, we will give thanks to you forever.
Amen.   Amen.

INVOCATION

Grant your light to illuminate our souls so we cannot miss your presence
with us, holy God. So confront us here that we will recognize you in the
midst of our daily work and in our leisure hours. Move us to disciplined
living and daring discipleship. Open our eyes and fill us with your Holy
Spirit, so we may respond gladly to your will rather than to our self-
concerned desires. Amen.

CALL TO CONFESSION

Child of God, why do you persecute the One who died for you? Why do
you treat your sisters and brothers with contempt? How is it that you defy
God by insisting that your way is the only way? Know that God is in this
place and calls you to account. Let us admit before God our misplaced
trust.

PRAYER OF CONFESSION

How can we stand before you, God of all people, for we have judged
others by our own standards, not yours, and lived by our own designs,
pretending we are faithful. We have deserted your way to follow our own
pursuits. We have denied our kinship with those who disagree with us.
We have loved the things of this world more than the One who says to us,
"Feed my sheep." Save us, O God, from our poor choices and pardon our
grievous errors. Amen.

ASSURANCE OF FORGIVENESS
God's anger is but for a moment, and God's favor is for a lifetime. God receives us where we are and empowers us to move toward who we should be. The God who transformed Saul, the persecutor of Christians, into Paul, the productive leader in their midst, is ready to bring out the best within us. Thank God and offer your praise.

COLLECT
We sense that you are waiting to communicate with us, God of heaven and earth. Break through the limitation of words written long ago to illuminate our way today. May the risen Christ inspire our prayers and activate our response to your word. Expand our love to enable us to follow wherever Christ leads, caring for all your flock. Amen.

OFFERTORY INVITATION
God has chosen us as instruments of mission. We carry good news, in word and deed, of a God who loves all people. Our gifts are a response of thanks and a symbol of our commitment. May we be inspired by God's generosity toward us.

OFFERTORY PRAYER
For sight when we are blind, hearing when we are deaf, and the assurance of your touch when we have ceased to feel, we give thanks, Sovereign God. We would extend to others all that we have received from your hand. Use these offerings of gratitude in our midst and far beyond the reach of our imagination. Amen.

COMMISSION AND BLESSING
Go out, looking for the good in other people;
reach out, seeing in others the potential God sees.
We go out as messengers of God's forgiveness
and proclaimers of God's faithfulness.
Dare to do things differently in work and play.
Take the risks of following where Christ leads.
We reach out to feed and tend at Christ's command,
valuing our sisters and brothers as God's own.
Praise God, O you saints of the Most High,
and honor the Lamb who was slain for us.
We will praise God in the depth of our being,
so that even the silence speaks of God's love.
Amen.   Amen.

(See hymns No. 54 and No. 55.)

Easter 4

Historic Message: Acts 13:15–16, 26–33
Psalm 23
Epistle: Revelation 7:9–17
Gospel: John 10:22–30

CALL TO WORSHIP
Unnumbered multitudes gather in many places
to praise the God whom Jesus revealed.
We are among the crowds responding in faith,
hungering and thirsting for bread and living water.
In our tribulation and in our triumphs
we are drawn to the throne of grace.
Blessing and glory and wisdom and thanksgiving
and honor and power and might be to our God.
The promises God made to our ancestors
are meant also for us and for today's world.
We have come to hear this good news
and to prepare ourselves to share it with others.

INVOCATION
O Shepherd of all who put their trust in you, restore our souls in this time of worship, for we are tired and needy. Lead us by still waters, on paths of righteousness. Comfort us in death's dark valley and take away our fears. Feed us and anoint us with your goodness and mercy in this time together, so that when we part we shall not doubt your continuing presence. Amen.

CALL TO CONFESSION
Before the throne of God we are fully known. We cannot hide our intentions or our actions from God. Before we can truly hear or accept the promises and commission of God we need to remove the barriers. Let us confess our resistance to the message of salvation and our tendency to hoard for ourselves what we have received.

PRAYER OF CONFESSION
O God of Abraham and Sarah, we have listened without hearing and heard your word without understanding. We have understood without heeding or following in your way. We have pretended to follow while our hearts were far from you. Heal the divisions within our lives, so we may relate with integrity to one another and to you. Amen.

ASSURANCE OF FORGIVENESS

Surely goodness and mercy shall follow us through all of life. God grants salvation for all eternity and claims us day by day. Let us walk as children of light, who rejoice in the Shepherd's loving guidance, and show gratitude for springs of living water.

COLLECT

Grant that we may hear your voice speaking our names and claiming us as your own, O God of our salvation. Open our ears to hear the law and the prophets, and the good news of their fulfillment in Christ Jesus. Satisfy our hunger and quench our thirst, that we may bear witness to your truth. Amen.

OFFERTORY INVITATION

How shall people hear the message of salvation, if no one reaches out to share it with them? How shall we be fully invested in sharing the message, if we withhold our treasure to secure advantages for ourselves? How will others recognize the Savior of humankind, if we have not allowed transformation from our own selfishness? Let us respond gladly and generously.

OFFERTORY PRAYER

Loving God, whose promises to us find their fulfillment in Jesus Christ, grant us to walk in the way of peace, giving thanks for every blessing you send. Accept the work of our hands and all the gifts we dedicate to your service. Amen.

COMMISSION AND BLESSING

God sends us out to do greater works
than we have yet accomplished.
We follow in faith where Christ leads,
knowing the water of life will be available to us.
The promises of God go with us every day,
and the love of God dwells among us.
God wipes the tears from our eyes
and grants rest when we are weary.
God offers us eternal life, beginning now,
inviting us daily to accept God's goodness and mercy.
Blessing and glory and wisdom and thanksgiving
and honor and power and might be to our God.
Amen.   Amen.

Benediction

(See hymn No. 56.)

Easter 5

Historic Message: Acts 14:8–18
Acts 16:11–15 (alt.)
Psalm 145:13b–21
Epistle: Revelation 21:1–6
Gospel: John 13:31–35

CALL TO WORSHIP

God is near to all who call upon God,
to all who approach the Almighty in truth.
We look to God, who supplies our food
and fulfills the desires of those who cry for aid.
God is faithful and gracious in word and deed,
raising and upholding those bowed down and fallen.
We seek God's kindness and justice
amid our tears and our hopes.
With open hands God welcomes us
and preserves us from wickedness.
Our mouths will speak the praise of God;
let all flesh bless God's holy name forever and ever.

INVOCATION

We gather in this place of prayer to worship you anew. This is a time like
no other and a gathering not to be repeated. Accept our expression of
faith and lead us in new ways. Open our hearts, that we may invite you to
dwell within us. Heal us, lest we use our limitations as an excuse for
inaction and unfaithfulness. Loosen our tongues to sing your praise.
Amen.

CALL TO CONFESSION

God has provided for us in ways that amaze us. How awesome is all God's
creation! God rightfully expects our grateful response to all this bounty.
Yet we seldom pause to give thanks or to ponder the wonderful deeds by
which life is sustained. Come to confess every violation of God's law of
love—those you remember and all of which you are unaware.

PRAYER OF CONFESSION

Generous Provider, you have loved us and met our needs, even when we
have ignored you and resisted your Word. We have not loved you or one
another as you command, but have looked for saviors in our own image
and have given our attention to those from whom we think we can gain.
We have closed our eyes to the suffering and pain we help to inflict on

some of your children. Forgive us and turn us around, lest our care and concern come too late to help other children whom you love. Amen.

ASSURANCE OF FORGIVENESS

Stand up on your feet and walk. God has healed your crippled spirits and helped you to feel the pain of your sisters and brothers. God satisfies you with food and gladness, so you can pass on the mercies of your Creator to others. God is your Alpha and Omega, the Source and the Ending of all things. Dwell in God's love as forgiven sinners.

COLLECT

We are as little children, aspiring to be fully present with Jesus. Enfold us in a love that we cannot help but share. Inspire us with a new heaven and a new earth we can experience today. Grant us priceless water from the fountain of life, that we may have something good to offer all who seek you. Speak to us now with a fresh and vital revelation. Amen.

OFFERTORY INVITATION

Our discipleship is revealed in our love for one another, and our love is made known in the opening of our hands to share God's good gifts. We are witnesses to God's care for all creation through our offerings. Let us give generously, as God gives to us.

OFFERTORY PRAYER

For your gracious faithfulness, for food and generous provision for all our needs, for every kindness we have received from your hand we give thanks, loving God. Use these expressions of our gratitude to wipe away tears, comfort those who mourn, and heal those afflicted in body or soul. Grant living water to extend our mutual ministry. Amen.

COMMISSION AND BLESSING

God goes with all who seek God's help,
with all who would give authentic witness.
> **We believe God will supply the food we need**
> **and fulfill the desire of our hearts for meaning.**
Our gracious and faithful God sustains us,
lifting the fallen and those weighed down with cares.
> **We cannot hide from God's justice**
> **or wander beyond the reach of God's kindness.**
The blessings of God are meant for all humanity,
so we go out to make them real to others.
> **Our mouths will speak the praises of God,**
> **and our deeds will tell of God's kindness.**
Amen.   Amen.

(See hymn No. 57.)

Easter 6

Historic Message: Acts 15:1–2, 22–29
                    Psalm 67
Epistle: Revelation 21:10, 22–27
Gospel: John 14:23–29

CALL TO WORSHIP

Let all the people join in praise to God,
whose face shines on us in our darkness.
God is gracious to us and blesses us;
let all the ends of the earth fear God.
Make known the ways of God through every land,
God's saving power among all nations.
God judges with equity and guides us.
Let everyone be glad and sing for joy.
The earth yields abundant harvests,
by which the people of God are fed.
God teaches us to live in peace;
let all the people rejoice and live their faith.

INVOCATION

We come, O God, out of our common need. Some of us pretend to know
your requirements for everyone else. Some of us ignore your purposes to
follow our own schemes. Some of us are troubled by upsetting words and
contradictory deeds. How we long for your truth, glorious God! Shine
your light on us to show us your way. Amen.

CALL TO CONFESSION

We whose ways have often denied the faith we profess come to the Ruler
of the universe to find renewed integrity. We who insist on our own way
open ourselves to the correcting inclusiveness of our Savior. Let us
confess our individual and corporate sins.

PRAYER OF CONFESSION

Almighty God, forgive our pretensions to righteousness through rigid
laws that restrict and divide rather than help people to grow. Forgive the
arrogance that puts others down and presumes our superiority. Forgive
our wayward pursuit of selfish pleasure and our unfaithfulness to you and
one another. We are sorry for the burdens others must bear because of us.
Help us, O God. Amen.

ASSURANCE OF FORGIVENESS

The Holy Spirit comes to cleanse and make whole, to lift burdens from our shoulders, to bring to our remembrance all that God teaches us. In Christ we receive God's peace, a peace that the world cannot give. Let not your hearts be troubled, neither let them be afraid.

COLLECT

Make your home with us, O God, and teach us to love. Send your Spirit to bring hope and peace. Expand our capacity to live with differences and to respect the beliefs of others. Move us to praise and rejoicing, and lift from us the troubles that weigh us down. Grant that we may walk in your light. Amen.

OFFERTORY INVITATION

We bring our offerings, that truth may prevail and love flourish among us. Let us be honest before our Creator as we respond in gratitude for God's blessings. Let our gifts be a genuine expression of love for sisters and brothers who need the help we can give. Sharing is a privilege and a blessing.

OFFERTORY PRAYER

For your witness to humankind in Jesus of Nazareth we give thanks. For the peace your Holy Spirit brings we rejoice. For your truth that persists and will not let us live comfortably in our deceit we are grateful. For your compassion that bids us share the bounty you provide we pledge our loving care and concern. Walk with us day by day. Amen.

COMMISSION AND BLESSING

Return to home and work and play
with a new vision of what life is intended to be.
We have seen the Holy City of God,
where temples are unnecessary and God is Light.
Let not your hearts be troubled,
neither let them be afraid.
Our names are written in the book of life,
and the peace of God rules in our hearts.
Let us live with one accord as Jesus' disciples,
willing to risk all in faithful obedience.
Let all the people praise you, O God.
Let all the ends of the earth serve you in awe.
Amen.   Amen.

(See hymns No. 58 and No. 59.)

Ascension Day
(or Easter 7)

Historic Message: Acts 1:1–11
Psalm 47
Epistle: Ephesians 1:15–23
Gospel: Luke 24:46–53
Mark 16:9–16, 19–20 (alt.)

CALL TO WORSHIP
Gather to experience the power of God
to lift us up beyond the bonds of earth.
Clap your hands, all peoples!
Sing to God with loud songs of joy!
Wait for the promises of God, and give thanks!
Open yourselves to the baptism of God's Spirit.
Sing praises to God, sing praises!
Sing praises to our Ruler, sing praises!
Receive power to become God's witnesses
in this place and to the ends of the earth.
Jesus Christ is alive and forgives our sin.
Jesus Christ lives and appoints us to share good news.

INVOCATION
We wait for your promises, O God, anticipating the power of the Holy Spirit. Help us to hear the witness of your faithful followers. Melt our hardness of heart and break through our unbelief. May our church be alive with Christ's presence and committed to the mission on which Christ sends us. Amen.

CALL TO CONFESSION
Have we lived by our doubts rather than trusted the Author of life? Have we responded as skeptics—rather than as believers—to news of the resurrection? Have we labeled others according to their sins rather than cast our lot with God's forgiveness and transforming power? Have we seen only the bad news of a decaying and cynical world when Christ calls us into the world to preach good news? We have much to confess.

PRAYER OF CONFESSION
We call on you, Creator of the universe, for we have doubted your personal interest in this planet. The news of an empty tomb evokes our doubts rather than our faith. We are not ready for the miracle of new life, in ourselves or in others. We are afraid of the forces of evil that lead to destruction, and we recognize some of them in ourselves. O God, turn us around, that we may be partners in your good news. Amen.

ASSURANCE OF FORGIVENESS

You shall receive power when the Holy Spirit has come upon you, and you will be witnesses to the gospel of Jesus Christ. God, the Ruler of earth, has raised Jesus from the dead and affirmed for all time the way of love and forgiveness. You are pardoned and reconciled, freed from the oppression of your doubts and skepticism. God helps you put aside unfair judgments and pessimism to embrace the good news. God empowers your witness to the ends of the earth.

COLLECT

Open to us the authority of your word and the reality of your love. Turn us from gazing into the heavens when you call us to witness on earth. Keep us from helpless resignation to earth's cruelty and hatred when the resources of heaven are available to us. Grant that we may serve the gospel of love as we grow in the likeness of Jesus Christ. Amen.

OFFERTORY INVITATION

We are called to be instruments through whom the realm of God becomes a reality on earth, not by our own energies, but as the Spirit baptizes and empowers. Our offerings are a symbol of our trust in God to shape the body of Christ on earth as a worthy carrier of good news.

OFFERTORY PRAYER

Loving God, you have melted our hardness of heart and penetrated our unbelief with your forgiveness and your commission. We believe you are sending us and our resources to do your work of peacemaking and salvation. May the programs and outreach of this church be worthy of our support, and may each of us be faithful bearers of your good news. Amen.

COMMISSION AND BLESSING

Christ Jesus, who burst the bonds of earth,
commissions us to share with all the power of God.
   The Holy Spirit has made us bold to speak
   and eager to share the good news.
The promises of God find fulfillment in you,
and the Spirit empowers your service.
   Christ is head over all things for the church,
   and we are witnesses to God's rule among us.
Go into all the world
and preach the gospel to the whole creation.
   We have known the blessings of God
   and are eager to pass them on to others.
Amen.   Amen.

(See hymn No. 60.)

Easter 7

Historic Message: Acts 16:16–34
Psalm 97
Epistle: Revelation 22:12–14, 16–17, 20
Gospel: John 17:20–26

CALL TO WORSHIP

God reigns; let all the earth rejoice;
let every nation be glad!
God brings righteousness and justice;
let all the earth see and tremble!
The heavens proclaim God's righteousness
and all the people behold God's glory.
We put aside all our idols to worship God
and give thanks and praise to God's holy name.
Light dawns for the righteous,
and joy for the upright of heart.
God is our Alpha and Omega,
the First and the Last, the Beginning and the End.

INVOCATION

Come, Lord Jesus, to bring the water of life to our thirsty souls. May this place of prayer provide the refreshment we need to confirm our faith and send us forth to do battle with the world. Wash our wounds, heal our divisions, and remove our hesitation to speak the truth, in love. Amen.

CALL TO CONFESSION

We do not often identify ourselves among the lawless or wicked or adversaries of God. Yet, under the veneer of respectability, we are often found in that company. Let us admit to God and to one another that we are far from realizing the potential God has entrusted to us.

PRAYER OF CONFESSION

Most high God, we confess that we have used others for our own gain. We benefit from the labors of many who are exploited and impoverished. We resist the rule of love and turn away from those who cry for help. We seek to settle differences with weapons of war rather than work for the unity you intend for your children. Take our misplaced loyalties and turn them around, so we serve your purposes instead of our own. Amen.

ASSURANCE OF FORGIVENESS

The water of life is ours without price, God's gift to all who are thirsty. The love of God in Christ comes to us, transforming the way we look at our surroundings and at other people. Receive the gift of forgiveness, that you and your household may know salvation, through Christ.

COLLECT
Help us to know our true selves, so we may be open to your Word and to one another. Our thirst for truth is not for ourselves alone, but that the world may believe. Take from us the idols that keep us from true worship, and the prejudices that cause us to misinterpret events and misunderstand people. Come, Lord Jesus! Amen.

OFFERTORY INVITATION
God repays us many times over for the good we have done, and we are grateful. God has preserved our lives, and for this we give thanks. One expression of our gratitude is the outreach to others that our offerings make possible. Let us give generously.

OFFERTORY PRAYER
Without thought of gain we return for the work of your church, O God, a generous portion of your goodness to us. Use these gifts to shake the foundations of evil and build new structures of peace. May they bring release to prisoners and offer sight to those enveloped in shadows. Unite us in one chorus of praise that echoes across this planet. Amen.

COMMISSION AND BLESSING
The world needs your work for unity and peace;
go out, proclaiming the good news of Christ.
We have known the love of God,
and that love sends us forth to serve.
Witness to our Creator, who is not defeated,
but always has the last word.
We seek for all access to the tree of life
and refreshment from the water of life.
God reigns; let the earth rejoice;
give thanks to God's holy name.
The light dawns for all who seek righteousness,
and joy fills the hearts of all who believe.
Amen.   Amen.

(See hymn No. 61.)

The Pentecost Season

Pentecost Sunday

Old Testament: Genesis 11:1–9
                  Psalm 104:24–34
Epistle: Romans 8:14–17
                  Acts 2:1–21 (alt. for OT or Epistle)
Gospel: John 14:8–17, 25–27

CALL TO WORSHIP

When the day of Pentecost had come
they were all together in one place.
    Suddenly a sound came from heaven
    like the rush of a mighty wind.
There appeared to them tongues as of fire,
distributed and resting on each one of them.
    They were all filled with the Holy Spirit
    and began to speak in other tongues.
All were amazed and perplexed,
asking, "What does this mean?"
    It shall be, on that great and manifest day,
    that whoever calls on God shall be saved.

INVOCATION

We call on you, gracious God, to pour out your Spirit on all flesh, that old and young may see visions and dream dreams. Lead us out of slavery to our fears and undue focus on our troubles. Prepare us here to do those greater works to which Christ calls us. May our worship be pleasing in your sight. Amen.

CALL TO CONFESSION

We who are never quite satisfied with the extent of God's revelation are called to account for the insights and gifts we have received. How have we used them? And how have we resisted the wonders of God's love? Let us confess our failures.

PRAYER OF CONFESSION

Creator of all, we confess that we have been more intent on building monuments to our own importance than on building right relationships with one another. We have been more eager to make a name for ourselves than to call on the name of the Lord. We have doubted your revelation and turned a deaf ear to your call. We take your commandments as suggestions to be rejected, and your love as indulgence that will never call us to account. Help us, God, for we cannot stem the tide of evil within and among us by our own efforts alone. Amen.

ASSURANCE OF FORGIVENESS

Whoever calls on the name of the Lord shall be saved. God's hand is open to give you all the good things you need. The works of Jesus Christ will be repeated in you; indeed if you ask anything in the name of Jesus, God will do it and empower you for still greater works. Receive the Counselor, the Holy Spirit, who will teach you all things. The peace of God is yours; let not your hearts be troubled or afraid.

COLLECT

Show yourself to us, gracious God, and guide us by your Spirit of truth, that we may hear and keep your commandment to love. Do not hide your face from us, but reveal yourself through the scriptures in fresh and vital ways. Let us not shrink from the mighty winds or tongues of fire that would invest us with power to speak and act in your name. Amen.

OFFERTORY INVITATION

As heirs of God, all things are ours. God makes it possible for us to be generous. Let us not shrink from the greater works to which we are called, but respond in creative ways to the possibilities given us to grow and serve in Jesus' name. Bring your gifts with joy.

OFFERTORY PRAYER

May these gifts carry forward the ministry you intend here in our church and community and wherever people are scattered on the face of the earth. May our open hands share your gifts and our open hearts reach out in love and peace. Show us how to use this offering to accomplish your purposes. Amen.

COMMISSION AND BLESSING

Be led by the Spirit as sons and daughters of God.
Let God turn visions to reality through you.
  I will sing to God as long as I live;
  I will sing praise to my God while I have being.
The Counselor, the Holy Spirit, will teach you,
and the Spirit of truth will dwell in you.
  May my meditation and my service
  be pleasing to God, in whom I rejoice.
Peace I leave with you, the peace of God;
let not your hearts be troubled or afraid.
  We will walk in peace and be peacemakers;
  we will let the Spirit dwell with us forever.
Amen.   **Amen.**

(See hymn No. 62.)

Trinity Sunday

Old Testament Proverbs 8:22–31
Psalm 8
Epistle: Romans 5:1–5
Gospel: John 16:12–15

CALL TO WORSHIP
Come, celebrate the wisdom God created
before the stars were born and set in place.
Before the planets cooled around our starlet,
wisdom ruled with God beyond all space.
Rejoice that God created earth in grandeur,
towering mountain, and the depths of seas.
Give thanks for fertile fields and flowing waters,
designed with wisdom, that we might be pleased.
The majesty of earth is all around us,
and infants sing the glory of the skies.
We tremble at the thought that human beings
have dominion over all that God supplies.

INVOCATION
Thank you, God, for the majesty of heaven and earth, for the amazing
expanse of space, and the intricate beauty of a flower. Far beyond all our
eyes can see you have created order and design we only dimly compre-
hend. Come to us now to re-create and re-order our lives. Amen.

CALL TO CONFESSION
How have we exercised the dominion entrusted to human beings by our
Creator? We who were "crowned with glory and honor" to manage the
resources of earth are called to give account of our stewardship. Come to
confess before God our neglect and misuse of our heritage.

PRAYER OF CONFESSION
Spirit of truth, we recognize the high hopes in which we were given birth
and the many ways in which we have failed others, ourselves, and you.
We have taken for granted the gift of life in all its variety of plant and
animal forms. We have scarred the face of the earth with our lust for
power and wealth. We have neglected the people you have invited us to
love, while worshiping at the altars of our own success. Forgive us, God,
and help us to change the habits that destroy. Amen.

ASSURANCE OF FORGIVENESS
When we are truly sorry for the brokenness we have caused, God offers

healing and forgiveness. We are justified by faith and have peace with God through Jesus Christ. The Spirit of truth will guide us into all the truth.

COLLECT

Grant your Word to guide us toward your truth. Send your Spirit to pour love into our hearts. Put us back in touch with the marvels of your creation, O God. Quiet our frantic pace as we ponder running waters, mountains, and stars in the sky. Help us to aspire to our true identity as your children. Amen.

OFFERTORY INVITATION

God has placed all things under our feet. That responsibility to care for all creation calls for our daily commitment to reach out helping hands. We celebrate that commitment in our offering. As we dedicate the fruits of our labor we also consecrate all the work we do to God's purposes for the earth and its people.

OFFERTORY PRAYER

Loving Creator, we bring these symbols of our stewardship, seeking your blessing on all the work we do. Grant us the depth of character truly to appreciate and care for all you have made. We dedicate to your service our time, our talent, and all the riches we accumulate. May what we share here be well used in ministry to one another and in outreach to the world. Amen.

COMMISSION AND BLESSING

Go forth once more to look at God's creation.
Open minds and hearts to the mystery of life.
   When I look at the heavens, the moon and the stars,
   what are human beings that God cares for us?
We are made a little less than God,
and crowned with glory and honor.
   We will seek to use wisely the dominion God grants,
   protecting all God's creatures from exploitation.
We are offered grace and peace,
as God's love is poured into our hearts.
   Grounded in God's loving care for us,
   we commit ourselves to compassionate care for others.
Amen.   **Amen.**

(See hymn No. 63.)

Pentecost 2
(May 29–June 4, if After Trinity)

Old Testament: 1 Kings 8:22–23, 41–43
Psalm 100
Epistle: Galatians 1:1–10
Gospel: Luke 7:1–10

CALL TO WORSHIP
Make a joyful noise to God, all the lands!
Come into God's presence with singing!
It is God who made us, and to God we belong;
we are God's people, the sheep of God's pasture.
Enter into worship in a spirit of thanksgiving;
serve God in praise and gladness.
God's steadfast love endures forever,
and God's faithfulness to all generations.
Grace to you and peace from God, our Creator,
and from our Savior, Jesus Christ.
God keeps covenant with us day by day,
showing steadfast love to all who serve.

INVOCATION
Gracious God, beyond all our thoughts of heaven and earth, there is no power greater than yours in all the universe. We worship One beyond our imagination, yet near to our hearts. You are so much more than we can know, yet so much closer than we have dared to explore. Receive now our humble praise. Amen.

CALL TO CONFESSION
When we come from our "far countries" to return to the embrace of a loving God, we are welcomed home. Let us come confessing our desertion, the failure of our trust, and our immersion in values that deny God's rule. Let us pray.

PRAYER OF CONFESSION
O God, we are not worthy of your presence with us. We have settled for the evil that maintains advantages for some at the expense of others. We have deserted the gospel in favor of the wisdom of the marketplace. We have sought human favor at the cost of our integrity. Our sins condemn us. Only you can save. Hear us and change us. Amen.

ASSURANCE OF FORGIVENESS
The steadfast love of God is not withheld from sinners. God's faithfulness

is not withdrawn when we violate our trust. Jesus Christ bore our sins to deliver us from this evil age. Although we are unworthy, our Savior heals and restores us to the faith. How good it is to be cleansed and renewed, to join the chorus of praise to our God!

COLLECT

Say again the word by which our lives become new, O God. In the stories of other times and places, confront us with who we are and lead us to what we may yet become. Deepen our trust in you and our love for one another. Keep us from hearing only what we want to hear, so the gospel may reach us in its fullness. Send your word to all the peoples of the earth, that all nations may stand in awe before you. Amen.

OFFERTORY INVITATION

Around this world many people are begging for the word of truth. Multitudes seek healing for body and spirit. Millions see no meaning in their lives. The church proclaims a Savior who knows our troubles first-hand. Our offerings extend that proclamation. Let us give gladly and generously!

OFFERTORY PRAYER

We whose faith is fragile marvel at your generous response to our needs, O God of love. You take the little we offer and turn it to great results. The more we give, the more your blessings abound, until we cannot count them all. Receive us as co-workers with Christ in the transforming work you seek to do throughout all the earth. Amen.

COMMISSION AND BLESSING

Walk before God with all your heart,
and dare to offer God's steadfast love to others.
God is faithful even when we are not,
and God's grace is for all people, everywhere.
Preach the gospel in every day and place
by the way you live and by what you say.
We seek not to please human beings,
but to be servants of Jesus Christ.
Grace to you and peace from God, our Parent,
and from Jesus Christ, to whom be glory forever.
We will make a joyful noise to God
as we seek to be faithful to the covenant.
Amen.   Amen.

(See hymn No. 64.)

Pentecost 3
(June 5–11, if After Trinity)

Old Testament: 1 Kings 17:17–24
Psalm 113
Epistle: Galatians 1:11–24
Gospel: Luke 7:11–17

CALL TO WORSHIP

Praise God, all you, God's servants.
Blessed be the name of our Sovereign.
From the rising of the sun to its setting
let the name of God be praised.
May God's life-giving power be known to all,
and God's compassion be told in every place.
God is high above all nations;
God's glory fills the whole universe.
The gospel of Jesus Christ turns us around,
and we become disciples and apostles.
Listen for the voice of God in Christ,
for God's Word comes when we least expect it.

INVOCATION

Lift us up into your presence, comforting God, for we are weighed down
by life's tragedies. So much that is wrong in the world seems to be, at
least in part, our fault. We blame ourselves, or other people, or you, for
the calamities that shake our existence. Help us to express our angers and
our fears, so we may be ready for the new life you offer. Amen.

CALL TO CONFESSION

God summons us from our false gospels and narrow horizons to see more
of eternal truth. Do we recognize the signs of death within us? Our
lukewarm faith may be keeping us from the delight and power of true
worship. Bring to remembrance, and confess, with me, all that separates
us from God.

PRAYER OF CONFESSION

All-knowing God, we shrink from acknowledging you, for when we do,
our sins are exposed. We block out your revelation and deny the word of
your prophets. We choose our own traditions in preference to the way of
Christ. We deal violently with those with whom we disagree, believing
that this is safer than your way of peace. O God, deliver us from our
arrogance and fear; forgive our waywardness, we pray. Amen.

ASSURANCE OF FORGIVENESS

God set you apart before you were born. In God's grace there is a place for you. Leave your past behind; it is forgiven. Embrace the new future Christ offers. Live and share the faith, now vital and alive in you.

COLLECT

God of the needy and deprived, we are all in need of your Word to turn our lives around for the better. We would entrust those most precious to us to your healing presence. Have compassion on us and on them. Entrust us now with your transforming good news. Amen.

OFFERTORY INVITATION

Often the poor receive special notice in the scriptures. Perhaps because they are more vulnerable than most, and aware of their need, they are also more open to the good news that points to life's meaning. We need not be poor to be grateful for God's bounty, nor do we have to be rich before we can share. Everyone can know the blessing of a generous spirit. You are invited to give as God has blessed you.

OFFERTORY PRAYER

For the precious breath of life, for the wonder of children, for prophets among us, for all the glory of creation round about us, O God, we give you thanks and praise. May our zeal for faithful witness be expressed through these offerings and in our daily lives. We offer your compassion to one another in these gifts and in our personal acts of kindness. Amen.

COMMISSION AND BLESSING

The miracles of God continue,
and some will take place in you.
The saving power of Christ goes with us,
and we are the ones who may be changed.
The Holy Spirit grants new life
and the opportunity for greater faithfulness.
Our church may be just a breath from greatness,
and we may be instruments of its renewal.
May others glorify God because of you;
may tears be dried because of your caring.
We will honor God with our praise
and serve God by helping others.
Amen.   **Amen.**

(See hymns No. 65 and No. 66.)

Pentecost 4
(June 12–18, if After Trinity)

Old Testament: 1 Kings 19:1–8
Psalm 42
Epistle: Galatians 2:15–21
Gospel: Luke 7:36—8:3

CALL TO WORSHIP
Our souls are filled with longing, O God,
for we are thirsty for your truth.
Sometimes we feel so alone and forgotten;
even in a crowd we feel abandoned.
The good we have done seems to count for nothing,
and the forces of evil seem to prevail.
The standards we uphold seem to be failing,
and we pursue high values without reward.
Why are you cast down, O my soul,
and why are you disquieted within me?
Hope in God, for we shall again praise God.
Rejoice, for Christ lives in us!

INVOCATION
When we feel that no one cares, show us the worth of our own lives and what we seek to do. When worship is flat and uninspiring, open our lips in songs of thanksgiving, and attune our hearts to the music. Meet us in this hour to give us a new perspective on life. Amen.

CALL TO CONFESSION
We have been forgiven, but the same sins recur. We resolve to live in newness of life, but the old patterns prove hard to break. Just when we think we are doing well a new view of ourselves reveals still greater need for forgiveness. Let us seek God's help.

PRAYER OF CONFESSION
O God, we are no better than our ancestors in the faith who tried to justify themselves through their good works. We compare ourselves with obvious sinners, and congratulate ourselves on our virtues. We exaggerate our own faithfulness while discounting the kind deeds of others. By what we do and what we neglect we fail to live as your children. We pray, O God, for your pardon. Amen.

ASSURANCE OF FORGIVENESS
God hears the longing of our souls for the living God. Forgiveness is ours,

along with reason for hope. Our faith in Christ is justified, and our Savior makes a home in our hearts. Because we have been forgiven much we are empowered to offer forgiveness to those who wrong us. Rejoice in God's steadfast love.

COLLECT

Help us to meet ourselves in the biblical stories we hear. In the discouragement of the prophet and the deep longing of the psalmist, speak to us. We join in Paul's struggles to express our faith in words, and in a woman's efforts shown by her deeds, a commitment she did not have language to express. Grant to us a saving faith, and peace the world cannot give. Amen.

OFFERTORY INVITATION

Does Christ mean enough to us that we will sacrifice what is most valuable to us to honor our Savior? Will we provide for the ministry of Jesus today out of our means? We are forever in debt to the triune God. Today we have the opportunity to repay a portion of what we owe, as we dedicate our offering to the mission on which Christ sends us.

OFFERTORY PRAYER

O God, we would support the work of those who stand courageously for your truth. We want to reach out in faithful witness to all who long for the living God. By our gifts we tell the world of our commitment and desire to serve. Multiply our contributions by your love, so your will may be accomplished among us. Amen.

COMMISSION AND BLESSING

Live as forgiven sinners, aware of God's mercy;
live as forgiving people, sensitive to others' needs.
We have good news to share: God's realm is near;
our faith has saved us and given us peace.
Live as disciples of Jesus, your Teacher and Guide.
Live as apostles of Christ, who saves and sends.
We have been crucified with Christ,
who now lives in us and among us.
All who admit the depth of their sin experience mercy,
and all who seek to be faithful are empowered.
God has granted food for body and soul,
and steadfast love to sustain us through each day.
Amen.   **Amen.**

(See hymn No. 67.)

Pentecost 5
(June 19–25, if After Trinity)

Old Testament: 1 Kings 19:9–14
                Psalm 43
Epistle: Galatians 3:23–29
Gospel: Luke 9:18–24

CALL TO WORSHIP
We gather, not as rigid keepers of the law,
but as responsible people of faith.
We come, not because of the law's restraints,
but as sons and daughters of God, through faith.
As many of you as were baptized into Christ
have put on the character and outlook of Jesus.
We are spiritual offspring of Sarah and Abraham,
heirs, with Christ, according to God's promise.
In Christ there is neither Jew nor Greek,
slave nor free, male nor female.
All are welcome in the household of God,
for we are all one in Christ Jesus.

INVOCATION
God of hosts, we aspire to equality and unity through faith in Jesus Christ. We seek to be people of covenant, bound to you and one another by promises made and faithfully kept. When we are discouraged, thinking that we alone are true to our vows, show us the larger community of committed people to whom we are linked in trust and caring. Amid wind and earthquake and fire sustain us, so when they are past we may hear your still small voice. Speak to us now in the silence of this hour. Amen.

CALL TO CONFESSION
The deceitful and unjust, whom we condemn, are not all "out there." Sometimes they are "us." The wicked, who throw down altars and slay God's prophets, include some of us with pious credentials. There are times when we avoid the cross at all costs rather than face its pain. For all this, and more, we need to find forgiveness.

PRAYER OF CONFESSION
O God, we confess that we deny the cross and take up ourselves. We are impressed with our own accomplishments. At the same time we are unable to grasp the full potential you have created for us. We blame others for our failures and envy the successes of our neighbors. Faith

becomes for us pious phrases instead of trust in the living God, and Jesus Christ becomes an oath, not a savior. Forgive us, God! Change us! Use us! In Christ. Amen.

ASSURANCE OF FORGIVENESS
God vindicates and defends us. God comes to us in unexpected times and places, seeking entrance into our souls. Jesus Christ died, loving us, giving all for our sakes. The barriers we erected against God and humanity are destroyed, so we can claim our oneness in Christ. Hope in God, and sing God's praise!

COLLECT
Send us your light and your truth, O God, and alert us to hear and keep your message. Speak powerfully, through words and silence, that your justice and true equality might prevail. Move us to deny ourselves, take up our cross daily, and follow where Jesus leads. Amen.

OFFERTORY INVITATION
God meets us amid mountaintop experiences and when we are hiding out in fear. Always, God walks with us, inviting us into partnership. Our offerings are one way we enlist in the work God calls us to do. Let us give proportionately, as we have been blessed, as good stewards. It is a glorious privilege to be generous.

OFFERTORY PRAYER
We come to your altar with exceeding joy, grateful that you are with us in all the storms of life, dear God. We want to lend our support to others facing trying days and difficult decisions. Use our offerings to that end, we pray, and equip us to be instruments of your truth and your love, in Jesus' name. Amen.

COMMISSION AND BLESSING
Go forth to live as covenant people;
God does not leave you alone.
  Send out your light and truth; let them lead us,
  let them bring us to your holy hill.
You are sons and daughters of God, through faith.
Baptized into Christ, you have put on Christ.
  We will praise you with the lyre, O God,
  for you are our Help and our exceeding Joy.
If any would follow Christ, they must deny themselves
and take up their cross daily.
  If we try to save our lives, we will lose them.
  Only as we lose our lives for Christ's sake will we find life.
Amen.   Amen.

(See hymns No. 68 and No. 69.)

Pentecost 6
(June 26–July 2)

Old Testament: 1 Kings 19:15–21
Psalm 44:1–8
Epistle: Galatians 5:1, 13–25
Gospel: Luke 9:51–62

CALL TO WORSHIP
The agendas of the world place many gods before us,
but today we seek the counsel of the One who is truly God.
We want to hear once more of a God who cares,
a God who has high expectations of us.
Let nothing stand in the way of our listening,
and no looking back prevent our following Christ.
For freedom Christ has set us free;
therefore, we will not submit to the yoke of slavery.
Let us celebrate the freedom that is ours in Christ,
turning away from temptations of the flesh that enslave.
We will not use people for our own ends,
but seek to love our neighbors as ourselves.

INVOCATION
God of our ancestors, we have heard of your wonderful deeds in freeing
people from bondage. Now we come to you seeking true freedom within
ourselves. We do not ask to be free of obligation or responsibility, but to
be able to lay aside the unnecessary burdens we carry. Our self-preoccupation, worry, and anxiety have blocked our ability to do and to be our
best. Come to us now in your saving and freeing power, that we may truly
worship and joyously serve. Amen.

CALL TO CONFESSION
The works of the flesh are plain, wrote Paul: fornication, impurity, licen-
tiousness, idolatry, sorcery, enmity, strife, jealousy, anger, selfishness,
dissension, party spirit, envy, drunkenness, carousing, and the like. In
Paul's list each of us will find at least one relevant word that describes our
separation from life in the Spirit. Let us confess our sin to God.

PRAYER OF CONFESSION
By our own efforts, O God, we have not succeeded in becoming your true
sons and daughters. We have misused our bodies and failed to give proper
nourishment to our spirits. We have not realized the best you have placed
within us nor brought out the best in others. We have taken you for
granted and failed to listen to your word. Forgive us and restore us to
right relationships with you, others, and the best in ourselves. Amen.

ASSURANCE OF FORGIVENESS
The fruit of the Spirit is love, joy, peace, patience, kindness, goodness, faithfulness, gentleness, self-control. You are forgiven, and the Spirit seeks a home within you. Trust the Spirit's leading. Walk by the Spirit, enjoying your new freedom in Christ. Let the fruit ripen within you; recognize its presence, and celebrate each experience that gives evidence of your growth in the Spirit.

COLLECT
Set before us the demands of discipleship, O God, even when we are not ready to hear and respond. Challenge us to put our hands to the plow and look ahead, walking by the Spirit and offering to the world the love, joy, and peace you intend. Curb our impatience when our faithfulness as a church does not seem to match that of our ancestors. Keep us gentle and kind, self-controlled, and abounding in good works. Amen.

OFFERTORY INVITATION
Jesus set his face to go to Jerusalem because he knew a witness to God's love needed to be made there. Where do we see a need for that witness today? To what extent will we support the needed proclamation? Jesus put life itself on the line. What are we prepared to give? Today's offering represents part of the answer we are called to make.

OFFERTORY PRAYER
O God, we are not here to make excuses, but to give substance to our commitment. We want to put you first in our lives, no matter what that costs. Here is the best we can offer today; bless it, we pray, in Jesus' name. Amen.

COMMISSION AND BLESSING
What are you doing here, people of God?
You have been forgiven and empowered to serve.
We are ready to venture once more into the world,
for we know God is with us; we are not alone.
Other people join you in the journey toward faithfulness.
Be on your way to win others to Christ.
We have been freed from slavery to the flesh;
the Spirit lifts us beyond the law's constraints.
Be led by the Spirit, walking in love, joy, and peace.
Practice patience, kindness, goodness, and gentleness.
The Spirit calls forth our faithfulness
and equips us with self-control.
Amen.   **Amen.**

(See hymns No. 70 and No. 71.)

Pentecost 7
(July 3–9)

Old Testament: 1 Kings 21:1–3, 17–21
Psalm 5:1–8
Epistle: Galatians 6:7–18
Gospel: Luke 10:1–12, 17–20

CALL TO WORSHIP
God hears our voices in the morning
and hearkens to the sound of our cries.
We enter the house of God to worship;
in awe and fear we stand before the eyes of God.
God knows the intention of our hearts
and is not deceived by actions that seem noble.
We are not here to boast, but to pray,
and to glory only in the cross of Jesus Christ.
God pours out steadfast love in abundance
and leads us in the ways of righteousness.
We have come to hear God's directions
and to be equipped to work in God's harvest.

INVOCATION
We seek peace in your house, mighty God—not a peace that wipes out
differences and eliminates conflict, but the peace of integrity within and
solid grounding in your love. We seek to be in touch with your concern
for all people. Send your Spirit to make of us a new creation. Amen.

CALL TO CONFESSION
How have we violated our neighbors—those whom we know and those
worlds away from our own experience? Where have we sold ourselves to
do what is evil in the sight of God? Have we sowed to our own flesh, and
boasted of accomplishments as if we did everything ourselves? Together
let us seek God's forgiveness.

PRAYER OF CONFESSION
Sovereign God, our false pride brings us to our knees before you, seeking
once more to be freed from the burden of our sin. We have grabbed for
ourselves what is rightly to be claimed by others. We have lived deceit-
fully, speaking lies and trying to re-order the world to revolve around us.
We have failed to share the bounty you have poured out on us, or to
witness convincingly to the good news of Christ for all people. Help us to
change, O God, as you forgive and offer us a new start. Amen.

ASSURANCE OF FORGIVENESS
God sweeps away the evil and unrepentant, but to those who are truly sorry for their sin and eager for new life in Christ, God offers mercy and peace. To those who are inclusive of others and their concerns, in outlook and decision making, God offers a new creation. Even the demons are subject to those who, in Christ, offer peace to the world.

COLLECT
By your Word, gracious God, open us up to your assignment. Show us what you would have us do. Lead us in your righteousness to bear the marks of Jesus, to glory in the cross, and to do good to all people. May we be bearers of your peace wherever we go. Amen.

OFFERTORY INVITATION
God bids us travel light on this journey through life. We make elaborate excuses for the vast accumulations most of us have undertaken instead. This is a good time to examine our motives, our relationships to our neighbors whose vineyards we covet and exploit, and our responsibilities to one another. The church of Jesus Christ seeks to re-order the world's priorities. Our offerings help us as well as all others we seek to help.

OFFERTORY PRAYER
We have heard your voice, O God, and are compelled to give from the rich abundance you entrust to us. We seek to do good to all people, to labor in the harvest, and to send out others. To do this gives us great satisfaction and joy. Thank you, God, for the marvelous privilege of giving. Amen.

COMMISSION AND BLESSING
God pours out on you an abundance of steadfast love,
and will lead you in all righteousness.
We are empowered by the love of God,
that we may not lose heart in our well-doing.
Peace and mercy be on all who walk with Christ.
The harvest is plentiful, but the laborers are few.
We accept our assignments in God's harvest
and seek to enlist others to labor with us.
The grace of our Lord Jesus Christ
be with your spirit, my friends.
The realm of God has come near to us;
we offer to all God's new creation.
Amen.   **Amen.**

(See hymns No. 72 and No. 73.)

Pentecost 8
(July 10–16)

Old Testament: 2 Kings 2:1, 6–14
　　　　　　　　Psalm 139:1–12
Epistle: 　　　Colossians 1:1–14
Gospel: 　　　Luke 10:25–37

CALL TO WORSHIP
Wherever we go we are in the presence of God;
we come together to celebrate what is always true.
God has searched us and known us;
God discerns our thoughts from afar.
We cannot go away from the Spirit of God;
there is no way we can flee from God's presence.
Before a word is on our tongues,
God knows what we are going to say.
No darkness can hide us or cover our activity,
for God penetrates the night and shines through it.
God lays a hand of blessing on us;
how wonderful is our Creator!

INVOCATION
God of the prophets, do not leave us alone, but visit us once more to intervene on our behalf. Part the waters that separate us from you so we may walk through unafraid. Grant us courage in this hour to examine ourselves before you and to open our lives to your direction. Lead us, we pray, from darkness to light. Amen.

CALL TO CONFESSION
We cannot escape the judgment of God, for our Creator knows all our thoughts and words and deeds. Yet God is ever ready to hear the honest groping of our souls for integrity and true communion with the Source of our being. Let us confess all that divides us and keeps us from bearing good fruit.

PRAYER OF CONFESSION
God, our Mother and Father, how often we have tried to escape your watchful eye. Whenever we measure ourselves by your intention for us we are found wanting. We have resisted change and growth. We have seen your suffering people—and passed them by. Your children cry out for mercy and compassion—and we harden our hearts and focus on more immediate concerns. We resent the intrusion of your word into the cozy

arrangements we have made for our own benefit. Save us from ourselves, we pray. Amen.

ASSURANCE OF FORGIVENESS
God delivers us from the power of evil. In Jesus Christ we have received redemption, the forgiveness of our sins. Give thanks to God, who reaches out to us as a patient Parent and offers us the opportunity to share in the inheritance of the saints in light.

COLLECT
Eternal God, who grants to us glimpses of eternity in the midst of time, teach us to love you with our whole being and to love our neighbors as ourselves. May your gospel bear fruit among us, as we grow in your truth, enabled by your Spirit. Equip us with the prophet's mantle, laying your hand on us in blessing, encouragement, and support. Amen.

OFFERTORY INVITATION
Life is a gift we have done nothing to deserve. The faith we have inherited has been won with the blood of saints and martyrs. People of faith have taken risks on our behalf. In gratitude we set aside a portion of our wealth to witness to God's saving action among us. Let us give with joy.

OFFERTORY PRAYER
May our offerings witness to your presence among the poor, the oppressed, and all seekers after truth. Bless us through our giving, as we have been enriched by your generosity. We give thanks for our inheritance and the chance to pass it on to others. Amen.

COMMISSION AND BLESSING
Grace to you and peace from God, our Father and Mother.
Know God's presence wherever you go.
    God besets us behind and before,
    laying on us a hand of blessing.
Go forth with faith in Jesus Christ
and with love for all the saints.
    God leads us through darkness to light,
    from despair to hope, from weakness to strength.
Extend the mercy and compassion of Christ
to all whom life has passed by.
    We have good news to share
    of life filled with meaning and joy.
Amen.   Amen.

(See hymn No. 74.)

Pentecost 9
(July 17–23)

Old Testament: 2 Kings 4:8–17
Psalm 139:13–18
Epistle: Colossians 1:21–29
Gospel: Luke 10:38–42

CALL TO WORSHIP
The Holy One prepares a place for us
and welcomes us to this time of worship.
We come with our anxiety and distractions,
wanting to be free of their oppression.
God counts each person precious and irreplaceable,
a unique creation, beloved and valued.
We would be rid of hostility and estrangement,
that we might be reconciled to God.
God meets us where we are
and inspires us by what we may become.
We come, daring to seek what we need,
believing the promises of God.

INVOCATION
Creator of all things, form us anew in the likeness of Christ. Open up to us possibilities we cannot imagine, and free us from self-imposed limitations. Help us explore the depths of faith and the heights of possibility, for wherever we go, you are with us. Unite us now in empowering worship. Amen.

CALL TO CONFESSION
What have we done with God's wonderful creation, of which we are part? Why is the image of God so marred among us that people cannot recognize whose we are? Let us recount the good we have neglected, the evil we have allowed, and the hostility we have expressed that alienate us from our Creator and from one another.

PRAYER OF CONFESSION
Sometimes, O God, we can see no reason to join in prayers of confession, for we believe we are the faithful ones, doing the right things. At other times we despair at our attitudes, our stinging words, our insensitivity to the feelings and needs of others. We live as if the world revolved around us, and soon become alienated from one another and from you. Our hostility leads to evil deeds and evil neglect. Forgive our anxiety and distractions, so we can focus once more on your intentions for us and mature daily. In Christ Jesus. Amen.

ASSURANCE OF FORGIVENESS

When we awake from our sin we realize that we are still with God. In Jesus Christ our reconciliation with God has already occurred. Forgiveness is real; we have received from God a new spirit. Let us continue in the faith, stable and steadfast, not shifting from the hope of the gospel. God reveals through us the good news in which we can grow and mature.

COLLECT

We come, O God, to sit at the feet of Jesus, seeking wisdom, energy, and inspiration. Sharpen our listening skills, for your thoughts are precious to us and in your way we find life. Reveal again your wonderful works that frame and expand our lives. Feed us and sustain our courage in the face of all life's troubles and toil. Amen.

OFFERTORY INVITATION

Throughout our lives we have depended on the generosity of others: parents, friends, teachers, church leaders, strangers. In many expected and unexpected ways God has provided for us, and we have been blessed. Now we can show our gratitude by sharing our abundance, even to the extent of suffering if need be, that our sisters and brothers may be rescued and given life.

OFFERTORY PRAYER

From our wealth we would equip all your saints for ministry, gracious God. Grant fulfillment to those whose lives seem incomplete, inspiration to your prophets, and purposeful activity to those who labor day by day in tasks that seem routine. May our gifts and all our efforts make known the riches of your glory. Amen.

COMMISSION AND BLESSING

Go forth to serve, as you are able,
but do not be distracted in your serving.
  We want to grow in faith, stable and steadfast,
  continuing in the hope of the gospel we have received.
Seek refreshment and nurture in quiet times,
when you can listen to the thoughts of God.
  How precious to us is the wisdom of God
  in which we can mature as followers of Christ.
Wonderful are the works of God in you,
and precious are all the days God grants you.
  In us the word of God comes alive anew
  and the wisdom of God inspires and teaches.
Amen.   Amen.

(See hymn No. 75.)

Pentecost 10
(July 24–30)

Old Testament: 2 Kings 5:1–15
Psalm 21:1–7
Epistle: Colossians 2:6–15
Gospel: Luke 11:1–13

CALL TO WORSHIP
Ask, and it will be given you; seek, and you will find;
knock, and doors will be opened to you.
Those who ask receive, and one who seeks finds,
and to those who knock it will be opened.
Come to praise the responsive love of God,
who meets us in our need, where we are.
We come, rejoicing in God's presence with us
and trusting God's steadfast love to direct us.
Seek the Holy Spirit to guide and protect;
God will give the Spirit to those who ask.
We who know how to give gifts to our children
are confident of God's gifts to us.

INVOCATION
Teach us to pray, loving God, that the longing of our hearts might find words, and the intent of our spirits result in faithful deeds. We would not dictate the manner of your appearance among us, but would be alert and receptive to your surprises. Prepare us in this hour for the joy of your presence and the fullness of life you intend. Amen.

CALL TO CONFESSION
Are we sometimes enraged because God does not do things our way? Do we reject God's children whose appearances or beliefs or practices differ from our own? Do we use power unfairly? Surely we have much to confess before the Ruler of the universe, as we seek forgiveness and newness of life.

PRAYER OF CONFESSION
Ruler of all worlds, we have tried to take charge of the earth as if it were ours to destroy. We have devoured its resources, tricked others out of their rightful claims, and deceived ourselves into believing that our ways are just. We have fallen prey to human traditions and philosophies that deny the fullness of life in Christ. Our lives do not acknowledge the

authority of Jesus Christ in our midst, for we choose to claim only those teachings we like and to practice only a few that are convenient and harmless. Forgive us, mighty God, and turn us from our destructive ways. Amen.

ASSURANCE OF FORGIVENESS
Buried with Christ in baptism, you have been raised with Christ through faith in the working of God, who raised Christ from the dead. God forgives our sin and makes us alive with Christ. God cancels the claims of the law against us, freeing us to accept newness of life. As we forgive those who are indebted to us we can realize the pardon God offers us. The gift of the Holy Spirit comes to God's children who ask. Rejoice in your new life in the Spirit.

COLLECT
Open to us your Word, gracious God, as we ask and seek and knock. Wash us in the fountain of your truth, that we may be clean and trust in your mercy. Bless us with fullness of life, and make us glad in your presence. We join in thanksgiving for all the gifts of your love. Amen.

OFFERTORY INVITATION
All our wealth cannot buy the mercy and favor of God. Yet God is pleased to use our gifts to spread good news that love is at the heart of the universe. In grateful response to God's love we bring our offerings of time and treasure, recognizing also the untapped talents we are called to invest in ministry.

OFFERTORY PRAYER
For your healing love, for the goodly blessings we enjoy, for life itself, we give thanks with these tokens of gratitude. Dwell in us, that we may be moved to make all of life an offering to your steadfast love. May we learn to give good gifts to all your children who need what we have to offer. Multiply our efforts to be faithful as you add others to our family of faith, in Christ's name. Amen.

COMMISSION AND BLESSING
Take the good gifts of this hour into the world
to use in your own life and to share.
   As the Holy Spirit has blessed us with new life,
   we seek to be a blessing to others.
Receive God's healing power day by day
as you take time for thought and prayers.
   In the strength Christ gives we reach out
   with love and forgiveness to our neighbors.
God grant you new life, today and always;

the steadfast love of God goes with you everywhere.
We receive all God's gifts with joy
as we celebrate the glory and majesty of God.
Amen.   **Amen.**

(See hymns No. 76 and No. 113.)

Pentecost 11
(July 31–August 6)

Old Testament: 2 Kings 13:14–20a
Psalm 28
Epistle: Colossians 3:1–11
Gospel: Luke 12:13–21

CALL TO WORSHIP
The world calls: eat, drink, and be merry;
take your ease; enjoy what you have accumulated.
But God calls: seek the things that are above;
know the glory of Christ, who is our Life.
Anger, wrath, malice, slander, and foul talk are of the earth.
Covetousness, fornication, evil desires, and lies mark idolatry.
But God offers us a new nature in Christ,
being renewed after the image of our Creator.
The world makes distinctions between Jew and Greek,
slave and free, those under the law and those who are not
But in Christ all are one and all are welcome;
there are no distinctions; we come to worship.

INVOCATION
We lift our hands toward your most holy sanctuary, God of all people,
praying that you will respond to our faithfulness. Hear the voice of our
supplication, for we are oppressed by some who do not honor your way.
Shield us from them, and give us strength to sing your song. We trust you
to give refuge and be our shepherd. Amen.

CALL TO CONFESSION
Before the majesty of God we know we are not as righteous as we had
imagined. We are mired in the popular views and practices of earth,
where we seek to be better than others, not sisters and brothers to them.
We have become rich in things and poor in soul. Let us confess our need
for forgiveness.

PRAYER OF CONFESSION

Gracious God, you have given us a heritage, and we have grasped it for ourselves, seeking to exclude those whom we judge less worthy. We have coveted what others have, and have hoarded what you entrust to us. Truthfulness eludes us, and anger rises easily within and among us. In our self-concern and our misuse of others there is idolatry. Spare your wrath, O God, and come to re-create us. We cannot put off the old nature and its practices without your help. Amen.

ASSURANCE OF FORGIVENESS

God has already acted in Jesus Christ to renew us after the image of our Creator. Christ lives in us, ready to lift our thoughts above. We are anointed with a new spirit and equipped with arrows of victory over our old ways. Let us trust God and marvel at what God is already accomplishing among us.

COLLECT

Lead us, O God, to appreciate the plenty you have entrusted to us and to ponder the meaning of this bounty for our shared life of faith. As you have raised us with Christ, help us to think, not according to our society's agenda, but as people already living in your realm, where all are loved and valued, and honesty reigns. May we hear your prophets when they have a word from you for our day. Amen.

OFFERTORY INVITATION

If our lives were to end tonight, would we be prepared to give good account of our stewardship? Or are we still pulling down our barns to build larger ones, while God says, "Fool! . . . the things you have prepared, whose will they be?" Let us share our treasures.

OFFERTORY PRAYER

These gifts represent the work of our hands: the abilities you have given us and our efforts to use them well. We share them here to support one another in our efforts to hear your will and do it. Help us as a church to make a faithful witness out of love for one another and you, and in service to the whole world. Amen.

COMMISSION AND BLESSING

Face the world a renewed people,
living in new and creative ways in Christ.
We dare to be faithful, pure, and generous,
meeting others with open delight in them.
Greet one another as sisters and brothers
who delight in bringing out each other's best.
We want to be honest, caring, and kind,
treating our neighbors as we would treat Jesus.

Reach out, not for what you can take, but give,
knowing the least of God's children also contribute.
We commit ourselves to Christ's way,
in which all know they are equally valued by God.
Amen.   **Amen.**

(See hymns No. 77 and No. 78.)

Pentecost 12
(August 7–13)

Old Testament: Jeremiah 18:1–11
Psalm 14
Epistle: Hebrews 11:1–3, 8–19
Gospel: Luke 12:32–40

CALL TO WORSHIP
Be watchful and ready;
the Human One is coming at an unexpected hour.
We are ready for Jesus Christ to enter our lives;
we would be servants and disciples.
You are offered a place in God's dominion,
a dwelling place in the community where God rules.
God's realm is coming and is already here.
We are becoming whom God wants us to be.
Faith is the assurance of things hoped for,
the conviction of things not seen.
The world was created by the Word of God,
made out of things that do not appear.

INVOCATION
Gracious God, we seek a homeland with you, where your promises find fulfillment and our intentions are faithfully lived. Mold us in your perfect design in this hour. Help us to listen carefully and act wisely. Keep us alert to discern your purposes in all we do. Amen.

CALL TO CONFESSION
Return, everyone, from your evil ways; amend your thinking and your doing. The foolish say in their hearts, "There is no God." They have gone astray and are corrupt. Sometimes that is our story, and we need to admit it. Let us confess our sin.

PRAYER OF CONFESSION
Amazing God, we do not think of ourselves as evil, yet we eat up your people as we eat bread. The poor are exploited by us more than helped. We declare our intention to build and instead tear down and destroy. We resolve to be alert to your presence and then sleep through the challenges you set before us. Forgive the sins we recognize and confess, and also the evil that lurks, unknown, within and among us. Amen.

ASSURANCE OF FORGIVENESS
Fear not, it is God's intention to forgive and to grant us opportunities to participate in God's realm. Trust God to mold a new you and a new world. God is within and among us, empowering us to take charge of our thoughts and deeds and to turn away from evil. The God in us delivers us from all that dehumanizes and diminishes our possibilities for fulfilling service. Praise God that today we can realize our best.

COLLECT
We are ready, O God, to open the doors of our lives to your transforming word and empowering presence. We believe you are ready to build and plant among us, shaping new realities for your faithful people. Turn us away from the foolishness of our doubts and the corruption of selfish deeds, that we may rejoice in your promises. Strengthen our convictions and increase our hope. Amen.

OFFERTORY INVITATION
What shall we give up for the reign of God's love among people? Jesus challenged: Sell your possessions and give alms, for where your treasure is, there will your heart be also. Let us invest ourselves in those causes in which we believe, through our offerings and our stewardship of all the gifts of God in our charge.

OFFERTORY PRAYER
With joy and gladness we dedicate our treasure and our hearts to celebrate your reign within us and in the community of your faithful people. Reshape us in your image and use us, we pray, to extend your love to all we meet, and to sisters and brothers we will never know. Amen.

COMMISSION AND BLESSING
God is still creating and re-creating in our world,
and we are privileged to participate in God's activity.
  **With faith and hope we venture forth with God,
  sensing anew our place in God's plans.**
Dare to obey, as did our spiritual ancestors,
for obedience to God is the road to perfect freedom.
  We are ready to test God's promises

and to rely on God's deliverance and blessing.
Seek after God with all your heart,
that you may act wisely and serve lovingly.
We invest our treasure and our hearts
in the life and mission to which the church is called.
Amen.   **Amen.**

(See hymns No. 79 and No. 80.)

Pentecost 13
(August 14–20)

Old Testament: Jeremiah 20:7–13
Psalm 10:12–18
Epistle: Hebrews 12:1–2, 12–17
Gospel: Luke 12:49–56

CALL TO WORSHIP
Come, you fearful and you faithful;
God dwells with you, not with your persecutors.
God sees our hearts and minds;
God knows the causes to which we are committed.
Sing to God; praise God all the day long;
God delivers the needy from the hand of evildoers.
We must speak up in God's name,
for God's Word is like a burning fire in our bones.
God rules forever and ever, though nations perish
and fires of division are cast upon the earth.
God hears the desires of the meek
and brings justice and strength to the oppressed.

INVOCATION
Sometimes, O God, we feel far from you. We feel deceived and mocked,
and powerless to respond. We are depressed by all we see around us in
your world and by your seeming lack of response to the evil that op-
presses so many. We suspect that people are out to get us, and they seem
to have no regard for your truth. We are denounced for our faith, even by
those who are closest to us. The convictions by which we seek unity seem
to divide us instead. Come, O God, to interpret our times to us and give
us strength to live in them. Amen.

CALL TO CONFESSION
The sins of others are apparent to us. Our own are somewhat hidden.

Sometimes we think that God should ask us for forgiveness, instead of the other way around. How easily bitterness overtakes us, clouding our sight, dulling our ears, and blocking our compassion. As individuals, and as a church, we seek the forgiveness that opens channels of communication and puts us in touch with a love far greater than any we can muster. Let us pray.

PRAYER OF CONFESSION
Loving God, our pride is hurt, and we want to lash out at those who oppose us. We want vengeance for all who have violated us or others too weak to defend themselves. Forgive us, God, for willing their hurt and destruction. What we desire for ourselves we seek also for them—the removal of anger and pain and violence—so all of us can begin to know your peace. Heal us, O God, so we have something to offer those whom we seek to help. Amen.

ASSURANCE OF FORGIVENESS
God tries the righteous and delivers the needy from the hands of evil-doers. God's ear is inclined to hear the desires of the meek and to strengthen their hearts. Lift your drooping hand and strengthen your weak knees. God is forgiving you and equipping you to live among the divisions of this world.

COLLECT
Help us, O God, to read your signs through the scriptures and in our everyday world. Surround us with that cloud of witnesses who can inspire us. Put us in touch once more with Jesus Christ, the pioneer and perfecter of our faith, who endured the cross with triumphant joy. Amen.

OFFERTORY INVITATION
Forget not the afflicted, the orphan, and the oppressed. God calls us to give attention and help to the needy. We are summoned to give account of our stewardship and of our efforts on their behalf. Let us worship God with offerings of self and substance to make faithful witness to the gospel.

OFFERTORY PRAYER
Despite all the distractions, we cannot avoid giving witness to the gospel. Your good news is a fire within us that cannot be put out. Use these gifts to strengthen the fainthearted and support the weak. We commit ourselves anew to strive for peace with all people. Amen.

COMMISSION AND BLESSING
Return to families, work, and leisure,
committed to the way of justice and peace.
   **We want to discern God's word and signs,
      that we may see clearly and serve faithfully.**
Be alert to the cloud of witnesses God sends,

That you may be empowered to run a good race.
We want to work with God and God's people
for a better world, responsive to truth.
God sees your hearts and minds
and will provide all the help you seek and need.
The grace of God rests on us
and will provide our vision and empowerment.
Amen. **Amen.**

(See hymn No. 81.)

Pentecost 14
(August 21–27)

Old Testament: Jeremiah 28:1–9
Psalm 84
Epistle: Hebrews 12:18–29
Gospel: Luke 13:22–30

CALL TO WORSHIP
Come from east and west, north and south;
join in songs of praise to the living God.
How lovely is your dwelling place, O God of hosts!
My soul longs, yea, faints for the courts of God.
God breaks the yokes of oppressors
and brings people back from their exile.
A day in your courts, O God,
is better than a thousand elsewhere.
God sent Jesus as mediator of a new covenant
to bring us all to God's way of peace.
I would rather be a doorkeeper in the house of my God
than dwell in the tents of wickedness.

INVOCATION
We come before you, God of hosts, in reverence and awe, for you are a consuming Fire. You are far greater than we can imagine, judging, transforming, and upholding. Grant us to enter by the narrow door and to walk uprightly today and every day. Bless our time together, that we may be a blessing to others we meet along life's way. Amen.

CALL TO CONFESSION
Warnings fall on deaf ears. We put off changes we know we should make. We resist the idea that we are sinners, despite the nagging suspicion that

our lives are not all they are intended to be. Come now to the only One who can purify and make whole. Let us admit before God our failures and our need.

PRAYER OF CONFESSION

Bring us back into true communion with you, O God, for we have broken covenant and wandered far from your truth. We have exiled ourselves from your guidance and direction, trying to chart our own course in our own way. We have not trusted you or believed that your way of peace is the way to life. Turn us around today, God, lest we come to destruction. Save us from ourselves. We want to be in tune with the truth you have created. Amen.

ASSURANCE OF FORGIVENESS

You have come to the city of the living God, to the assembly of the firstborn in heaven, to the God whose judgments are just and perfect. To all who seek to walk uprightly God offers forgiveness and fulfillment. But to some who put off commitment God may say, "I do not know you. Depart from me, all you workers of iniquity." God grant that the doors to life may open to us, for we truly want the new day God offers.

COLLECT

We are ready to listen, O God, for one who is speaking your Word. May the strength of your living presence permeate this assembly as we listen, beyond words, to the movement of your Spirit in our midst. Break the yokes that bind us to old ways, that we may hear and heed the prophets' word of peace. Amen.

OFFERTORY INVITATION

Do not miss the opportunity to give that is ours today. We are a free people, who share from a deep sense of gratitude, not out of compulsion. We have found a home with God, which we would humbly offer to other people, a strength in the service of God, which is a joy to share. We are amazed at the outpouring of good things from the hand of God. What a privilege now to be givers ourselves.

OFFERTORY PRAYER

For the joy of sharing in your new covenant in Jesus Christ and being a part of your unshakable realm in our midst, we give thanks, mighty God. For turning our self-concerned values upside down so love may become the rule of life, we rejoice with hymns of gratitude. For your generous gifts to us, which we now return and dedicate to your service, we sing our appreciation and praise. Amen.

COMMISSION AND BLESSING

Go now to the east and west, the north and south,
to live the peace of God among its skeptics.

We carry the blessing of the Almighty
among those who are not yet free to love.
No one need live in exile, a stranger to God's realm;
God is in the midst of us, creating and re-creating.
In God's love we go from strength to strength,
for we are privileged to share in God's work.
Find the strength for your service in this house of prayer
and in your daily walk and talk with God.
Our hearts and flesh sing for joy to the living God.
God pours out good things on us day by day.
Amen.   Amen.

(See hymn No. 82.)

Pentecost 15
(August 28–September 3)

Old Testament: Ezekiel 18:1–9, 25–29
           Psalm 15
Epistle: Hebrews 13:1–8
Gospel: Luke 14:7–14

CALL TO WORSHIP
Come in humble gratitude and longing
to sit at the feet of the Divine Majesty.
   We come, seeking the righteousness of God,
   hardly daring to stand in God's presence.
All are invited to the feast of God;
come all you poor, maimed, lame, and blind.
   How shall we sojourn in the tents of God,
   or dwell on God's holy hill?
Jesus Christ bids us come, today and forever,
as people were summond long ago.
   We will not fear what people may do or say,
   for the Sovereign God, our helper, welcomes us.

INVOCATION
Across the generations we gather, Holy God, to learn your way, to hear
your judgment, and to renew our relationship with you and one another.
We come, seeking the faith to those who have gone before us in righteousness and truth. Lead us by your Word to walk in your statutes and
observe your ordinances. Amen.

CALL TO CONFESSION

We are a people of faith who know that God gives us responsibility for our own conduct. The way we treat others reflects on our relationship with God. We are called to be just, but beyond that to feel with others what they are suffering, and to be kind. We are far from this ideal and so come to confess our need.

PRAYER OF CONFESSION

Gracious God, how can we turn from the immorality that plagues us on every side? We pursue our own gain and selfish pleasure without regard to the cost to others. In our cleverness we rob others unwittingly. We love money and use people. Our tongues twist the truth and tear down our neighbors. We break commitments when our feelings change. In setting personal goals we build idols that separate us from you. O God, show us the destructiveness of our ways and divert us from the calamity we are creating. O God, we implore your help as we seek to change our ways. Amen.

ASSURANCE OF FORGIVENESS

We are assured that when we turn away from the wickedness we have committed and do what is lawful and right, we will be saved. Therefore, having considered and reversed the direction of our lives, we will surely live, by God's grace. Let us walk blamelessly before God, speaking truth from the heart and reaching out to others in humble compassion.

COLLECT

Challenge us again with a word that points us beyond where we are in the direction you would have us go. Link us together, parents and children of every generation, in the quest for righteous living. Reveal to us the depths of love, and teach us truly to love one another. Help us to reach out to those from whom we can expect no thanks or return favors. Amen.

OFFERTORY INVITATION

Our God has been very generous with us, forgiving us again and again, and providing us with resources beyond our own need. We are cautioned to keep our lives free from the love of money and to be content with what we have. God will not fail or forsake us as we divide our portion with others. Let us give, with thanks.

OFFERTORY PRAYER

Great God, who has given us all things, grant us discernment to use well all that we receive from your hands. May we as individuals and as a church be faithful in our investment of the resources entrusted to us, showing hospitality to strangers, reaching out to those in prison, and standing with those who are abused and mistreated, in Jesus' name. Amen.

COMMISSION AND BLESSING

Move out, in the faith of your ancestors,
to honor and love all God's children.
Jesus Christ continues to walk with us,
the same yesterday, today and forever.
Empowered by God's forgiving love in Christ,
recognize all other people as sisters and brothers.
We do not aspire to rule over others
or to sit in high places of honor.
God offers life abundant to those who shun iniquity
and seek to walk in the ways of justice and peace.
We look to our Creator for daily guidance;
God is our helper; we will not be afraid.
Amen.   **Amen.**

(See hymn No. 83.)

Pentecost 16
(September 4–10)

Old Testament: Ezekiel 33:1–11
                 Psalm 94:12–22
Epistle: Philemon 1:1–20
                 Hebrews 13:8–16, 20–21 (alt.)
Gospel: Luke 14:25–33

CALL TO WORSHIP

Grace to you and peace from God our Father and Mother
and from the Sovereign Jesus Christ.
Because we have been strengthened by the grace of God
we are here to offer our sacrifices of praise.
God will not forsake or abandon us,
but promises justice to the upright of heart.
If God had not been our help,
our souls would have dwelt in silence.
God is our stronghold and refuge;
the steadfast love of God upholds us.
When the cares of our hearts are many
the consolations of God cheer our souls.

INVOCATION

Although you are with us every day, God of all worlds, we come together to know your presence more fully in this special place set aside for worshiping you. We are here not only to be taught, but also to be chastened. We are here not only to remember, but also to be renewed. We are here not only to celebrate our freedom, but also to be strengthened in the living out of our responsibilities. May our worship be genuine and our discipleship complete. Amen.

CALL TO CONFESSION
The way of life God sets before us is not easy. The expectations God has of us challenge all that is superficial and routine. We are called to grow in faith, and to share it, to be ambassadors for Christ in our daily lives, to be sentries who sound a warning against the wickedness we see around us. Let us confess how limited our response has been.

PRAYER OF CONFESSION
O God, our transgressions and our sins are upon us, and we waste away because of them. We see evil all around us, but we do not oppose it, and sometimes we are part of it. We have not shared the judgment and warnings you make plain to us because we do not wish to offend or seem self-righteous. The blood of others is on our hands, and that is even more frightening than our personal guilt. O God, how can we be forgiven and find the life you intend? Amen.

ASSURANCE OF FORGIVENESS
As I live, says the Sovereign God, I have no pleasure in the death of the wicked, but that the wicked turn from their ways and live. God does not abandon us in our failures or give up on us when we go our own way. When, by our neglect, we ally ourselves with systems and institutions that oppress, God calls us to new responsibilities, teaches us new ways, and strengthens us by grace we do not deserve. We are forgiven; let us live and serve as forgiven people.

COLLECT
Rescue us from our slavery, Sovereign God, so we may be your ambassadors, refreshing the hearts of your saints. Teach us when to blow the trumpet on your behalf, and how to bear the abuse Jesus endured. May the church be alive in our homes and in this sanctuary, as we listen daily for your word of truth. Amen.

OFFERTORY INVITATION
Do not neglect to do good and to share what you have, for such sacrifices are pleasing to God. We bring our gifts because God has enabled our sharing and calls us to reach out with good news for others. We cannot be disciples if we cling to our possessions. Therefore, we make these offerings of gratitude of our own free will, in response to God's love in Christ.

OFFERTORY PRAYER

For the devotion of our ancestors who kept faith alive and passed it on to us, for neighbors and friends who remember us in their prayers, for the church that provides nurture and support for the work of ministry that engages us all, we give thanks. Bless and multiply these gifts, that the world may be served. Amen.

COMMISSION AND BLESSING

The God of peace go with you into the world,
equipping you for the work God calls you to do.
Jesus Christ, the great shepherd,
lives with us in eternal covenant.
Listen for the will of God and dare to follow it,
that God may be praised in the good you do.
We are ambassadors for Jesus Christ,
that the hearts of saints may be refreshed through us.
Grace to you and peace from God our Father and Mother,
and from the Sovereign Jesus Christ.
Discipleship is more important to us than all else;
we take up our own cross to follow where Christ leads.
Amen.   Amen.

(See hymns No. 84 and No. 85.)

Pentecost 17
(September 11–17)

Old Testament: Hosea 4:1–3; 5:15—6:6
            Psalm 77:11–20
Epistle: 1 Timothy 1:12–17
Gospel: Luke 15:1–10

CALL TO WORSHIP

Let us return to God who heals and binds up,
that we may recall God's constant presence.
We will call to mind the deeds of God
and remember God's wonders of old.
Press on to know the God of lightning and thunder,
whose judgments crash in on our murderous ways.
God has redeemed our ancestors
and led them gently like a flock.
God pursues us wherever we go

and searches for us when we are lost.
We rejoice in God's steadfast love
that draws us near in the company of friends.

INVOCATION

Immortal, Invisible, God over all, we quake before your creative energy, so far beyond our knowing and evident beyond our willingness to perceive. We live in your presence, whether or not we acknowledge you, and we are subject to your rule, whether or not we choose to follow your way. Encounter us in this hour, that we may not mistake our prejudices and preferences for your will. Through Christ. Amen.

CALL TO CONFESSION

Christ came into the world to save sinners. This news is not just for other people. It is for you and me, for we are the ones whose knowledge of God has failed to grow and whose faithfulness is suspect. We are the lost ones whom God seeks. Let us pray.

PRAYER OF CONFESSION

O God, we prefer to sit in judgment of others rather than look at our own misdeeds. We can see lying, killing, stealing, and adultery when others do it, but we find it hard to identify such sins in ourselves. We are quite content to wander away, following our own pursuits, until we find ourselves in difficulty. Then we expect you to rescue us. O God, have mercy. Take away the burden of guilt we rightly carry, and raise us up to a new life in which we have strength to resist temptation and to do your will. Amen.

ASSURANCE OF FORGIVENESS

You have already received the mercy God pours out in Christ Jesus. God revives us in our weariness and raises us up to a new life. God heals our brokenness, binds up our wounds, and patiently teaches us a new and better way. The grace of God overflows, so you may know faith and love. Receive God's gifts with joy!

COLLECT

We rejoice, loving God, that you receive sinners and join us as a real and available presence wherever we are. Thank you for valuing us as if you had no other concern and for granting us strength to serve you. We return to you now, with all our attention, that we may know your Word and live it. Amen.

OFFERTORY INVITATION

God seeks our steadfast love rather than ritual deeds, our growth in knowledge and relationship to our Creator more than token contributions that only conceal from ourselves the poverty of our commitment. Come, then, to make a true offering that calls forth a dedication of self not before realized.

OFFERTORY PRAYER

Thank you, God, for your wonderful creation that continues to unfold before our eyes. Grateful that you have brought us to this hour, we accept your mercy and seek to respond to others with the generosity you have shown us. Receive our offerings as symbols of our larger commitment as undershepherds and disciples. We would join you in celebrating each addition and each return to the family of faith. Amen.

COMMISSION AND BLESSING

Our God, who celebrates who we are,
turns us from ourselves to a world in need.
We go out to share the patience of God
with those who usually exasperate us.
Christ appoints us to serve in difficult places,
challenging the false values of our world.
We go out to live what we profess
and to profess what we really believe.
God rejoices in the lost who are found
and strengthens us with overflowing mercy and grace.
We venture into new experiences
in the confidence that God cares for us.
Amen.   Amen.

(See hymns No. 86 and No. 87.)

Pentecost 18
(September 18–24)

Old Testament: Hosea 11:1–11
              Psalm 107:1–9
Epistle: 1 Timothy 2:1–7
Gospel: Luke 16:1–13

CALL TO WORSHIP

God calls us from whatever oppression we face;
cry out to God in your time of trouble.
God loves us even when we rebel
and reaches out to us while we are fleeing from God.
Praise the goodness of God; give thanks,
for God's steadfast love endures forever.
God does not give up on us or forsake us,
for God is the Holy One in our midst.

The compassion of God is warm and tender;
God heals us again and again beyond our knowing.
  God satisfies the thirsty with living water
  and fills the hungry with good things.

INVOCATION
Our voices join in supplication for all who gather here and for all your children. As we are blessed by your presence, bless also your people gathered in other places and all who are alone. May the rulers of all nations be open to your authority and responsive to universal realities. Purge us all of greed and party spirit and make of us honest and faithful stewards of your good earth. In Jesus' name. Amen.

CALL TO CONFESSION
When we are called to give account of our management of God's resources, we become aware of our acquisitive nature and the exploitation of much that is entrusted to our care-taking. Let us be honest with God and with one another as we admit our fondness for privilege and our habit of using others for our own ends. Join me in confessing our sin.

PRAYER OF CONFESSION
Deliver us, gracious God, from the stress of our unfaithfulness. You are the Source of all we have and all we are, yet we turn away from you and ignore you as if there were no reality beyond ourselves. We waste all that you have entrusted to us and destroy resources meant for future generations. We have become so enslaved to things that we cannot serve you with integrity and wholeness. Forgive us, O God, and rescue us from this way of death. Amen.

ASSURANCE OF FORGIVENESS
In warmth and tender compassion God responds to us, not with anger that is justified from a human point of view, but with love that is unmerited. God does not seek to destroy us, but to lift us up in steadfast love to recognize a new and better way. It is God's will that all people be saved and find fulfillment in a quiet and peaceable life, godly and respectful in every way. You are freed from your past to serve the living God.

COLLECT
Equip us by your word to be faithful in little things, that we may grow into a much more extensive stewardship. Show us the tasks to which you appoint us, and grant us the courage and determination to fulfill our assignment. We recognize that we are still little children, learning to walk. Be with us as a Parent to encourage us along the way and lift us up when we fall. We need the warmth of your love every day. Amen.

OFFERTORY INVITATION

We who burn incense to the idols of our common life are called instead to offer sacrifices of self and the fruit of our labor on the altar of the one true God. Give thanks to God whose steadfast love endures forever. Give practical expression of your gratitude to the One who satisfies your hunger and thirst every day.

OFFERTORY PRAYER

Accept, we pray, this expression of our stewardship. By this offering we would renew our pledge to acknowledge you in all things and serve you with all we have. May we handle faithfully the wealth you have given us, so we may also relate with integrity to people whose lives touch our own and to unseen sisters and brothers who need our help, in Christ. Amen.

COMMISSION AND BLESSING

Go out to use the wisdom of this world
to the honor and glory of the living God.
We would serve God, and not mammon.
May our love be faithful and our caring true.
Be stewards of your time and all you possess,
investing yourself for the salvation of all people.
We will testify to God's steadfast love
and rejoice in God's wonderful works to humankind.
God promises deliverance in times of distress
and arms of love when help is needed.
We join in prayers for one another
and for all who seek to lead in our world.
Amen.   Amen.

(See hymn No. 88.)

Pentecost 19
(September 25–October 1)

Old Testament: Joel 2:23–30
              Psalm 107:1, 33–43
Epistle: 1 Timothy 6:6–19
Gospel: Luke 16:19–31

CALL TO WORSHIP

God, who dwells in unapproachable light,
is present and available to us here and now.
God, who is more than we can ever imagine,

reveals to us, here and now, glimpses of eternity.
We are all children of one God, who loves us all,
poor and rich, old and young, powerless and powerful.
God richly furnishes us with everything to enjoy
and calls us to live for the good of all.
Let us be glad and rejoice in our God.
Let us praise God, who deals wondrously with us.
Give thanks to God, for God is good;
God's steadfast love endures forever!

INVOCATION

Source of all goodness, we know we have been blessed with abundant opportunities. Everything necessary for life in all its fullness has been made available to us. You have dealt wondrously with us. Pour out on us now, we pray, an extra measure of your spirit to expand our vision, enlarge our dreams, and help us to speak and live your truth. Amen.

CALL TO CONFESSION

Desiring to be rich in the things of this world, we fall into temptation. Our craving for more and more things distorts our priorities. How can we aim at righteousness, godliness, faith, love, steadfastness, gentleness when we are worried about possessions? Let us dare to examine ourselves before God, from whom comes everything we enjoy.

PRAYER OF CONFESSION

O God, we brought nothing into the world and can take nothing out of it. Yet, while we are here, the things of this world become terribly important to us. We find it hard to believe your promises that we will eat in plenty and be satisfied, for we know of many for whom this is not true. We love money and the things money can buy. We want to feast on the abundance of this earth. We think that when we are truly rich we can become generous, but we never have enough to risk truly liberal sharing. O God, if this is keeping us from you, show us a better way. Give us a new perspective from which to view what is really important in life. Have mercy on us, we pray. Amen.

ASSURANCE OF FORGIVENESS

God pours contempt on princes but raises the needy out of affliction. When we recognize our need and seek God's help we can count on God's gifts. God deals wondrously with all of us, pouring out spiritual blessings that help us deal with life as it is. Relationships with God and with our sisters and brothers become more important to us when we welcome Jesus Christ into our lives. Let us be the church, the Body of Christ in our world!

COLLECT

Remove, O God, the chasm we have created between ourselves and your will for all people. Speak through the scriptures, so we may hear the cries of the poor, oppressed, and troubled. Set our hopes on you and focus our concern on what is most important in your eternal purposes. Grant us wisdom to heed your Word and to consider, above all else, your steadfast love. Pour out your spirit to bring us new life. Amen.

OFFERTORY INVITATION

God has dealt wondrously with us. How shall we respond? We receive living water when life seems like a desert. We are fed and clothed from the abundance God makes possible. We are called to do good, to be rich in good deeds, to be liberal and generous. Let us respond as people who see and feel the plight of sisters and brothers whom we have the resources to help.

OFFERTORY PRAYER

O God, you have made us very rich, and we are grateful for your trust in us. With our offerings we recognize the responsibility you place on us to be liberal and generous in our giving and in good deeds. We find it hard to leave behind our concern for getting ahead. Help us to trust you and truly to dedicate our all to your purposes, as we are able to discern them. Amen.

COMMISSION AND BLESSING

God has sustained and fed us here,
but God also confronts and challenges us.
  We cannot leave this place the same as we came,
  for God has encountered us here.
God offers comfort and contentment to those who trust,
but God also warns of the lure of riches.
  We cannot put our trust in things
  and still love God as first priority in life.
Dare to receive and walk in the Spirit,
believing the promises of God to provide for us.
  God has held us in steadfast love;
  we dare to trust God to walk with us and help us.
Amen.   **Amen.**

(See hymn No. 89.)

Pentecost 20
(October 2–8)

CALL TO WORSHIP
Come to God with whatever faith is yours;
seek good and not evil that you may live.
We come to rekindle the gift of God within us
and to re-examine our commitments and actions.
Seek the whole of truth, and God will be with you;
give heed to the way that is blameless.
We want to be faithful and to walk with integrity,
to give our best to the tasks God sets before us.
Grace, mercy, and peace be yours today,
from Creator, Christ, and Holy Spirit.
The triune God calls us to loyalty and justice
and gives us a spirit of love and self-control.

INVOCATION
Our timid spirits seek the empowerment of Christ's self-giving love as we listen for your Word to us, O God. We would remember one another in prayer, giving thanks for the heritage of faith that has brought us to this hour. May we serve you without expectation of reward and with enthusiasm for the truth entrusted to us by the Holy Spirit. Amen.

CALL TO CONFESSION
Who are those who trample on the poor, build ever larger houses, and provide for their own comfort and security as if these things were central to life? Who turns away from truth when its implications are costly? Who practices deceit or utters lies? Through your own words, or in the words we say together, confess your guilt to God, so its ravages can be halted.

PRAYER OF CONFESSION
O God, we have turned your justice to wormwood and betrayed the very people you have called on to help. We enjoy the fruits of others' labors without giving them just compensation. We pursue arrogant power to keep our privileges and practice deceit to gain our own ends. Save us, we pray, from our poor choices, our willful disobedience, and our unconscious denial of your way, through Christ. Amen.

ASSURANCE OF FORGIVENESS

Seek good and not evil, that you may live. God looks with favor on the faithful in the land. In Jesus Christ death is abolished and life and immortality are brought to light. We are saved by God's grace, not by our works, but what we do testifies to God's redeeming love within us. Let us receive with joy the gift of forgiveness, being empowered thereby to sing new songs of praise and thanksgiving.

COLLECT

Increase our faith, O God of revelation, that we may dare to deal with difficult matters. So fill us with your truth that we will not be ashamed to share its demands or its promises. If suffering must come, grant us insight and strength to endure. Point our thoughts beyond ourselves so we may know and serve you well for all your children. Amen.

OFFERTORY INVITATION

Let us come to this time of giving, not out of guilt, but in anticipation of the good we can do and of the joy to be experienced both by us and by those whom we help. May our offerings and our lives bear testimony to the purposes of God, revealed in Jesus Christ.

OFFERTORY PRAYER

May your truth be proclaimed through our offerings. May lives be changed as your light is shared. May our sisters and brothers feel the touch of your hand and find new hope in which to live. O God, may this high moment of giving be crowned with our renewed commitment to be servants of Jesus Christ, whose way we seek to follow. Amen.

COMMISSION AND BLESSING

Do not be ashamed to testify of your faith in God
or to suffer for the sake of the gospel.
    Our salvation points us to our holy calling,
    through which God's purpose may be realized.
The Holy Spirit entrusts you with God's truth
and sends you out to share it with joy.
    We know the One whom we have believed,
    and want to share the faith and love we have.
God looks with favor on those who are faithful.
May you continue in God's presence, in honest service.
    God has blessed us through our parents
    and through the power of love to transform.
Amen.   **Amen.**

(See hymn No. 90.)

Pentecost 21
(October 9–15)

Old Testament: Micah 1:2; 2:1–10
                 Psalm 26
Epistle: 2 Timothy 2:8–15
Gospel: Luke 17:11–19

CALL TO WORSHIP
From our busy world, with all its temptations,
we gather to listen and renew our commitment.
This is not a place of rest, but of refreshment;
in this community of faith we are challenged.
God's steadfast love is before our eyes;
let us walk in faithfulness before our Creator.
With Christ we are called to die, but also to live;
with Christ we can endure, that we may also reign.
God is faithful and ready to show mercy;
God restores and heals; let us give thanks.
Sing aloud a song of thanksgiving;
let us tell of all God's wondrous deeds.

INVOCATION
In confidence and trust we draw near to you once more, O God, that you may test our minds and hearts. We have sought to walk uprightly, with integrity in all we do. As we gather we begin to experience your glory in our midst. Hear our songs of thanksgiving as we testify to all you are doing for us. Amen.

CALL TO CONFESSION
God, who knows our every thought and deed, is surely a witness against us. God sees our wickedness, oppression, and pride. God knows how we preach what we do not practice. How shall we find forgiveness unless we face honestly the evil we condone and the good we neglect?

PRAYER OF CONFESSION   (KEITH KARAU)
There is more wickedness in us than we like to admit. We want what isn't ours. We are jealous of those who have more than we. We want to keep others in their places, lest they become more important. Sovereign God, have mercy on us. Let your Spirit move in and through us, that we might be forgiven and become responsible, caring disciples of Jesus. Amen.

ASSURANCE OF FORGIVENESS
In Christ, God offers mercy, forgiveness, and healing, even when we are

ungrateful. By faith we are made whole, that we might rise with Christ and serve with the faithful. Let us respond as people who know God's approval and seek to live up to it. Praise God!

COLLECT
How shall we grow in faith if we forget to express our gratitude? How shall we rise with Christ if we are not ready to die with Christ? How shall we hear your Word if we are ashamed to be seen with a Bible in our hands? How shall we trust you, God, if there is no integrity in us? O God, let us hear even the word we do not wish to hear, and the challenge we would just as soon forget. Amen.

OFFERTORY INVITATION
Sometimes it is when our portion in life is greatly reduced that we learn to be thankful for little things. Sometimes it is an unexpected blessing—a healing for which we could scarcely have hoped—that overwhelms us with gratitude. Whatever other good reasons you have for giving, this is primarily a time to say "thank you." We do this materially and with our lives.

OFFERTORY PRAYER
We praise you with our offerings and with time and effort devoted to your purposes, gracious God. By your mercy we have been healed and by your love we are blessed day by day. In Christ we have been introduced to life in its fullness. Grant us to enjoy simple things as Jesus did, and to live with others in mutual caring, respect, and helpfulness. We would live and endure with Jesus Christ. Amen.

COMMISSION AND BLESSING   (KEITH KARAU, ADAPTED)
God's word has begun our worship and praise;
now God's word launches our service.
   We are scattered in the world
   to share what we have discovered here.
God has been the actor in the drama of our lives;
now we are sent out to act in God's name.
   We go out to touch and heal
   in gratitude for what has been done for us.
May the blessing of God surround us;
may the strength of God uphold us.
   May the voice of God speak in and through us.
   May the will of God be accomplished among us.
Amen.   Amen.

(See hymns No. 91 and No. 92.)

Pentecost 22
(October 16–22)

Old Testament: Habakkuk 1:1–3; 2:1–4
Psalm 119:137–44
Epistle: 2 Timothy 3:14—4:5
Gospel: Luke 18:1–8

CALL TO WORSHIP
Come once more to learn of our God,
whose testimonies are righteous and faithful.
We are gathered to hear what God would say to us,
to catch the vision God places before humankind.
Turn away from those who teach what you want to hear
and listen instead for the truth of God.
We turn to the scriptures God inspired,
that we may be equipped for every good work.
Be persistent in your quest for God's precepts
and in your cries for help when God seems silent.
We seek to live by faith and hope
and to fulfill the ministry to which God calls us.

INVOCATION
(KEITH KARAU)

You hear us, all-listening One, when we pray. You come to us when we call out. You show us the right things to do and call us back when we have gone our own way. Open our hearts during this hour of worship, that we might discover afresh your righteous ways for our living. Help us to persist in our prayers and stand firm in working for the truth you are teaching. Come and be with us during this time of worship and praise. Amen.

CALL TO CONFESSION
(KEITH KARAU)

Some fall away and abandon the teachings of God; others of us only deceive ourselves, thinking we are righteous and good. During these moments God is helping us to look closely at ourselves, so we might see what we are meant to be. Let us confess our sinfulness.

PRAYER OF CONFESSION
(KEITH KARAU)

Righteous God, we distort far too easily the truth and wisdom you have set before us in life. We listen when it is easy; we ignore what is hard; we select what is convenient to hear and expedient to do; we give up when life is difficult. We find ways to feel good about our prejudices and make excuses for our failures. Holy One, have mercy on us. Set your truth firmly before us until we see and, seeing, become the people of Jesus' way. Amen.

ASSURANCE OF FORGIVENESS
We are assured that God will speedily vindicate those who persist in their prayers, who cry out to God in faith even in the midst of trouble and anguish, when violence and destruction seem to reign. We are forgiven by the One in whom we trust, who grants us a vision of what life is intended to be.

COLLECT
We come in faith to listen to sacred writings from the past, which you inspired, O God. Teach us, correct us, train us for the good works you would have us do. Grant us patience with one another, and with all your children, to go with our zeal for the truth. Amen.

OFFERTORY INVITATION
Growing people are giving people. Praying people have their horizons expanded, so they want to help less advantaged sisters and brothers People who have been forgiven want to express their gratitude. We are growing, praying, forgiven people who believe it is possible for individuals and groups and nations to change for the better. To that end we worship with our offerings.

OFFERTORY PRAYER
Because you have heard and answered our cries for help we give thanks Because you have granted us a measure of understanding we want to learn more. Because we have found your promises to be sure we want to share them with others. Because we have experienced the truth of the scriptures, and believe them to be a guide and correction for all of us, we commit ourselves anew to making them known. Stretch us and our offerings to do more than we would have thought possible, to extend the reign of Christ among us. Amen.

COMMISSION AND BLESSING
God has placed a vision before us
and bids us go to realize its fulfillment.
> **We will take our stand for righteousness**
> **and live according to the faith we have received.**
God equips us for every good work
through the inspiration of the scriptures.
> **We will remember the precepts of God**
> **whenever we feel belittled and afraid.**
God is faithful to us and ever available,
adding to the understanding of all who seek to learn.
> **We will seek God's truth above all lesser claims**
> **and share what we learn with patient enthusiasm.**
Amen.   Amen.

(See hymn No. 93.)

Pentecost 23
(October 23–29)

Old Testament: Zephaniah 3:1–9
Psalm 3
Epistle: 2 Timothy 4:6–8, 16–18
Gospel: Luke 18:9–14

CALL TO WORSHIP
In the name of God we welcome all who come.
trusting or faithless, faithful or rebellious.
We come because we know our lives are incomplete;
perhaps if we listen, there will be good news for us.
Seek the God of righteousness and justice,
who comes, unfailing as the dawn, every morning.
We wait for God to be revealed,
daring to open our lives to God's correction.
God, who greets us in the morning, sustains us
through the day and through the night.
We seek to call on the name of God
and to serve God with one accord.

INVOCATION
We cry aloud to you, O God, as we approach your holy hill in awe and reverence. Who can escape your judgment or stand before your righteous anger? Change our thoughts and our speech, and transform our actions. Melt our pretenses and false pride, that we might worship with genuine humility and openness to your correction. In the service of Christ Jesus Amen.

CALL TO CONFESSION
We are part of the cities that oppress, the people who listen to no voice but their own, the prophets who congratulate rather than correct, the priests who profane the sacred. It is against us that God's judgment comes. Who will repent and find life?

PRAYER OF CONFESSION
Sovereign God, it is hard to admit that all is not well with us, for we spend so much effort convincing ourselves and others of our significance. Even our religious practice is pursued more to cover over the blemishes than to heal our wounds and transform our actions. We trust in ourselves and the things we have accumulated rather than in unseen, eternal realities. Rescue us, O God, from the evil that has crept in to dominate our souls.

Deliver us from forces outside ourselves that have no claim on us and no ultimate power. God, be merciful to us, for we are sinners. Amen.

ASSURANCE OF FORGIVENESS

God cuts off the nations that go their own way, but to the cities that accept correction God offers a new day. The person who turns from the eager pursuit of corruption will know the re-ordering of life made possible in Jesus Christ. God delivers us from our enemies, stands by us in our weakness, and saves us for the heavenly dominion. Praise God, from whom all blessings come!

COLLECT

Stand by us, gracious God, fortifying us with your strength to hear and proclaim the message you set before us. Grant us the humility to see ourselves in a perspective larger than our self-concern. Let us hear words of judgment as surely as we discern reassurance and hope. Remold us according to your purposes, and sustain us in the face of trial and temptation, that others may be blessed, even through us. Amen.

OFFERTORY INVITATION

How shall we tithe for the service of God all that is already God's gift to us? How shall we share what is grossly misbalanced in our favor? Will we justify our greed, or seek justice for all? These questions will find answers, not in our words, but in our deeds. Let us give thanks and answers with our offerings.

OFFERTORY PRAYER

For your mercy when we least deserve it, for your understanding when we fail again in our best intentions, for your strength when there is nothing left within to sustain us, we give thanks, loving God. Our gifts express our dependence on you and our desire to further your reign among us. Bless and multiply our tithes and offerings. We pray in Jesus' name. Amen.

COMMISSION AND BLESSING

God sends us forth as equals,
saints and sinners, every one of us.
  We have been strengthened to fight the good fight,
  to finish the race, to keep the faith.
Go out to see life in new ways
because you have let God break through to you.
  We have been granted purity of speech
  and cleansing of our motives.
The God of mercy exalts the humble
and blesses all who respond in faith.
  Let us call on God's name every day

and respond as we are loved, in God's service.
Amen.   **Amen.**

(See hymn No. 94.)

Pentecost 24
(October 30–November 5)

Old Testament: Haggai 2:1–9
Psalm 65:1–8
Epistle: 2 Thessalonians 1:5–12
Gospel: Luke 19:1–10

CALL TO WORSHIP
Today salvation has come to this house of prayer;
receive this gift with gratitude and joy.
God's Spirit abides among us;
we will not fear, but will take courage.
God repays with affliction those who afflict others
and grants rest to those who are afflicted.
God fills us with good resolve,
that we may do the work of faith with power.
God invites us to this time of learning
to celebrate our mission to all people.
God sends us out to seek and save the lost.
May we become worthy to respond to this call.

INVOCATION
Gracious God, draw us near to experience your goodness. Abide among
us to still our fears, as heaven and earth are shaken. Grant us courage to
look at our world and its people in new ways, through the eyes of Jesus
Christ. Help us to see the potential transformation you envision for us,
and for sisters and brothers we are tempted to reject. Unite us all in
worship and praise. Amen.

CALL TO CONFESSION
All flesh is summoned before God on account of sins. Our continuing
pursuit of our own agenda, before all other considerations, may exclude
us from awareness of God's presence and bring us the punishment of
eternal destruction. We come to examine ourselves before God, not out of
fear, but with a vision of God's promises.

PRAYER OF CONFESSION

O God, despite our best intentions our sins prevail over us and our transgressions are many. The things of this world tempt us to defraud. We cut corners for our own advantage. The wrongs we could address do not move us to action. The gospel is not a priority with us, and Jesus Christ does not fit into our busy lives. O God, we shut you out and do not know you—not because you are unavailable, but because we do not seek you. Come to us now in our need, for all is not well with us and we feel oppressed by conditions we face. Walk with us and bring us to dwell with you, in Jesus Christ. Amen.

ASSURANCE OF FORGIVENESS

When our transgressions prevail over us God forgives. When we are afflicted God grants rest. God delivers those who ask, and offers salvation, not because of our deserving, but in response to our sincere request. God says to each of us, as Jesus said to Zaccheus, "I must stay at your house today." Let us receive the Eternal One with joy.

COLLECT

Eternal God, who sent Jesus to seek and save the lost, we want to be found by you today. Let us hear once more your assurance of salvation, the hope for healing and wholeness that you offer to the ends of the earth and to us. Turn us away from all the destructive forces we devise. Grant us courage to accept your call and fulfill it with joy. Amen.

OFFERTORY INVITATION

All silver and gold belong to God. It is God who grants prosperity. How do we answer God's generosity? Surely with joy and imitation, giving as we have been blessed, with a song in our hearts.

OFFERTORY PRAYER

Through what we give, bless those who are poor. Grant to the fearful, courage; to the oppressed, deliverance; to the confused, new clarity and direction. May the programs and outreach supported by these gifts make you known in ways that are uplifting and transforming. Amen.

COMMISSION AND BLESSING

Take courage, people of faith; God is with us.
God abides among us and prospers our journey.
Praise is due to God, who hears our prayers.
Praise we will give through the days ahead.
Strength and courage are gifts from God,
that we may do the work to which God calls us.
Morning and evening we shout for joy,
and moment by moment we are empowered.
Jesus Christ is glorified in your words and deeds,
by the grace of God, whose promises are true.

Today salvation has come to this house.
We are made whole to fulfill God's call.
Amen.   **Amen.**

(See hymn No. 95.)

Pentecost 25
(November 6–12)

Old Testament: Zechariah 7:1–10
              Psalm 9:11–20
Epistle: 2 Thessalonians 2:13—3:5
Gospel: Luke 20:27–38

CALL TO WORSHIP
We are bound to give thanks to God
for all our brothers and sisters in the faith.
The love of God draws us together,
and the gracious deeds of God evoke our praise.
God chooses us all for salvation,
to confirm in us the truth of the gospel.
In the glory of Jesus Christ, our Savior,
we are tied to one another in love.
God has promised to strengthen us,
and we know God is faithful in all things.
The Spirit of the living God is in our midst,
enlivening all we say and do.

INVOCATION
We come to you, living God, as a resurrection people, chosen by you to
reveal truth we ourselves have not fully perceived. In spite of our dullness
the brilliance of your saving grace is expressed through us. Even when
our religious observances are self-centered you use our praise to multiply
the kindness and mercy you would bring to light. Be gracious to us now,
that we may be fully alive to you and one another. Amen.

CALL TO CONFESSION
How often we sink into the pits of our own making. Again and again we
are snared in the work of our own hands. We become the wicked and evil
people we are set to guard against. We have flawed the gifts that come
with our humanity and fallen before our human frailties. Let us be honest
with God and one another as we confess our sin.

PRAYER OF CONFESSION (KEITH KARAU)

We admit, holy God, that we want this life of ours to go easily. We do almost anything to avoid pain and discomfort. We look the other way when people are hurting; we refuse to stand up for right even when we hear you calling us; we like to think that we are in charge of our own lives and that you will give us all we want. Forgive our foolish understanding of you. Lift our vision and help us to discover the power to walk faithfully through every difficult moment. Amen.

ASSURANCE OF FORGIVENESS

God has chosen to save us, to deliver us from wickedness, to strengthen us in the faith, and to guard us from evil. We are not bound by the deaths we inflict on ourselves or condemned to dwell in the deep mire of apathy, self-concern, and willfulness. God is beginning an abiding transformation in our midst. The Word of God will triumph in us; sing praises to God!

COLLECT

Catch our attention, living God, as you speak to us once more through and beyond the recorded word. Make yourself known to us, that our hearts may be comforted and your work firmly established within each one. Firmly root us in your love, that we may have the energy needed to reach out in kindness and mercy to our neighbors. Expand our view of neighbor to include those who are alone or alien or poor, and those whom we might otherwise label as enemies. Live in us today and always. Amen.

OFFERTORY INVITATION

Our giving is invited because we need this discipline as much as programs need our support. Our giving is expected because we cannot truly worship God without giving concrete expression to our gratitude. Our giving is a joy to us because we have known the comfort and strength of a faithful God in whose love we can live confidently in all times and places. This is the high point of our worship.

OFFERTORY PRAYER

We give thanks that you are saving us and leading us to the steadfastness of Christ. To you we dedicate these offerings, that the needy shall not be forgotten or the poor perish for lack of water and food we can provide. May these gifts answer the cries of the afflicted and bring hope to many who seek the blessing of your Spirit. Amen.

COMMISSION AND BLESSING (KEITH KARAU, ADAPTED)

Go forth into life, praising God,
giving thanks for the love you have received.
  We rejoice that God has chosen us
  and is saving us by the Spirit's power.
Be strengthened by God's love and favor
to tell among all people the gracious deeds of God.

We will stand firm in the gospel
and hold to the truths we are taught.
Show forth the kindness and mercy of God,
made known to us day by day as we walk with Christ.
We will see and serve Christ in our neighbors;
God is with us as we go forth into life.
Amen.   Amen.

(See hymn No. 96.)

Pentecost 26
(November 13–19)

Old Testament: Malachi 4:1–6
           Psalm 82
Epistle: 2 Thessalonians 3:6–13
Gospel: Luke 21:5–19

CALL TO WORSHIP
The sovereign God of all nations summons us;
all of us are offspring of the most high God.
As children of the Eternal One
we seek realities that are yet unseen.
God calls us away from speculation to life's realities:
people are suffering and dying for their faith.
Some are persecuted and betrayed;
some are delivered up and imprisoned.
For many, the foundations of life are shaken
and there is no justice or hope to be seen.
We come to hear from the divine council,
that we might rise up on the healing wings of God.

INVOCATION
God of right and justice, speak to us in ways we cannot ignore, lest we be
led astray by other voices. Enlist us in meaningful work among the least
of your children. Keep us from unproductive idleness that ignores the
tasks, small or large, you intend for us to do. Strengthen our ties with
parents and children, that we may grow in understanding and mutual
support. Amen.

CALL TO CONFESSION   (KEITH KARAU)
It is so easy to get caught up in the world around us that we cannot hear
the voice of God or feel the presence of all that is holy. Let us look closely

now, that we might see ourselves in the presence of God. Let us confess our sinfulness.

PRAYER OF CONFESSION (KEITH KARAU)
We confess, O God, that we are ignorant about your ways. We allow wickedness to shape and control us. We do not stand for the justice you have called us to share. We do not care enough about those who are poor or give ourselves to the extent you invite. We like to think others should care for us, that life should be easy and free of real work. Help us, Holy One, to see ourselves in comparison to Christ. Amen.

ASSURANCE OF FORGIVENESS (KEITH KARAU)
God still rules the world with justice. God offers fresh new possibilities, even to those who have ignored the way of faithful living. God gives us life through the forgiveness of our sins. Let us go and live as servants of the faithful God.

COLLECT
We open our minds and our wills to direction from your word, mighty God. Grant us wisdom and courage to face a confused and frightening world. Put us in touch with those segments of our human family that are most vulnerable, and show us how to be most helpful. Engage all our senses in the work and witness you expect of us. Amen.

OFFERTORY INVITATION
Most of us have worked hard to earn a living. We have invested our talents and energies to support ourselves. Many of us are, or have been, responsible partners in developing a creative, supportive family unit. God asks us to invest some of the resources we have accumulated in the larger family of humankind. The weak and needy are part of our family too.

OFFERTORY PRAYER
Most high God, we bring our offerings with mixed feelings. Sometimes we are resentful that we have to work so hard while others live in idleness. Why does it fall on us to provide for others who do not appreciate our efforts? Then we remember your goodness to us when we are undeserving, and the blessing of being needed and able to help. We would not be weary in well-doing, for you have not wearied in your provision for us. Thank you, God, for your generosity that helps us to endure all things. Amen.

COMMISSION AND BLESSING
Go out to live and work and witness;
do not be weary in well-doing.
We face another week, grateful for meaningful tasks
and for people who share their lives with us.

Rescue the weak and needy;
deliver them from the hand of the wicked.
   We reach out to others with help, not judgment,
   remembering how God has met our needs.
Receive the gifts God offers you;
dwell in the wisdom God imparts.
   Our spirits leap in response to God,
   who helps us endure and triumph.
Amen.   **Amen.**

(See hymn No. 97.)

Pentecost 27
(November 20–26)

Old Testament: 2 Samuel 5:1–5
                    Psalm 95
Epistle: Colossians 1:11–20
Gospel: John 12:9–19

CALL TO WORSHIP
With hearts full of reverence and praise
we bow before the Maker of all our days.
   Let us come into God's presence with thanksgiving,
   making a joyful noise to the Rock of our salvation.
The heights of mountains and depths of earth
belong to our God, who gave us birth.
   Wherever we go, God strengthens our hand
   while leading in ways we do not understand.
Life in God's peace grants our churches fresh breath,
and joy that endures through our life, and in death.
   We are people of God's pasture, sheep of God's hand,
   who worship the one who formed sea and land.

INVOCATION
In joyful noises and hymns of praise we sing out our gratitude for the gift
of life, for companionship along life's pathways, for the covenant that
draws us together in faith and service. Empower us once more to stand
against evil as we explore the heights and depths of possibilities you offer
us. Dwell in us, so Jesus Christ may be revealed in our deeds and words.
Amen.

CALL TO CONFESSION

God is angry with those who ignore the way of peace, whose hearts are closed to God's indwelling presence and to their neighbors' needs. Come now to let God melt all that is hard and resistant within you, that light may dawn once more to awaken your spirits and grant new life.

PRAYER OF CONFESSION

Deliver us, O God, from dependence on sensational happenings and emotional outbursts that masquerade as faith experiences. Meet us in the tough times when trust is shaken and life's meaning is obscured. Cut through our resistance to your sovereign rule, that we may discern your handiwork among the principalities of earth and through the far reaches of space. Draw us to yourself, to partake of eternity here and now. Amen.

ASSURANCE OF FORGIVENESS

God has delivered us from the power of evil to dwell in the dominion of Jesus Christ, where sins are forgiven and faith is strengthened. God qualifies us to share in the inheritance of the saints of light, granting endurance and patience with joy. Be glad that God renews and heals, pardons and empowers.

COLLECT

Expand our capacity to understand your word for our times, loving God. Call us out of the tombs of our truncated hopes and limited vision, that we may live out our discipleship with enthusiasm and faithfulness. Stretch us, strengthen us, lead us, as our cups overflow with opportunity. Amen.

OFFERTORY INVITATION

Our inheritance from God evokes our thankfulness, and our gratitude inspires us to share the gifts we have received. Let us bring our tithes and offerings to extend the possibilities for reconciliation and peace.

OFFERTORY PRAYER

May these gifts extend the songs of our lips into a symphony of thanksgiving to the Rock of our salvation. May we do our part with faithfulness so that all our congregations together can accomplish significant work among your people. We dedicate these tokens of esteem for Christ, who is our Head, whose life and ministry we not only remember, but also seek to live. Dwell with us, building your perfect peace among us, we pray. Amen.

COMMISSION AND BLESSING

We are not only the sheep of God's flock,
but also a people called to be shepherds.
In covenant God equips us to serve,
strengthening us for patient endurance.

Go forth in joy to share your inheritance,
as saints who are living in the light of God's love.
**We will forgive as we have been forgiven
and trust others as we have been trusted.**
God grants you this day understanding and peace
as you follow Christ, who reconciles you to God.
**Hosanna to the One who is Head of the church
and welcomes us as members of the Body of Christ.**
Amen.   Amen.

(See hymn No. 98.)

Other Special Occasions

Presentation
(February 2)

Old Testament: Malachi 3:1–4
Psalm 84
Psalm 24:7–10 (alt.)
Epistle: Hebrews 2:14–18
Gospel: Luke 2:22–40

CALL TO WORSHIP
Awareness of God's presence may come suddenly.
Can we endure the Mighty One in our midst?
How dare we stand before the glorious Ruler,
who bursts through our temples and our techniques?
The Powerful Light forces us to open our eyes,
and the messenger whom God sends speaks to us.
We hear the voice of Jesus from our common humanity,
yet also as our faithful High Priest.
Blessed are those who find strength from their Creator,
who are inspired and empowered by the Spirit.
We long to experience the saving gifts of God
and the assurance we need to face each day.

INVOCATION
Gather us, O God, to meet Jesus in this hour. In the perfect humanity of
the Nazarene we see ourselves as you intend. In that faithful life of long
ago we sense who we could be. Now in this place our souls find a home
away from the frantic pace and the din of competing claims. How lovely is
your dwelling place, O God of hosts! We will ever sing your praises.
Amen.

CALL TO CONFESSION
The Refiner and Purifier bids us come to renew our covenant with God
and with one another. We leave behind the tents of wickedness, so we will
know this is the house of God. Here we seek forgiveness and renewal, for
we are ready to turn from temptation and sin. God is listening for our
sincere prayers.

PRAYER OF CONFESSION
Hear our prayers, Sovereign God, for we are afraid. We have tried so hard
and so often to walk uprightly, but we have failed again. We have given in

to temptation, staining your image within us. We have wandered away from the community of faith, even while you are calling us to come home. Forgive us, God of hosts, that we may find a place at your altar and at your table. Amen.

ASSURANCE OF FORGIVENESS

God will forgive and purify all who come with contrite hearts. Trust in the One who sent Jesus to earth as one of us. When we are tempted we can remember that Jesus shared the same temptations, and overcame them. As the Christ, Jesus made expiation for our sins. We need not be bound by the brokenness and wrong we have caused. God has already forgiven us. Accept that forgiveness, and live the new life God offers.

COLLECT

Fill us with your wisdom, O God, and grant renewed trust and vigor. Deepen our devotion as we accept your salvation and your peace. Lift us up, freeing us to praise you in spirit and flesh, with eyes and ears and voices, with heart and mind and strength. Amen.

OFFERTORY INVITATION

Our offerings are pleasing to God when we give from the heart. God does not withhold from us any good thing we need. Let us not withhold what belongs to God: our tithes, our offerings, ourselves.

OFFERTORY PRAYER

We ask you to accept these offerings, gracious God, and to work with us until our sacrifices are pleasing to you. Keep us from being satisfied with less than our best efforts to help all people see your salvation. May we walk in your light and live by your word, as conveyors of your peace. Amen.

COMMISSION AND BLESSING

According to the word and purposes of God:
Depart in peace, to serve wherever you go.
 Our eyes have seen the salvation God prepares
 for all people, near and far.
Shine as lights for the whole world to see;
sing praises for all the earth to hear.
 We dwell in the arms of God, who blesses us
 and sends us out to deliver others from bondage.
Go out with prayers on your lips;
know that God hears, understands, and answers.
 We go from strength to strength
 as God blesses us day by day.
Amen.   Amen.

(See hymn No. 99.)

Annunciation
(March 25)

Old Testament: Isaiah 7:10–14
Psalm 40:6–10
Epistle: Hebrews 10:4–10
Gospel: Luke 1:26–38

CALL TO WORSHIP
Let us gather according to the word of God,
that God's law may be written on our hearts.
We delight to do your will, O God,
for with you all things are possible.
We rejoice once more in God's steadfast love,
and sing of the faithfulness of our Creator.
We share good news of deliverance
and celebrate the salvation that makes us whole.
Whatever God asks of us, we will do;
wherever God leads, we will follow.
We will not put God to the test
or weary the One who has done so much for us.

INVOCATION
Eternal Spirit, come to us as you came to Mary long ago. May Jesus
Christ live anew through us, in the way we respond to your love and in
the way we treat one another. Help us to see in the circumstances and
people around us more and more opportunities to minister in the name
and for the sake of your Child. We have come to do your will, gracious
God. Reveal to us your intentions for this community of faith. Amen.

CALL TO CONFESSION
While our lips proclaim our faith and devotion, we know deep within that
we are not fulfilling God's intent for us. God is not as real to us as are the
distractions of the marketplace. We let partial dedication substitute for
full commitment. Yet God does not abandon us to our selfish and limited
pursuits, but ever calls us into a new and right relationship. Let us seek
the forgiveness and favor of God.

PRAYER OF CONFESSION
Loving God, we want to live faithfully in response to the path you have
set before us in Jesus of Nazareth. We confess that we have not lived up to
our intent. We have strayed from your way, pursued lesser loyalties,
misrepresented your truth, and misused other people. We have tried to
earn for ourselves what you have freely given. We are truly sorry for our

sins. Cancel them, we pray, and wipe clean the slate of our lives, giving us new freedom to respond authentically to your favor. Amen.

ASSURANCE OF FORGIVENESS

The Holy Spirit comes to us with freeing power. We are not limited by our past, but are liberated from all that diminishes the image of God within us. We have been sanctified through the body of Jesus Christ offered once for all. Let us cast aside all our fears, to respond boldly to our forgiveness and acceptance. Let us dare to be fully Christian.

COLLECT

We listen for your greeting, most high God, for you call us by name and give us tasks to do. We have come to hear your word and do your will. We would not weary you with our endless chatter or put you to the test with demands for a sign. Simply let us walk with Jesus and learn from Christ to be the people you want us to be. Amen.

OFFERTORY INVITATION

This day let your offerings speak a powerful message. We are ready to support the ministry of this church with our tithes and our time, our offerings and ourselves. We are prepared to reach out in new ways, to sacrifice our self-interest, that the purposes of God might be realized in our midst and beyond our individual reach. Let us give with joy.

OFFERTORY PRAYER

In gratitude for the gift of Jesus Christ we bring all we have to share. We thank you for Immanuel, the assurance that you are with us in all circumstances. We bring these gifts in response to your unlimited generosity. We dedicate them to your service. May these resources and our lives accomplish your purposes. Amen.

COMMISSION AND BLESSING

The Child of the Most High reigns among us;
let us follow wherever Jesus leads.
We want to be disciples who continue to learn
and ambassadors of good news who delight to serve.
We have been favored by God in many ways;
now we go out to vindicate God's investment in us.
We will not fear to witness to our faith
or to risk ourselves for the gospel's sake.
God sends us out into the world
and assures us of favor to overcome our fears.
We will not hide God's saving help in our hearts,
but will speak of God's faithfulness and salvation.
Amen.   Amen.

(See hymn No. 100.)

Visitation
(May 31)

Old Testament: 1 Samuel 2:1–10
Psalm 113
Epistle: Romans 12:9–16b
Gospel: Luke 1:39–57

CALL TO WORSHIP
Praise God, all you servants of the Most High;
bless the name of God now and for evermore.
From the rising of the sun to its setting,
may the name of God be praised.
The glory of God is chanted above the heavens
and the deeds of God are known through all the earth.
God has filled the hungry with good things
and has sent the rich empty away.
God has blessed the barren with children
and has given life to those who were discouraged.
Our hearts exult in God,
and we rejoice in the salvation we are offered.

INVOCATION
God of all holiness, Rock of our salvation, we dare to approach you in humility and expectation. As you have fed us with all good things, strengthen us now by your Word. Make us rich in all that really matters. We bless and praise your name, and our spirits rejoice in the opportunity to serve you. Amen.

CALL TO CONFESSION
Come, all who are arrogant and proud; come, all you mighty ones who aspire to thrones. Come, all who put their faith in riches and are poor toward God. Come, all who neglect the good and perpetuate evil. God awaits our confession.

PRAYER OF CONFESSION
Great God of all people, we are tired of pretending to be strong when we really feel weak and inadequate. Behind our smiling, confident front you see the ash heap inside us. The appearance of riches mocks the poverty of our souls. We long for genuine communion with you, but we have not been willing to pay the price of disciplined prayer and openness to your cleansing, empowering love. We beg forgiveness. Guide our minds and our feet in new directions, and set us on fire with your empowering Spirit. Amen.

ASSURANCE OF FORGIVENESS
God pours out mercy on all who are truly sorry for their sin and offers a new and vital relationship with the Eternal. All who hunger for genuine love and harmony and hope will find transformation in daily prayer and openness to the Spirit. God girds the feeble with strength and guards those who are faithful. Rejoice, and let your speech and actions reflect God's forgiveness.

COLLECT
We hunger for your Word. Visit us, O God, that we may discern your presence in exciting and powerful ways. Increase our affection for one another within this faith community, so we may be strengthened to reach out in love to all your children. Fill us with the will and capacity to praise you, rejoicing in your salvation. Bring us to life, and grant the joy of faithful service. Amen.

OFFERTORY INVITATION
God weighs our actions, not just our words. Our offerings give feet to our faith. They carry the word where our steps cannot go. They support causes that lift people from hopeless despair to life abundant. Let your gifts reveal the depths of your devotion.

OFFERTORY PRAYER
May these gifts make possible the sharing of your mercy, the feeding of the hungry, the empowerment of your saints for ministry. May all who give know your blessing and all who receive be moved to thanksgiving for all your bounty. Keep us faithful in the tasks you set before us. Amen.

COMMISSION AND BLESSING
Carry your praise of God into your daily living;
let word and deed show your devotion.
God has girded our lives with new strength
and will guard our feet as we go out to serve.
Feed the hungry, and love people to life;
outdo one another in showing mercy and honor.
God has set us on fire with zeal for goodness;
we will offer hospitality to all God's children.
God goes with you among all who would persecute you,
empowering you to bless even your enemies.
We will not fear, for God is present everywhere.
May God's name be praised in all we do!
Amen.   **Amen.**

(See hymn No. 101 and also hymn No. 65.)

Holy Cross
(September 14)

Old Testament: Numbers 21:4b–9
Psalm 78:1–2, 34–38 (alt.)
Psalm 98:1–5
Epistle: 1 Corinthians 1:18–24
Gospel: John 3:13–17

CALL TO WORSHIP

Come, children of God, to meet the One sent by God;
Jesus came to live among us and die for us.
Jesus is our Hope for eternal life,
the One who shows us how to live for others.
Listen for the words that open our understanding,
for the parables that unfold life's mysteries.
We have entered into covenant with God,
who is our Rock and our Redeemer.
Remember God's steadfast love and faithfulness;
make a joyful noise to God, all the earth!
We will sing a new song to God,
whose works among us are marvelous indeed.

INVOCATION

O God, in whom strength is revealed in the midst of weakness, look on us
with your favor. We have stumbled in our impatience and grown weary in
our futile search for wisdom. We have turned away from the defeat of the
cross, little sensing its victory. We turn to you now, knowing there is no
other place to find help. Lead us through the shadows to the light of
Christ. Amen.

CALL TO CONFESSION

We who have been complainers and scoffers are invited to confess all we
have done to separate ourselves from God. We who have asked for signs in
order that we might believe are humbled before the cross, the ultimate
sign of God's love. Let us seek the power and wisdom of God.

PRAYER OF CONFESSION

We have sinned, for we have spoken against God. We have lied to God
with our mouths and our maneuvers. We flatter our Creator with pious
words and deny the cross with shallow allegiance. Our complaints drown
out our thanks, and our folly demeans God's wisdom. We have caused
others to stumble because we are such faithless disciples. Forgive us,
God, for we cannot face ourselves as we are. Amen.

ASSURANCE OF FORGIVENESS

Look on Christ and live! God loved the world so much that Jesus was sent to live as the Human One, fully in tune with all the limits we face, yet triumphant over them. Through Jesus, salvation and wholeness come to us. In Christ we can know the power of God and the wisdom of God. Let us turn away from lesser claims.

COLLECT

In the name of Jesus, who was lifted up on the cross for us, we come to learn about life. Inspire the preaching of your Word and the hearing of our souls. Lead us beyond the folly of what our heads tell us to the truth that our hearts so dimly discern. Teach us in every way to honor you and to live in your steadfast love. Through Christ. Amen.

OFFERTORY INVITATION

No offering will ever be an adequate response to God's love in Christ. Our Creator knows that; so do we. God asks us to give according to our means, to take pleasure in sharing, as we have been blessed. May the love of God in Christ Jesus be our first motive for giving, and our second a desire to help those whose needs God helps us see.

OFFERTORY PRAYER

O God, before whom our cleverness is nothing, we ask you to direct the management of possessions we hold dear and projects we support. As we claim for ourselves your promise of eternal life, entrust to us occasions to pass on the good news of your gift. We are grateful for your steadfast love and faithfulness, revealed most fully in Jesus Christ, crucified and risen. Amen.

COMMISSION AND BLESSING

The One whom God sent goes with us
into the wilderness and deserts of life.
  When life is difficult and the way is not clear
  we sense that we are not alone.
Jesus bids us live as people of eternity,
who embrace God's foolishness over worldly wisdom.
  We would not choose the way of the cross,
  but we will not flee from it, if necessary.
A compassionate God empowers our loving service
and directs our words and deeds in new ways.
  We will be true to our covenant with God
  as our work and worship declare our praise.
Amen.   Amen.

(See hymn No. 102.)

All Saints
(November 1, or First Sunday in November)

Old Testament: Daniel 7:1–3, 15–18
Psalm 149
Epistle: Ephesians 1:11–23
Gospel: Luke 6:20–36

CALL TO WORSHIP
Praise God in the assembly of the faithful;
sing to God a new song, and dance for joy.
God is our maker, the Ruler over all things.
We take pleasure in our praise and service.
God takes pleasure in those who are faithful
and adorns the humble with victory.
God meets us in our anxiety
and interprets to us what we do not understand.
God calls us to a fresh and abiding hope
and imparts to us the good news of salvation.
God is merciful to all who live in love
and seek to do good to all people.

INVOCATION
With all the saints of every time and place we come to worship you, God Most High. We praise your glory and rejoice in the wisdom you reveal to us. Enlighten us once more in this time of adoration and blessing. Fill us with hope, even when conditions around us seem only to hurt and destroy. Help us to do good and show mercy, expecting nothing in return. Meet now our personal needs, as you minister to your church. Amen.

CALL TO CONFESSION
Despite our best intentions our days have been marred by thoughts and actions that pull us away from God and distort our relations with people. We need to be restored to integrity and self-respect, freed of the burden of our mistakes. Honest confession and the acceptance of forgiveness from God can turn our lives around. Draw near to God in silence to receive this precious gift. . . .

PRAYER OF CONFESSION
. . . Hear, O God, our deep longing to be more in tune with your purposes. We have cursed you when we are destined and appointed to praise you. We have sought the riches of this world while our spirits are impoverished and undeveloped. We grab for ourselves what should be shared, to satisfy our own hungers. We offend others when our own wants

are involved but are often cowardly in our witness for causes that apply the gospel to issues of our day. Prayer for our enemies, doing good to them, and loving them, is asking more of us than we are prepared to do. O God, forgive us, and turn us toward your way. Amen.

ASSURANCE OF FORGIVENESS
God is merciful to all who truly seek a new way of life. If you have come in genuine penitence and desire to try God's way rather than your own, be assured that you are forgiven. You are freed to sing a new song, to leap for joy, to treat others as you wish to be treated.

COLLECT
We hunger, O God, for more than bread. Feed us now with that spiritual food that lends a new taste and zest to lives grown stale and unimaginative. Teach us to care and to act from a love that demands nothing in return. Fill us with hope for Christ's reign in our midst, as we accept the ways of Jesus as a guide to our own conduct. Amen.

OFFERTORY INVITATION
Our inheritance in Christ Jesus is guaranteed. What more do we need? We who are rich, whose hunger is met with good food, whose thirst is quenched with purified water, who enjoy many resources that entertain us and make life easier, need one thing more—to share generously from our abundance that we, and others, might truly live. Our gifts are meant to share Christ with the whole human family.

OFFERTORY PRAYER
We give from the abundance of your gifts to us, merciful God. We reach out to the beggar and to those too proud to beg, with equal concern and compassion. We dare to minister to the needs of our enemies as well as our friends. We would share the riches of the gospel with all. Amen.

COMMISSION AND BLESSING
Go out into the world to do good,
expecting nothing in return.
   As we wish that people would do to us,
   we will do to them, with love in our hearts.
Go forth to praise God in the world
as we together have praised God in the sanctuary.
   Day by day we will seek God's revelation
   and live by the wisdom God imparts.
Receive from God the hope to which you have been called,
that you may live as forgiven and forgiving saints.
   By the grace of God we sinners are also saints,
   empowered to love with boldness and joy.
Amen.   **Amen.**

(See hymns No. 103 and No. 104.)

Thanksgiving Day

Old Testament: Deuteronomy 26:1–11
Psalm 100
Epistle: Philippians 4:4–9
Gospel: John 6:25–35

CALL TO WORSHIP

Come into God's presence with gladness and singing,
for God has brought us safely to this day.
God has been with us in all our travels through life,
even when we did not realize God's care.
God is the Author and Chief Actor in our life stories
and has given us all good things to enjoy.
Through toil, affliction, and oppression
we have known God's steadfast love and faithfulness.
In everything by prayer, supplication, and thanksgiving,
let your requests be made known to God.
~~We are here to learn what we must do~~
~~to be doing the works of God.~~ *We come to offer*
our gratitude and to praise God.

INVOCATION

When we remember all the good we have received from your hand,
Sovereign God, we are moved to deep thanksgiving and praise. Our
anxieties are turned to gratitude when we trust in you to provide. You
have given us the bread of life to nourish our souls, even as we have
received bread to eat from your bounty. Grant us now pure thoughts and
lofty motives as we seek the mind of Christ. Amen.

CALL TO CONFESSION

Jesus knew that some people were followers of the way only for their
personal gain. Others were merely curious or superstitious. It is ever so.
We take the name of Christian out of mixed motives, embracing the faith
as much to be seen as to serve. Let us confess before God our fragmented
lives.

PRAYER OF CONFESSION

Generous and loving God, we confess that our energies are invested in
labor for food that perishes rather than for what endures. Our thirst is
never satisfied because we do not taste enough of the pure water you
provide. We have failed to set our thoughts on what is true, honorable,
just, and pure. We have ignored what is lovely, gracious, excellent, and
worthy of praise. O God, forgive, and turn us to your way. Amen.

ASSURANCE OF FORGIVENESS

Jesus said, "I am the bread of life; whoever comes to me shall never hunger, and whoever believes in me shall never thirst." If we have come in sincere repentance and faith, trusting the power of God to transform us, we will find wholeness and assurance. Live, then, as children of God, in the steadfast love that endures forever.

COLLECT

Break before us the bread of heaven, that we may partake and live. Help us to see Jesus, that we may grow as disciples. Keep our hearts and minds attuned to Christ, so we will know your peace. As you have walked with us through the past, accompany us into the future, shaping our thoughts to appreciate truth, justice, purity, and excellence. Amen.

OFFERTORY INVITATION

The Israelites were commanded to take first of all the fruit of the ground as an offering of thanks to God. So, too, the first claim on all we earn is the tithe for charity and the sharing of the gospel. We are called to do the works of God, to pass on the true bread from heaven. Give, not according to what others are giving, but in proportion to the blessings God has bestowed on us.

OFFERTORY PRAYER

Great God, we give thanks that you have brought us out of our times of great difficulty to the enjoyment of many gifts we do not deserve. We rejoice in all the good you have granted us and our loved ones. Our thanksgiving prompts our praise and gladness. Hear our joyful noise as we summon others to partake of the bread of heaven. Amen.

COMMISSION AND BLESSING

Go your way rejoicing in God's continuing presence
and sharing the gifts you have received from God.
**God hears our requests and responds to our cries;
we will not be anxious, for God is with us.**
Meditate on whatever is true, honorable, and just;
think of whatever is pure, lovely, and gracious.
**God lifts our thoughts to what is highest and best
and leads us in paths of excellence.**
The peace of God that passes all understanding
keep your hearts and minds in Christ Jesus.
**The God of peace will be with us
as we seek to do what we have learned from Christ.**
Amen.   Amen.

(See hymn No. 105 and also hymn No. 64.)

Appendix of Related Hymns

How many times have you consulted the topical index of your hymnal to select the right hymn to go with a sermon or worship theme only to be disappointed? In a day when sensitive pastors try to speak in ways that are inclusive of all people, regardless of age, gender, race, or disabling conditions, have you shared my disappointment at the exclusive language so often used in hymns? Some of my old favorites contain words that now seem to stick in my throat.

I started writing hymns to address both concerns during my sabbatical early in 1986. Most of the lyrics I have authored are based on the scriptures that appear in the new ecumenical lectionary. At the bottom of most of the hymns in this appendix you will find the scripture references that inspired them. Sometimes only one of the biblical passages for the day was used; at other times all four suggested readings have influenced the content.

Each hymn may be sung to a familiar tune. The name of the tune I had in mind while writing is in parentheses to the upper right of the text. Consult the index of tunes in any good hymnal to locate most of these. If the name of the tune does not appear there, or you want to substitute a tune that is more familiar to your congregation, look next in the metrical index of your hymnal. The meter I used (number of syllables in each line) is noted above and to the right of each hymn's words. For most hymns, especially the short meter (6.6.8.6.), common meter (8.6.8.6.), and long meter (8.8.8.8.), there are a number of tunes from which to choose. Test out your selection ahead of time to make sure that the words and music are a good match.

There are 115 new hymn texts in this volume. Most are lectionary-related. A few at the end are for special occasions, such as wedding anniversaries, times of receiving new members, dedication of facilities that make a church more accessible, communion, and the birthday of Martin Luther King Jr. I invite you to try out all the hymns in worship. See the copyright page at the beginning of this book for permission to use these hymns. For any other authorization contact The Pilgrim Press.

As I add to the "standard repertoire" of hymnology, I am aware that the musical forms so familiar to my ears may not address many would-be worshipers in a meaningful way. My challenge to contemporary musicians and authors is that you try your hand at creating new ways so that we can together sing our praise to God and celebrate the oneness we discover in Christ's service.

Hymns for the Advent Season

1. Make Known Your Ways

First Sunday of Advent—C

8.8.8.8. *(L.M.)*
(DUKE STREET)

LAVON BAYLER

Make known your ways, O God Most High,
Lead us and teach us to rely
On steadfast love and faithfulness,
As Christ draws near our lives to bless.

Remember not, O God of Truth,
Sins we committed in our youth.
Wipe out transgressions of each day,
That we might walk Christ's humble way.

God of Salvation, make us strong;
For you we wait our whole life long.
Keep us from shame and treachery
As we look up, the Christ to see.

With all your saints, O God so near,
We bring our thanks that you appear
In Word-made-flesh for all to see
Glimpses of your eternity. Amen.

(Psalm 25:1–10; 1 Thessalonians 3:9–13; Luke 21:25–36)

2. Hear the Voice

Second Sunday of Advent—C

7.7.7.7.
(SEYMOUR)

LAVON BAYLER

Hear the voice of our distress,
Crying from the wilderness,
From all rough and crooked ways,
Seeking meaning for our days.

Hear John call us to confess
All the ways our sins oppress.

Listen now, prepare the way
For a new and better day.

Hear of valleys lifted high,
Mountains crumbling in reply.
Tears of sorrow dissipate
When the crooked is made straight.

Hear our prayers as love abounds,
Breaking forth in joyous sounds.
Let the earth glad songs employ,
Greeting Christ with shouts of joy. Amen.

(Malachi 3:1–4; Psalm 126; Philippians 1:3–11; Luke 3:1–6)

---

3. Give Thanks to God

Third Sunday of Advent—C   10.10.10.10.
                                                (LANGRAM)

LAVON BAYLER

Give thanks to God; rejoice with all your heart.
Call on God's name; make known God's mighty deeds.
Sing your thanksgiving; let God's love impart
Strength and salvation, meeting all your needs.

Have no anxiety, for God is near,
Caring for those the world has oft ignored.
Open your eyes to see, your ears to hear,
Human community, by God restored.

Let all your prayers reflect your thankfulness;
Know here the peace our Savior's love has brought.
Think on the pure and lovely things that bless
Life, gracious, just, and true that Jesus taught.

Learn once again to live in love and trust,
In every circumstance to be content.
Christ gives us strength to do whate'er is just,
So let us live each day by God's intent. Amen.

(Zephaniah 3:14–20; Isaiah 12:2–6; Philippians 4:4–13)

4. Bear Fruits of Penitence

Third Sunday of Advent—C

6.6.8.6. *(S.M.)*
(DENNIS)

LAVON BAYLER

Bear fruits of penitence;
No special priv'lege claim.
For God will raise, in faithfulness,
New folks to bear Christ's name

Ask not, "What shall we do?"
When God has made it plain.
Good things in life are ours to share,
That all may know God's reign.

May saints no longer steal
By hoarding what God gives.
While others dwell in poverty,
No rich one truly lives.

Let all whose lives are blest
By water's cleansing touch
Be transformed by the Spirit's fire
And wealth no longer clutch.

May John's good news inspire
Anticipation here,
That Christ may come with cleansing pow'r,
To make God's purpose clear. Amen.

(Luke 3:7–18)

---

5. Come to Bethlehem

Fourth Sunday of Advent—C

8.6.8.6. *(C.M.)*
(ST. AGNES)

LAVON BAYLER

Come, let us look to Bethlehem,
God's chosen one to see.
Watch for the branch from Jesse's stem,
Sensing God's majesty.

Celebrate now Christ's advent sure,
For those of low degree.
God will lift up the faithful poor,
Off'ring security.

No more shall neighbor's scorn confound,
Nor tears be daily bread,
As human souls with joy abound,
When by our Savior led.

May all pretense be washed away
By Jesus' offering,
As Advent brings the glorious day
Of pride's dismantling. Amen.

(Micah 5:2–4; Psalm 80:1–7; Hebrews 10:5–10; Luke 1:39–55)

Hymns for the Christmas Season

6. O Blessed Hope

Christmas Eve/Day—A, B, C

7.6.7.6.D.
(LANCASHIRE)

LAVON BAYLER

O blessed hope, appearing
With justice for the world,
And peace for all the nations
In wondrous birth unfurled.
Look now upon your people,
With burdens sore weighed down,
And lead them from the shadows
To honor Christ's renown

By grace we come rejoicing,
Led to a manger crude,
For we who heard your angels
Would sing our gratitude.
To all a child is given,
Whose peace and counsel stands
A beacon through the cent'ries,
For all of earth's vast lands.

We testify, Creator,
To right and justice giv'n,
To all your chosen people
From whom no truth is hidd'n.
May we renounce our passion
For worldly fame and wealth
And, zealous for good deeds, serve
In ways that lead to health. Amen.

(Isaiah 9:2–7; Psalm 96; Titus 2:11–14; Luke 2:1–20)

7. Prepare the Way

Christmas Day—A, B, C   8.6.8.6.D. (C.M.D.)
(Additional Lections, First Set)   (MATERNA)

LAVON BAYLER

Prepare the way, clear paths of stones,
That people here may see
The great redeeming work of God
That brings salvation free.
Let earth rejoice and coasts be glad
That, born in Bethlehem,
The Savior of the world appears
To seek, and not condemn.

A holy people, called to be
God's saints, who share good news
Of righteousness and justice born,
Earth's darkness to diffuse,
Come forth this day as messengers
To praise and glorify
Our God, who reigns with truth and grace,
And will our needs supply.

All glory be to God, whose love
Pours out the hope for peace,
That adversaries' warlike ways
Throughout the world may cease.
The heavens proclaim God's righteousness
And idols put to shame,
For light and joy this day emerge
To honor Jesus' name. Amen.

(Isaiah 62:6–7, 10–12; Psalm 97; Titus 3:4–7; Luke 2:8–20)

8. Come, O Word

Christmas Day—A, B, C   *8.7.8.7.D.*
(Additional Lections, Second Set)   (BRADBURY)

LAVON BAYLER

Come, O Word of God, to save us;
Shine into our deepest night.
Let the Word of Life enlighten
All our paths, and give us sight.
    Refrain:
    Blessed Sovereign, hear your people
    As they reach for truth and grace.
    Speak again to pour out mercy,
    And all forms of sin erase.

May we be your faithful children,
Born anew by God's own will.
Help us see the Word among us
Making folks disciples still.
    Refrain

Send us forth to bring good tidings.
Send us out to publish peace.
Free our lips for joyous singing;
May our spirits find release.
    Refrain

Judge us with your righteous fairness,
Holy Child, whose way we claim.
Pour out now the oil of gladness,
Setting all our hearts aflame.
    Refrain

(Isaiah 52:7–10; Psalm 98; Hebrews 1:1–12; John 1:1–14)

9. We Come to Praise

Christmas 1—C

LAVON BAYLER

6.6.4.6.6.6.4.
(TRINITY)

We come our God to praise;
Great are God's works and ways
To those who trust.
Give thanks with all your heart,
And ne'er from truth depart.
Let humble service start
In causes just.

Jesus, with insights new,
Traveled with parents to
Jerusalem.
List'ning and questioning,
Asking and answering,
Elders understanding,
Spent days with them.

In height, and favor too,
Young Jesus daily grew,
Showing God's love.
As Samuel long before,
Sought for the truth of yore,
Giving forevermore
Loyalty above.

God, help us grow in grace
And Jesus' footsteps trace
In covenant.
Our hatreds disavow,
Show us forbearance now
With kindliness endow;
Your wisdom grant. Amen.

(1 Samuel 2:18–20, 26; Psalm 111; Colossians 3:12–17; Luke 2:41–52)

10. Go Quickly

January 1 (New Year)—C   8.8.8.8. *(L.M.)*
                                                          (OLD HUNDREDTH)

LAVON BAYLER

Go quickly to the streets and lanes;
Extend God's word to hills and plains.
Call forth all people from afar
To heed the light of Jesus' star.

Our God has called us from the womb
And named us to disperse the gloom
That blinds the selfish to God's light,
Which we discern when Christ lends sight.

Make ready for the banquet feast
That God in Christ brings to the least;
The poor and maimed and blind and lame
Are gathered in our Savior's name.

As God reveals the mystery
Of grace poured out for you and me,
We know that we cannot deserve
The role of saints who preach and serve.

Yet God accepts us as the heirs
Of Christ who, for our use, prepares
The church with wisdom from on high
That we our God might glorify. Amen.

(Isaiah 49:1–10; Ephesians 3:1–10; Luke 14:16–24)

---

11. May God Bless

January 1—Jesus and Mary—A, B, C   8.7.8.7.
                                                              (RATHBUN)

LAVON BAYLER

May the Lord God bless and keep you,
May God's face upon you shine,
Lift God's countenance upon you,
Grant you peace, by God's design.

May God's saving pow'r be given
To all nations of the earth,
As God judges all with fairness
And proclaims each person's worth.

God is gracious; sing your praises.
May you know true peace and joy.
May God guide you and protect you,
And no enemy destroy.

May the Lord God bless and keep you,
May God's face upon you shine,
Lift God's countenance upon you,
Grant you peace, by God's design. Amen.

(Numbers 6:22–27; Psalm 67)

---

12. When God's Time

January 1—Jesus and Mary—A, B, C   7.7.7.7.7.7.
                                                                      (DIX)

LAVON BAYLER

When God's time had fully come
And the angels went away,
Shepherds ran to Bethlehem,
Waiting not for break of day,
There to worship and adore
And their newfound trust explore.

At the name of Jesus, bow
Common folks and rulers great,
Praising God for freedom sent
Through a love o'ercoming hate.
Come to worship and adore
And your newfound trust explore.

Let all tongues confess the truth,
Once so vividly expressed,
Through salvation's simple act,
By the child whose presence blessed.
May we worship and adore
And, in trust, our faith explore.

Now, in fear and trembling, rise;
Make your pilgrimage today.
In obedience to God's call,
Follow in the shepherds' way.
Worship Christ with all your hearts
In the trust God's love imparts. Amen.

(Galatians 4:4–7; Philippians 2:9–13; Luke 2:15–21)

---

13. O Sing Aloud

Christmas 2—A, B, C   8.6.8.6.D.
                                                        (CAROL)

LAVON BAYLER

O sing aloud with gladness, and
Proclaim, give praise, and say,
Our God has brought from sadness all
The people of God's way.
God gathers from the farthest parts
Of earth, the blind and lame,
With goodness touches all our hearts
And calls us each by name.

Keep us from stumbling, Gracious God,
And dry our tear-filled eyes.
May we find comfort in your Word
And in your strength arise.
With consolation lead us back,
Redeemed from all our foes.
Supply the courage that we lack
To face life's hardest woes.

By brooks of water we are led;
Along straight paths we walk.
From God's abundance we are fed
With food and gentle talk.
Our Shepherd would our gifts employ
And each response enhance.
Let faces show a radiant joy
As weary rise to dance. Amen.

(Jeremiah 31:7–14)

Hymns for the Epiphany Season

14. Now Arise and Shine

Epiphany—A, B, C

10.8.10.8.8.8.
(MARGARET)

LAVON BAYLER

Now arise and shine, for your light has come,
And the glory of God breaks forth.
From the shadows that hide life's tedium
God proclaims your abundant worth.
Rejoice, and be glad together
For the light that no woes can blur.

Lift your eyes to see, and be radiant;
Lift your hearts to rejoice and sing.
God, in peace, restrains all the violent,
That all lands may, with justice, ring.
Rejoice, and be glad together
For the light that no woes can blur.

May God's ruler live while the sun endures,
And defend the cause of the poor.
May deliv'rance come as God reassures
That the needy may live secure.
Rejoice, and be glad together
For the light that no woes can blur. Amen

(Isaiah 60:1–6; Psalm 72:1–14)

15. Proclaim the Mystery

Epiphany—A, B, C

7.6.7.6.D
(WEBB)

LAVON BAYLER

Proclaim the glorious myst'ry
That God, in Christ, reveals,
And share this revelation
With all whom Jesus heals.
Partakers of the promise,

We join in songs of praise,
As members of one body,
Rejoicing through our days.

O grant your church new insight
To venture day by day,
That, growing toward Christ's stature,
We may not miss God's way.
As ministers appointed,
The least of all your saints.
May we discern your riches
And give without constraints.

As those appointed stewards
Of your abundant grace,
As prophets and apostles,
We serve the human race.
By wisdom now empowered,
By faith made strong to teach,
We venture forth in boldness
The whole wide world to reach. Amen.

(Ephesians 3:1–12)

---

16. When Christ Was Born

Epiphany—A, B, C   *8.8.8.8. (L.M.)*
                              (DEUS TUORUM MILITUM)

LAVON BAYLER

When Christ was born in Bethlehem,
Came magi to Jerusalem
To seek the ruler of the Jews,
For stars, they said, had brought the news.

The troubled king consulted scribes
To hear who prophets' word describes:
A governor for Israel
Shall Judah's shadowed gloom dispel.

The magi, summoned secretly,
Were sent to Bethlehem to see
The child, to worship and adore,
And bring to Herod word once more.

Continuing, with star to guide,
They came at last to Jesus' side.
Gifts—gold and myrrh and frankincense—
They gave in acts of reverence.

Then, warned by God of king's deceit,
They sought their journey to complete
And Herod's order disobey,
By going home another way. Amen.

(Matthew 2:1–12)

---

17. When Jesus Was Baptized

Epiphany 1—Baptism of Jesus—C

7.6.7.6.D
(ST. HILDA)

LAVON BAYLER

When Jesus Christ was baptized,
The heavens opened wide.
God's gift of peace was re'lized
By those at Jesus' side.
"This is my Child, beloved,
The one with whom I'm pleased."
May all the world's unwanted
Find their rejection eased.

Send fire to re-ignite us
And peace to make us whole.
May serving you delight us
And help us to console
Your people, faint of spirit,
The poor, and those who mourn.
Grant truth to those who fear it,
That new life may be born.

Empower your baptized children,
Great God of all the earth.
May we be warmed and filled, when
The Spirit grants us worth.
Confront us with the myst'ry
Of Christ, the truth revealed.

Stay with us through our hist'ry,
That we may all be healed. Amen.

(Isaiah 61:1–4; Psalm 29; Acts 8:14–17; Luke 3:15–17, 21–22)

---

18. How Precious Your Love

Epiphany 2—C

10.10.10.10.10.10.
(YORKSHIRE)

LAVON BAYLER

How precious is your steadfast love, O God,
By which we see your bright salvation's light.
Led by that love, by various gifts well shod
We venture forth to serve with great delight.
We cannot silence keep, or take our rest,
For you have summoned us to give our best.

Clothed in your righteousness, by faith attired,
We strive to be your church, one neighborhood.
Claimed by your Spirit, we have been inspired
To seek for each and all the common good.
Christ calls our names, and all whom Jesus brings
Take refuge in the shadow of your wings.

We feast upon abundance in your house
And drink fresh water from the fount of life.
Each brings the gifts by which our God endows
Our common ministry amid earth's strife.
Wisdom and miracles our God expands
And works of healing by the prophet's hands.

Led by the Spirit, we acclaim Christ Lord
Of all we do and ev'ry word we say.
Called as disciples, we, with one accord,
Each use our special gifts along life's way.
Some utter wisdom, some interpret speech,
While, by the Spirit's pow'r some preach and teach. Amen.

(Isaiah 62:1–5; Psalm 36:5–10; 1 Corinthians 12:1–11)

19. At a Marriage Feast

Epiphany 2—C

LAVON BAYLER

7.7.7.7.7.
(HENDON)

At a marriage feast one day
Jesus faced a host's dismay,
Heard his mother's firm request
And the jars of water blessed.
May our hearts be changed by Christ.

Do what Jesus tells you to;
To his mission he'll be true.
'Though reluctant to impress,
Jesus met the host's distress.
May our hearts be changed by Christ.

When the steward of the feast
Tasted wine, the best, not least,
Awe-filled servants knew the source,
And the bridegroom felt remorse.
May our hearts be changed by Christ.

Seek the miracles within,
That, with Christ, we may begin
Our true mission to enjoy
And full energies employ.
May our hearts be changed by Christ. Amen.

(John 2:1–11)

---

20. We Stand in Awe

Epiphany 3—C

LAVON BAYLER

6.6.8.6.D. (S.M.D.)
(DIADEMATA)

We stand in awe before
The word that you inspired,
Creator of the Universe,
Whose works we have admired.

You make us one indeed,
Yet grant us gifts unique,
That each of us may undertake
Your true intent to seek.

Clear us from hidden faults,
Great God whose word is law,
And keep us back from arrogance
Lest we from truth withdraw.
Your precepts grant us sight
Our errors to discern.
We turn to you for strength and light
Your simple joys to learn.

Grant us attentive ears
And take us by the hand,
That we may Christ's disciples be,
And truly understand
The ways that you intend
For each of us to go.
Then lend us courage to respond
And your good news to show.

May we one body be
In our variety,
That hands and eyes and other parts,
While different, may agree
To seek the common good,
And care for each and all,
That in our work and worship we
May answer Jesus' call. Amen.

(Nehemiah 8:1–4a, 5–6, 8–10; Psalm 19:7–14; 1 Corinthians 12:12–30)

---

21. As Jesus Worshiped

Epiphany 3—C   10.10.10.10.
                                                      (MORECAMBE)

LAVON BAYLER

As Jesus worshiped on each sabbath day,
We come together now to sing and pray.
Open to us the scriptures' full intent,
That we may live by what is excellent.

As Jesus taught, empower us to teach;
Loosen our tongues your great good news to preach.
Touch us and cleanse, that we in turn may heal
And by our love and care your word reveal.

As Jesus freed the captive and oppressed,
We are encouraged now to give our best.
Show us anew the gifts your love imparts;
Open our eyes, O God, and lift our hearts. Amen.

(Luke 4:14-21)

---

22. We Trust and Praise

Epiphany 4—C

6.4.6.4.6.6.4.4.
(LOVE'S OFFERING)

LAVON BAYLER

You are our refuge, God,
In life's distress.
Incline your ear to us,
Rescue and bless.
Fill us with hope today;
Guard us from error's way.
We trust and praise.
We trust and praise.

You knew and formed us, God,
E'en from the womb.
You consecrated us,
Caused us to bloom.
You make no point of age,
But each one's gifts engage.
We trust and praise.
We trust and praise.

We hear you calling us
To lead and speak.
You send us forth to serve,
Others to seek.
From fear deliver us,
As we your word discuss.
We trust and praise.
We trust and praise.

May we your builders be,
Serving with grace,
Affirming others' strengths,
Doubts to erase.
As you continually
Strengthen our prophecy,
We trust and praise,
We trust and praise. Amen.

(Jeremiah 1:4–10; Psalm 71:1–6)

---

23. Faith, Hope, and Love

Epiphany 4—C   *8.6.8.6. (C.M.)*
                                              (WINCHESTER OLD)

LAVON BAYLER

With faith and hope and love we come,
Intent upon our quest
To be, with Christ, more venturesome,
Pursuing what is best.

We would not be as noisy gongs
Or clanging cymbals bold,
For all of life to God belongs,
And God, with love, upholds.

Prophetic powers are not enough
And faith is incomplete,
If we use knowledge to rebuff
The people whom we meet.

True love is patient, kind, and true,
Rejoicing in the right.
It does not childish ways pursue,
Nor arrogance invite.

No jealousy or boastful talk
Will mar the coming days,
For love endures along life's walk,
Not rude, resentful ways.

Grant understanding, and forgive
All care that just pretends.

Perfect in us the will to live
In love that never ends. Amen.

(1 Corinthians 13)

---

24. I Thank My God

Epiphany 5—C   *8.6.8.6. (C.M.)*
                                                      (ST. ANNE)

LAVON BAYLER

I thank my God with all my heart
And joyous anthems raise,
As people moved by faith, take part
In singing hymns of praise.

Bow down, all rulers of the earth,
For we are not in charge;
Yet God, in love, still grants us worth
Our vision to enlarge.

God's faithfulness includes us all
And goes to any length,
That we may answer when God's call
Requires our soul and strength.

The lowly poor, by troubles faced,
Will find deliverance.
By God's concern we are embraced
And giv'n a second chance.

God's purposes will be fulfilled,
For steadfast love endures,
Assisting us to grow and build.
God, grant us to be yours! Amen.

(Psalm 138)

25. Holy Are You

Epiphany 5—C

LAVON BAYLER

8.8.8.8. (*L.M.*)
(PENTECOST)

Holy are you, O God of hosts,
Far greater than our proudest boasts.
You live in majesty untold;
Earth cannot all your glory hold.

Foundations shake when you are heard;
Sins are exposed before your word.
People with unclean lips cry out,
Reaching for truth beyond their doubt.

Cleansing forgiveness touches us,
Saving from sin so perilous;
All of our guilt is washed away,
And we prepare for your new day.

Purged by your Spirit, we rejoice,
And once again we hear your voice:
Whom shall I send, and who will go?
Send us, O God, your love to show. Amen.

(Isaiah 6:1–8)

26. By Grace You Called

Epiphany 5—C

LAVON BAYLER

7.6.7.6.D.
(MEIRIONYDD)

By grace you called disciples;
By faith did they respond.
O Jesus Christ, your summons
Calls us to move beyond
Our narrow expectations,
Content with second best.
May we, like Simon Peter,
Our trust in you invest.

Launch us upon our journey,
With you, O Christ, to guide.
We listen for your teaching
And in your love abide.
As you have died to save us,
We dare to risk our all,
And leave behind our treasures
To answer when you call.

Now, awed by your appearance
To us, the least and lost,
We dare to claim the promise
Our sins cannot exhaust.
Remove the fears that bind us
In doubt and apathy,
That we may be apostles,
By grace empowered, set free. Amen.

(1 Corinthians 15:1–11; Luke 5:1–11)

---

27. Come, O God, to Bless

Epiphany 6—C   8.7.8.7.8.7.
                                                    (REGENT SQUARE)

LAVON BAYLER

Come, O God, to bless and heal us,
For we trust in you alone;
Human beings cannot save us
From the evil we have known.
By your law we grow and prosper
As Christ claims us as your own.

In our hunger you have fed us,
In our poverty you bless.
You are here when people hate us,
Tending to our deep distress.
Come, to turn our tears to laughter,
Overcoming bitterness.

We are blessed who heed your counsel,
Turning from our sinful ways.
In our prayer and meditation
You have moved our hearts to praise.

Lifted by Christ's resurrection,
We rejoice through all our days. Amen.

(Jeremiah 17:5–10; Psalm 1; 1 Corinthians 15:12–20; Luke 6:17–26)

---

28. Gracious God, We Trust

Epiphany 7—C

7.7.7.7.
(MERCY)

LAVON BAYLER

Gracious God, we trust in you,
Take delight in all you do,
Wait with patient hearts to hear
All the truth your Word makes clear.

Let not evil triumph now
As before your wrath we bow.
Turn us from our angry ways
Lest we miss this chance to praise.

We are still before your power
As we worship in this hour.
Feed our hunger, quench our thirst,
As we seek to put you first.

We would wait for you, O God,
As through life we daily plod.
Let the meek possess the land
As they prosper at your hand.

Add to all the good we do
Confidence in serving you.
May our hearts' desires be known,
Loyal to your truth alone. Amen.

(Psalm 37:1–11)

29. Your Ways

Epiphany 7—C

LAVON BAYLER

6.6.8.6. (S.M.)
(FESTAL SONG)

Your ways are not our own,
O Gracious God Most High.
Yet we would follow in your paths
And on your love rely.

Christ teaches us to bless
The ones who curse and harm,
To turn the other cheek when hit,
Attackers to disarm.

How shall we show your love,
Your pardon to reflect?
You bid us share as we are blessed
And give what we expect.

Forgiveness is our joy,
Receiving, giving, too.
Keep us from judgments hard and cruel,
That we may dwell with you. Amen.

(Luke 6:27–38)

30. Reveal the Mystery

Epiphany 8—C

LAVON BAYLER

7.6.7.6.D.
(GREENLAND)

Reveal to us the myst'ry
Of seeds that sprout and grow
From soil that you have watered
And light that you bestow.
The hills break into singing,
And trees shall clap their hands
As your amazing purpose
Spreads out to many lands.

Reveal to us the myst'ry
Of Christ who died and rose,
Whose grave was sealed, then broken
In ways no mortal knows.
Your work makes glad the nations,
Our lips reflect the joy
That issues forth in praises
E'en death cannot destroy.

Reveal to us the myst'ry
Of life beyond the grave,
Of death consumed by vict'ry
Of those Christ came to save.
We give you thanks, Creator,
As you our lives renew.
In steadfast love abounding,
We labor strong and true. Amen.

(Isaiah 55:10–13; Psalm 92:1–4, 12–15; 1 Corinthians 15:51–58)

---

31. Please Teach Us

Epiphany 8—C   *11.11.11.11.*
                                                   (ST. DENIO)

LAVON BAYLER

Please teach us, O Jesus, disciples to be,
Reflecting our Teacher that others may see
Your goodness and kindness in all that we do,
And faithful profession from hearts that are true.

Grant sight to disciples, lest blind lead the blind,
And all stumble badly while seeking to find
The truth that you offer, the help you provide.
Be with us, O Savior, to lead and to guide.

Remove from our eyes all the logs that are there,
That when we see specks we may not be unfair,
But offer our help, being humbly aware
That only your pardon enables our care.

Create in us goodness that none can dispute,
That out of your treasure our lives may bear fruit,
Which sweetens and nourishes all whom we meet,
Inspiring us all, your good news to repeat.

Now help us to build on the rock that is sure,
On sturdy foundations that hold and endure.
When storms break around us with pow'r to destroy,
Let none shake our confidence, none wreck our joy. Amen.

(Luke 6:39–49)

---

32. Show Us Your Glory

Last Sunday After Epiphany—C

10.10.10.10.
(SONG 24)

LAVON BAYLER

Show us your glory, God, beyond this world:
Transcendent majesty through space unfurled.
All of your universe bespeaks your pow'r;
Come to us now to reign within this hour.

Let all your people tremble at your word;
Let us be still that truth may here be heard.
Come to establish justice where we live,
That we may seek its reign through all we give.

Change and empow'r our minds and hearts today;
Grant us true freedom deep within, we pray,
That we may turn from underhanded ways,
Opening all our lives to honest praise.

Lead us by hope; our ministry renew
Through Christ, the chosen one, whose word is true.
Keep us awake to all that you reveal
As you reach out, our wounded hearts to heal. Amen.

(Exodus 34:29–35; Psalm 99; 2 Corinthians 3:12—4:2; Luke 9:28–36)

Hymns for the Lenten Season

33. Receive Our Treasures

Ash Wednesday—A, B, C

LAVON BAYLER

7.6.7.6.D.
(AURELIA)

Receive our valued treasures,
O God of love and grace,
And may our hearts take pleasure
Christ's footsteps to retrace.
Hear now our prayers in secret,
Enhance the fast we keep,
That, sounding not a trumpet,
We now true faith may reap.

Let piety be honest
And alms be generous,
As human greed we protest
And join an exodus
From our misplaced reliance
On treasures of the earth.
May we find true abundance
As heaven grants rebirth.

Have mercy, gracious Sovereign;
Create clean hearts within
That follow your new pattern
And turn from selfish sin.
Whatever hazards face us
May we triumphant be,
As you accept and change us
For your eternity. Amen.

(Joel 2:1–2, 12–17a; Psalm 51:1–12; 2 Corinthians 5:20b—6:10; Matthew 6:1–6, 16–21)

34. Tempt Us Not

Lent 1—C

LAVON BAYLER

7.7.7.7.7.7.
(REDHEAD NO. 76)

Tempt us not to grasp for bread,
God, by whom we're loved and fed.
Help us worship you alone,
In whose mercy we are known.
Keep us from the tempter's power
As we celebrate this hour.

Here we know your word is near,
Granting comfort, hope, and cheer.
Written on our lips and hearts
Is the grace your love imparts.
May we no distinctions know,
That, in trust, we all may grow.

Be our refuge day by day,
And deliver us, we pray,
From all troubles that befall,
When we seek to heed your call.
Lead us safely in your way,
Hour by hour and day by day. Amen.

(Psalm 91:9–16; Romans 10:8b–13; Luke 4:1–13)

---

35. Gather Your Children

Lent 2—C

LAVON BAYLER

8.8.8.8. (L.M.)
(HESPERUS)

Gather your children 'neath your wings,
God, by whose name creation sings;
Keep us from evil day by day,
As we ascend your mount to pray.

Protect us from our enemies;
Hear our petitions, heed our pleas.

From anxious toil turn us away,
Lifting us up to praise and pray.

Build now within, and all around,
Life in your covenant profound.
Shield us, O God, from thoughts that stray
Far from your purpose, when we pray.

Gather your children to profess
Ways you reach out to change and bless.
May we in Jesus Christ, your heir,
Know the companionship of prayer. Amen.

(Genesis 15:1–12, 17–18; Psalm 127; Philippians 3:17—4:1; Luke 13:31–35; 9:28–36)

---

36. We Hear God Call

Lent 3—C   6.6.8.6. (S.M.)
                                                            (SOUTHWELL)

LAVON BAYLER

We hear God call today,
And turn aside to see
The bush that burns but does not die,
And power that sets us free.

We stand on holy ground,
Our shoes removed in awe,
Before the One who sends us forth
To rescue by God's law.

We witness to God's truth
Before all worldly pow'r.
To free so many now oppressed,
Equip us in this hour.

We follow where you lead,
O God, the great "I Am!"
For you deliver us each day
From anger, fear, and sham. Amen.

(Exodus 3:1–15)

37. That Sabbath Day

Lent 3—C

8.6.8.6.D. (C.M.D.)
(ALL SAINTS NEW)

LAVON BAYLER

That sabbath day when Jesus healed,
And helped a woman be
A person, not a crippled one,
We, too, were healed, set free.
For Christ has touched our lives with hope,
And straightened us to stand,
Rejoicing in the One whose love
We dimly understand.

As parents nurture and forgive,
Our God extends a hand
To sinners, drowning in despair,
Their lives on sinking sand.
With mercy that surpasses all
The bounds of "common sense,"
God reaches out to lift us up
And grants new confidence.

O bless our God while life shall last,
Bless God with heart and soul.
With steadfast love and mercy crowned,
Stride forth toward freedom's goal.
Extend to all we meet the love
That sent us on our way,
Rejoicing in the chance to share
Good news of Christ each day. Amen.

(Psalm 103:1–13; Luke 13:10–17)

38. Happy Is One

Lent 4—C

LAVON BAYLER

10.10.10.10.
(TOULON)

Happy is one who finds recourse in God,
Who tastes of goodness God has offered free.
In their distress the poor who cry are heard;
And, saved from shame, each face shall radiant be.

O magnify the One True God with me;
Let us exalt together God's great name.
God has delivered us from all our fears,
That new creation we may now proclaim.

God was in Christ in reconciling love,
Saving from sin and moving us to praise.
Souls, sore afflicted, join in glad response,
Singing God's song of blessing all their days.

We are ambassadors for Christ today,
Boasting in God, who, through us, makes appeal
To all who see with only human eyes,
That we may know God's righteous commonweal. Amen.

(Psalm 34:1–8; 2 Corinthians 5:16–21)

39. Who Receives from God?

Lent 4—C

LAVON BAYLER

8.7.8.7.D.
(IN BABILONE)

Who receives from God the manna?
Who shall at Christ's table meet?
Surely sinners are excluded;
They do not deserve a seat.
Yet God blesses them with bounty
And, with love, a welcome gives.
Come, rejoice, make merry with us,
For my child, once dead, now lives.

Who receives from God a blessing?
Who will know a Savior's grace?
Faithful ones may take for granted
They deserve a favored place.
But our God is all compassion,
Welcoming the penitent.
Come, rejoice, with song and dancing,
At my pardoned child's event.

Who will join the feast of heaven
In our God's eternal realm?
Who will know the fruits God offers
When despair would overwhelm?
Those returning with confession,
Broken by effects of sin,
Seeking only to be servants,
Hear the welcome, "Please come in." Amen.

(Joshua 5:9–12; Luke 15:1–3, 11–32)

---

40. Lead Us by Love

Lent 5—C   *6.4.6.4.6.6.6.4.*
                                           (ST. EDMUND)

LAVON BAYLER

Lead us in ways made new,
That we may live;
Guide us to follow you,
Truly to give.
Counting all things as loss,
Jesus endured the cross;
Like Christ, we serve and trust
In causes just.

Lead us to waters pure
When there is drought,
That we may shout your praise
Beyond our doubt.
Restore our fortunes here;
Grant us to laugh and cheer,
As from the seeds we've sown
Harvests are grown.

Lead us in righteousness
This worship hour.
May we, through suffering,
Learn Jesus' power.
Forgetting former days,
Open to Jesus' ways,
We seek the goal above:
Living by love. Amen.

(Isaiah 43:16–21; Psalm 126; Philippians 3:8–14)

---

41. Come Once Again

Lent 6—Palm Sunday—A, B, C   6.6.8.6. *(S.M.)*
                                                      (ST. THOMAS)

LAVON BAYLER

Come once again in peace,
O Jesus Christ, today.
As once you entered David's town,
Bring hope along our way.

We raise our songs of praise
And add our loud applause,
Then turn away from earth's acclaim,
Enlisting in your cause.

Together, we will stand
Against the hate and shame
That led from donkey's back to cross
The One whom we proclaim.

Grant true humility
That does not grasp for fame,
But empties self as you once did
To glorify God's name.

May each day God has made
Awaken us with joy,
That we may teach as we've been taught
And all God's gifts employ.

In our obedience
We do not wish for death,

Yet seek to share God's love with all
As long as we have breath. Amen.

(Isaiah 50:4–9a; Psalm 118:19–29; Philippians 2:5–11; Luke 19:28–40)

---

42. We Behold Your Passion

Lent 6—Passion Sunday—C   *6.5.6.5.D.*

LAVON BAYLER

We behold your passion, Jesus Christ, today,
In our feeble fashion, Following your way.
Visiting your table, Taking cup and bread,
Asking "Are we able?" We are filled with dread.

"Who shall be the greatest?" We still ask today.
It may be the frailest Who discern your way.
Only those who serve you, Through all trials and pain,
Know your humble purview And your final reign.

While your lips are praying That we may not fail,
Christ, we hear you saying, We will drive the nail,
By a word deny you, By a kiss betray,
Sleepily defy you As you seek God's way.

Foll'wing at a distance, As they mock and beat,
Seeing no resistance, Feeling your defeat,
We, O Christ, feel broken, For we, too, betray.
Make us more outspoken Followers today.

As we're drawing near to Seek your way to live,
From the cross we hear you, "Gracious God, forgive."
Come, O Christ, to save us From self-centered ways,
Lest our wealth enslave us. Lift us up to praise! Amen.

(Luke 22:14—23:56)

43. Your Steadfast Love

Monday of Holy Week—A, B, C

LAVON BAYLER

6.4.6.4.D.
(BREAD OF LIFE)

Your steadfast love, O God, Fills all the sky.
We see your righteousness Like mountains high.
All living things you save Find refuge near,
And when your judgment comes, They have no fear.

You grant abundant feasts As we unite,
Eating and drinking here To our delight.
Yours is the life we know, Your light we see,
Bringing your saving love, Costly and free.

Now take us by the hand In covenant.
Call, in your righteousness, Each celebrant
To serve with faithfulness, In causes just.
Teach us to share your gifts, In you to trust.

As you have given sight, Now set us free;
Help us to open eyes So all may see.
Bring forth your justice here, Using our hands;
Send us to do your work In many lands. Amen.

(Psalm 36:5–10; Isaiah 42:1–9)

---

44. Come, O Christ

Tuesday of Holy Week—A, B, C

LAVON BAYLER

7.7.7.7.4. with Refrain
(CHAUTAUQUA)

Come to worship, humbly bow.
See the cross before us now.
Shall we turn away in shame?
Or its victory proclaim
In Jesus' name?
Refrain:
Come, O Christ, among us,
Come in this hour.

Grant that we may follow you,
Bearing fruit in service true.
Come now, in power.

God has chosen lowly ones,
Timid daughters, feeble sons,
Foolish to all worldly eyes,
Strengthened now to realize
God's fresh surprise.
Refrain

Walking in the light of day,
We behold Christ's faithful way,
Knowing death cannot contain
One who steadfast will remain
Through loss and pain.
Refrain

(John 12:20–36; 1 Corinthians 1:18–31)

---

45. O Sovereign God

Wednesday of Holy Week—A, B, C   7.6.7.6.D.
                                                    (LANCASHIRE)

LAVON BAYLER

O Sovereign God, sustain us,
And teach us day by day,
That we may help the weary
Find rest along life's way.
Awaken us to meet you,
And open up our ears,
That when we're shamed and taunted
We may not break, in tears.

O Sovereign God, come with us,
And help us all to stand,
Against all adversaries,
For freedom in the land.
Let no one be dishonored
Or none be brought to shame
Who seek for your salvation
In precious Jesus' name.

O Sovereign God, surround us
By witnesses so great,
Ancestors in the spirit,
Who did not stoop to hate.
We face the race before us
As Jesus faced the cross.
O may we not grow weary,
But find true joy, not loss.

O Sovereign God, still meet us
At Jesus' table, spread
For us and our salvation
With common wine and bread.
O keep us from betraying
Or putting to the test
The One who came to save us
And show us all life's best. Amen.

(Isaiah 50:4–9a; Psalm 70; Hebrews 12:1–3; John 13:21–30)

---

46. Fill Our Hearts

Maundy Thursday—C   *8.7.8.7.D.*
(ST. ASAPH)

LAVON BAYLER

Fill our hearts with expectation
As with Christ we here commune,
Not as guests, but as disciples,
Knowing death comes all too soon.
Grant us confidence and courage,
With a faith sincere and strong,
Holding fast to hope within us,
Singing in the face of wrong.

Jesus calls the least and greatest
That your will may here be known.
Gracious God, we now would render
Hymns of praise to you alone.
Breaking bread with one another,
To your holy realm draw near,
We accept the cup of suff'ring,
For your love o'ercomes our fear.

You have put your law within us
In a covenant made new
By the faithfulness of Jesus,
To whose love we would be true.
We would ever meet together
With encouragement and trust,
Doing good as Christ has taught us,
Serving you through causes just. Amen.

(Jeremiah 31:31–34; Psalm 116:12–19; Hebrews 10:16–25; Luke 22:7–20)

---

47. Draw Near with Confidence

Good Friday—A, B, C   6.6.9.6.6.8.
                                                 (SCHÖNSTER HERR JESU)

LAVON BAYLER

Draw near with confidence,
Mercy and grace to find,
Here at the feet of our great High Priest.
Jesus, the child of God,
Welcomes the lame and blind
And all in need, from great to least.

Christ knows our weaknesses,
Tempted as we have been,
Learning obed'ence through suffering.
Perfect in prayer and praise,
Christ pleads for us again
While giving life as offering.

Source of Salvation, come,
Making your home within
Each human heart that confesses need.
Jesus, we would obey,
Turning away from sin
To love and serve in word and deed. Amen.

(Hebrews 4:14–16; 5:7–9)

48. Jesus, We Follow

Good Friday—A, B, C

LAVON BAYLER

11.11.11.6. *(Irregular)*
(INTEGER VITAE)

Jesus, we follow to the garden, weeping,
Fearing the powers who your life are seeking.
Help us to put away swords that, in every day,
Threaten your peaceful ways.

Jesus, we follow to the dreary courtyard,
Seeking to hide amid the crowds there lurking.
Help us to stand again our faith confessing;
You are the one we serve.

Jesus, we follow to the time of trial,
Hearing you speak of truth by you embodied.
Help us to choose your way above all others,
And never crucify.

Jesus, we follow to the hill of suff'ring,
Feeling again your pain and deep compassion.
Keep us from fleeing in our fear and anger,
But grant us useful tasks.

Jesus, we follow to another garden
Where there is laid to rest our dreams now broken.
Help us to hear again words you have spoken.
Revive our wounded souls. Amen.

(John 18—19)

Hymns for the Easter Season

49. On This Day

Easter Sunday—C

8.7.8.7.D.
(HYMN TO JOY)

LAVON BAYLER

On this day of resurrection
You, O God, make all things new.
Come again to those who, frightened,
Wonder at your larger view.
You have changed our expectations,
Turned our weeping and distress
Into hope beyond all measure
And a joyous eagerness.

We who, unbelieving, doubted,
Hurry now to see the tomb,
Dazzled by the wondrous splendor
Here erasing fear and gloom.
You have chosen those receptive
To surprises and good news
As your messengers among us.
How can we your love refuse?

Grant us daring to be building
For the future you have planned,
When, in Christ, each day is precious
And each place a holy land.
Wolf and lamb shall feed together
As your word of peace resounds
Through that realm where death is conquered,
Love presides, and trust abounds. Amen.

(Isaiah 65:17–25; 1 Corinthians 15:19–26; Luke 24:1–12)

50. Teach Us Again

Easter Sunday—A, B, C

LAVON BAYLER

8.8.8.8.
(MARYTON)

Teach us again, Impartial God,
Always to do what you deem right,
That all who fear and honor you
Will find acceptance in your sight.

Preach once again good news of peace
That Jesus brings for ev'ry land.
May those oppressed find quick release,
And those defeated once more stand.

Send once again your Spirit's power,
Bringing your healing love for all.
May we be witnesses this hour
In answer to our Savior's call.

Judge once again our faithfulness
As day by day we seek to share
All of the ways that Christ will bless
Those who forgive and truly care. Amen.

(Acts 10:34–43)

51. God of Music

Easter Evening—A, B, C
(Honoring Jane Chipman)

LAVON BAYLER

7.7.7.7.D.
(CHIPMAN)

ROBERT HANSON

God of music, hear our praise
For your great and mighty ways.
Free our songs to soar above,
Giving thanks, returning love.
Praise we now with harp and lyre,
Trumpet blast and joyous choir.
All the creatures of the earth
Join in hymns to praise your worth.

Cymbals' crash and roll of drums
Praise your strength that overcomes
Chains of iron and swords of hate,
Calling us to celebrate.
In your love we join the dance
Of your joyous celebrants,
Praising all that you have done,
Giving thanks for vict'ries won.

Hear we now glad organ sounds,
Telling us your love abounds,
Not alone within this place,
But for ev'ry land and race.
For musicians who inspire
Glad response to tongues of fire,
God of music, hear our praise
And continue to amaze. Amen.

(Psalm 150 [and 149])

---

52. The Sun Was Sinking

Easter Evening—A, B, C

6.6.8.6.D. (S.M.D.)
(LEOMINSTER)

LAVON BAYLER

The sun was sinking low;
The day was nearly spent,
As two disciples on the road
Reviewed a sad event.
A stranger joined them there
And asked about their tears.
They told of Jesus and their hopes,
Destroyed 'mid soldiers' jeers.

Death marked life's end, and yet
Disturbing rumors flew.
Some women saw an empty tomb,
And their reports proved true.
O foolish ones, take heart,
Why mourn the one who died?
Did you not know the Suff'ring One
By God is glorified?

When they arrived at home,
The stranger stayed to sup,
And they beheld God's Chosen One
In broken bread and cup.
Did hearts not burn within
And suffering make sense,
When Jesus shared the bread of life,
Interpreting events?

Back to the upper room,
They hurried through the night,
And there beheld the Human One
Once more, by sound and sight.
The One Unknown still comes
To walk with us today.
We may not see, but we can feel
Christ's presence on life's way. Amen.

(Luke 24:13–49)

---

53. My Peace Be with You

Easter 2—C

10.10.11.11.
(LYONS)

LAVON BAYLER

My peace be with you, says Jesus to all.
My peace be with all who answer my call.
As God our Creator has sent me to serve,
So I send disciples and strengthen their nerve.

Receive now the Spirit, holy and true.
Forgive others' sins as Christ forgave you.
Dare now to believe what your eyes have not seen,
And trust our Sustainer for times in-between.

We cannot be still when others resist
The message of Christ, and bid us desist
From speaking the Name or proclaiming in deeds
The wonderful love that fulfills all our needs. Amen.

(John 20:19–31; Acts 5:27–32)

54. Sing Praises to God

Easter 3—C

LAVON BAYLER

8.6.8.6.8.6. (C.M.)
(CORONATION)

Sing praises to the living God,
O you, God's saints below,
For God, though angry, spares the rod
And blesses as we grow.
God's favor brings us morning joy,
Last night's tears to destroy.

Hear now, O God, and gracious be,
Our Helper and our Guide,
From our depression set us free
And in our souls preside.
Accept the thanks we offer now;
In gratitude we bow.

You turn our grieving into dance,
Great God of time and space.
You overlook our arrogance
And do not hide your face.
May we, rejoicing as you bless,
Extol your faithfulness. Amen.

(Psalm 30:4–12)

---

55. Discouraged Fishermen

Easter 3—C

LAVON BAYLER

8.8.8.8. (L.M.)
(CANONBURY)

Discouraged, doubting fishermen,
With empty nets and grieving hearts,
Found wholeness in their working when
They took the risks that faith imparts.

When Jesus said, "Cast out your net,"
And bid them come with him to eat,

They dared respond, though wond'ring yet,
At Jesus' triumph o'er defeat.

Do you, my servant, love me more
Than any marvels of the earth?
Then feed my sheep, my lambs restore
To recognition of their worth.

When angry, threat'ning Saul went out
To punish followers of the way,
His firm resolve could bear no doubt
Until, struck blind, he had to pray.

And then, dependent on God's grace,
He heard the risen Christ implore:
Let loving service now replace
Your hate, and persecute no more.

When Jesus meets us on our way,
Our view is changed, our lives made new.
Christ opens eyes and fills our day
With new horizons to pursue. Amen.

(John 21:1–19; Acts 9:1–20)

---

56. Come, Walk with Christ

Easter 4—C   *10.10.10.10.10.10.*
                                              (FINLANDIA)

LAVON BAYLER

Come, walk with Christ, who robes and purifies
Those washed in news of God's forgiving love.
Hear once again from prophets and the law
The word of One who reigns with God above.
Our God has raised the Child to save us all
And grants us comfort whate'er may befall.

Come, walk with Christ, through valleys drear and dark;
Fear not the evil that confronts your days.
For God has spread a table here for you
To show your enemies more loving ways.
In pastures green, with water for your quest,
The shepherd bids you, come aside and rest.

Come, walk with Christ, when scoffers hurl questions
And unbelievers put you to the test.
Let neither death nor life itself confound,
For with God's mercy you are daily blessed.
May faithful witness shine through ev'ry nerve
And goodness follow you where'er you serve. Amen.

(Psalm 23; John 10:22–30; Acts 13:15–16, 26–33; Revelation 7:9–17)

---

57. Love All

Easter 5—C

6.6.6.6.6.6.
(LAUDES DOMINI)

LAVON BAYLER

See God's new heaven and earth,
Where people know their worth
And share a larger view.
Those blessed seek ways to give,
This new command to live:
Love all as Christ loves you.

Our Gracious God upholds
Those suffering and old,
Life's meaning to pursue.
For body and for soul,
God offers food and goal:
To love as Christ loves you.

God helps us all to see
Our full humanity,
When care for all is true.
Those stronger help the weak
As they together seek
To love as Christ loves you.

With thankful hearts we praise
The One who fills our days
With loving tasks to do.
Our attitudes are healed
Within God's plan revealed:
Love all as Christ loves you. Amen.

(John 13:31–35; Revelation 21:1–6; Psalm 145:13b–21; Acts 14:8–18; 16:11–15)

58. Be Gracious, God

Easter 6—C

7.6.7.6.D.
(ST. THEODULPH)

LAVON BAYLER

Be gracious, God, to bless us,
And shine upon your earth.
Make known your ways among us,
O God, who gave us birth.
Grant insight in all nations,
And let them see your pow'r.
Let all the people praise you,
O God, within this hour.

Glad nations sing with joy, for
Your ways, O God, are just.
Let all the people praise you,
For in your word we trust.
You judge your people fairly
And come within to guide.
We bow in awe and wonder
As you with us abide.

Let all the people praise you,
For earth has yielded food,
And you, O God, have blessed us
And selfishness subdued.
We pray that ev'ry nation
Will worship you in deed,
And may the love of others
Be central to their creed. Amen.

(Psalm 67)

---

59. O God, Whose Love

Easter 6—C

8.6.8.8.6.
(REST)

LAVON BAYLER

O God, whose love is meant for all
Who love and keep your word,

Grant peace among us now, we pray,
That we may lead no one astray
Through burdens grown absurd.

We would not limit your design
To reach all humankind,
Or seek to keep some people out
Whose practices are less devout
Than those we have in mind.

You call us, God, to stay away
From idols we create,
To live in purity of soul,
That we may, faithful, reach your goal
And overcome all hate.

O God of glory, be the light
By which all nations walk.
Bring us to glory day by day
And carry falsehood far away
From all our deeds and talk. Amen.

(John 14:23–29; Acts 15:1–2, 22–29; Revelation 21:10, 22–27)

---

60. We Have Faith

Ascension Day (or Easter 7)—A, B, C   8.7.8.7.8.7.7.
(CWM RHONDDA)

LAVON BAYLER

We have faith in you, our Sovereign,
And your pow'r to change our lives.
May we with your saints bear witness
To the hope on which life thrives.
Singing praises, singing praises,
We will celebrate your reign.
We will celebrate your reign.

Pour on us your revelation
That, through centuries, amazed.
Send your Spirit now upon us,
That we may, with Christ, be raised.
Bearing witness, bearing witness,
We will share your love with all.
We will share your love with all.

May the slow of heart be prompted
To respond in word and deed,
Sharing news of your forgiveness,
Ev'rywhere that Christ may lead.
Blessing others, blessing others,
We will glorify your name.
We will glorify your name. Amen.

(Psalm 47; Mark 16:9–16, 19–20; Luke 24:46–53; Acts 1:1–11; Ephesians 1:15–23)

---

61. Make Us One

Easter 7—C
LAVON BAYLER

8.7.8.7.D.
(HYMN TO JOY)

Make us one in Christ our Savior
Who has bid all nations, "Come."
Quench our thirst and lift our spirits
To be bold and venturesome.
You have freed us from our prisons,
Opened doors and shown the way.
May we love as you have loved us
As we work for you today.

Help us stand for truth and justice
Even in the face of pain.
May we fight against oppression
'Though we have no hope of gain.
In the face of opposition
We would join in hymns of praise,
Thanking you for staying with us
Through both good and evil days.

You are Alpha and Omega,
Our beginning and our end.
May all earth rejoice and tremble,
Seeking ways that you intend.
We, your righteousness proclaiming,
Worship and exalt your name.
May your table now unite us
In one common, holy aim. Amen.

(Psalm 97; John 17:20–26; Acts 16:16–34; Revelation 22:12–14, 16–17, 20)

Hymns for the Pentecost Season

62. Come, Holy Spirit

Pentecost Sunday—C

LAVON BAYLER

6.6.8.6.D. (S.M.D.)
(TERRA PATRIS)

Come, Holy Spirit, come
And set our tongues on fire.
Move us to speak so all may hear
The message you inspire.
Our children prophesy,
And wonders never cease.
Both old and young new vision see
And seek your way of peace.

Come, Holy Spirit, come
With sound of mighty wind.
Blow through each troubled heart and soul,
And all our fears rescind.
Earth trembles at your word.
All creatures, great and small,
Look up to you for food and drink,
And you provide for all.

Come, Holy Spirit, come
And reign within our hearts.
Empower us to do your works
With love your breath imparts.
Adopted as God's heirs,
We serve with Christ today,
And witness bear, through suffering,
That all may learn your way. Amen.

(Psalm 104:24–34; John 14:8–17, 25–27; Acts 2:1–21; Romans 8:14–17)

63. How Shall We Praise You?

Trinity Sunday—C

LAVON BAYLER

11.10.11.10.9.12.
(TIDINGS)

Creator God, majestic in your wisdom,
By which the depths of earth and sea were made,
When we look up at heaven's glorious grandeur,
Marveling at a million suns displayed,
How shall we praise you, tell of your grace?
Grant us to know your truth in ev'ry day and place.

Spirit of Truth, declare to us the future;
Guide our dominion over sea and land.
When we are tempted to misuse creation
Bring us in touch with all your love has planned.
How shall we praise you, tell of your grace?
Grant us to know your truth in ev'ry day and place.

In Jesus' name we seek relief from suff'ring
While we endure and character is formed.
Give us the hope that will not disappoint us;
Pour out your love by which our faith is warmed.
How shall we praise you, tell of your grace?
Grant us to know your truth in ev'ry day and place.
Amen.

(Psalm 8; Proverbs 8:22–31; John 16:12–15; Romans 5:1–5)

64. We Make a Joyful Noise

Pentecost 2—C

LAVON BAYLER

8.6.8.6. (C.M.)
(SERENITY)

We make a joyful noise today
To you, Great God most high.
For you have promised, when we pray,
That you will e'er be nigh.

The wrong within us makes us fear

We cannot worthy be,
And yet, with pardon, you draw near
And from our sins set free.

Your faithfulness transcends all time;
Your steadfast love endures.
O keep us in your grace sublime,
Against all sins' allures.

May all earth's people learn your name
Through gospel rightly heard.
Among us make your rightful claim;
To all reveal your word.

We know that you have made us all;
We owe our lives to you.
We want to answer when you call
And do as Christ would do.

With gladdened hearts we join the song
And keep your covenant.
All praise and thanks to you belong
For healing that you grant. Amen.

(1 Kings 8:22–23, 41–43; Psalm 100; Luke 7:1–10; Galatians 1:1–10)

---

65. Praise the Name

Pentecost 3—C

8.7.8.7.D.
(HYFRYDOL)

LAVON BAYLER

Praise the name of God, most holy;
Bless God's name forevermore.
Praise whene'er the sun is rising;
At its setting still adore.
God is high above all nations,
And God's glory fills the skies.
Who like God reigns o'er creation?
Who but God can be so wise?

Praise our God, who lifts the needy,
Raising poor folk from the dust.
God, who blesses those most lowly,
Teaches us, by faith, to trust.

We shall sit among the nobles,
Hope restored and lives made whole.
God, who grants the barren children,
Lifts these saints toward heaven's goal. Amen.

(Psalm 113 [also used for Visitation—May 31—A, B, C])

---

66. Weep Not, My People

Pentecost 3—C   9.8.9.8.9.9.
                                                          (ST. PETERSBURG)

LAVON BAYLER

Weep not, my people, in your losses;
Death cannot take your joy away.
Grieve not, with anger, at life's crosses,
Nor let earth's sinful ways dismay.
God's love is stronger far than evil
And overcomes all human peril.

Breath comes again at God's commanding,
By God's compassion ever true.
Fear not, for God with you is standing
And in misfortune sees you through.
God visits us in Christ our Savior,
Pouring out love our lives can savor.

Take heart, for Christ's transforming presence
Reveals God's truth along life's road.
Traditions are no more our ref'rence,
Nor halls of pow'r our prime abode.
The gospel turns our hate and worry
Into a witness to God's glory. Amen.

(1 Kings 17:17–24; Luke 7:11–17; Galatians 1:11–24)

67. Why Are You Cast Down?

Pentecost 4—C

7.7.7.7.D.
(SPANISH HYMN)

LAVON BAYLER

Why are you cast down, my soul?
Why disquieted within?
Is there no one to console?
None to praise your origin?
"Where's your God?" detractors chide,
"Where does your Creator hide?"
We will never be alone;
Jesus Christ has made God known.

Has my God forgotten me?
Is my faithfulness for naught?
Shall I flee my enemy,
Live in exile, lost, distraught?
Is our God in ev'ry place,
Reigning through all time and space?
Yes, we'll never be alone;
Jesus Christ has made God known.

Will the wrong that we have done
Cut us off and isolate?
Will there be no champion
For the cause of love o'er hate?
Will our God once more forgive,
Teaching us with joy to live?
Yes, the God by whom we're known
Will not leave us or disown. Amen.

'1 Kings 19:1–8; Psalm 42; Luke 7:36—8:3)

68. O Send Out Your Light

Pentecost 5—C

LAVON BAYLER

11.11.11.11.
(ST. DENIO)

O send out your light and your truth; let them lead,
Through pain and oppression and hatred and greed.
Tear down all the barriers that warp and divide;
Give promise of justice with you by our side.

Come quickly to save us, forsaken and lost,
Amid fire and earthquake and seas tempest-tossed.
Tear down ev'ry idol we seek to erect,
And grant times of silence in which to reflect.

Cast down and disquieted, hope, O my soul,
For God sends a Savior to heal and console.
In covenant, God will your cause vindicate,
Confound all your enemies, lift ev'ry weight.

We listen and wonder at your still small voice
That promises refuge and bids us rejoice.
O send out your light and your truth; let them lead,
And make us responsive to others in need. Amen.

(1 Kings 19:9–14; Psalm 43)

69. What Is Faith?

Pentecost 5—C

LAVON BAYLER

6.5.6.5.
(MERRIAL)

What is faith, but trusting
God, in Christ revealed?
Who has justified us,
And forgiveness sealed?

Who is Christ, but Savior,
Dying for our sin?
Facing love's denial,
Our true life to win?

Who are Christ's disciples?
Not ones bound by law,
But those free and open,
Holding God in awe.

Who are sons and daughters
With the crucified?
All who, taking crosses,
In God's love abide.

Who will follow Jesus?
Those who self deny,
Risking life and fortune
God to glorify.

Who is first among us?
Neither slave nor free.
Christian love unites us
In equality.

What is faith, but living
In community,
Trusting one another
And the God who frees? Amen.

(Luke 9:18–24; Galatians 3:23–29)

---

70. God of All Times

Pentecost 6—C   *8.8.8.8. (L.M.)*
                                                       (FEDERAL STREET)

LAVON BAYLER

God of the past, be ours today;
Ancestors told us of your deeds.
Send now your Spirit, lead the way;
Speak to our hearts; inspire our creeds.

God of the present, meet us here;
Remove the yoke of slavery.
Let your realm be our new frontier,
As in your love we're called, set free.

God of the future, make us strong
In all your Holy Spirit's fruit;

As we to Jesus Christ belong,
Love, joy, and peace be our pursuit.

God of all times, grant faithfulness,
Gentleness, patience, self-control.
Fill us with good and kindliness,
Reaching the depths of ev'ry soul. Amen.

(Psalm 44:1–8; Galatians 5:1, 13–25)

---

71. While Foxes Have Holes

Pentecost 6—C

6.6.8.6. (S.M.)
(ST. MICHAEL)

LAVON BAYLER

While foxes have their holes
And ev'ry bird a nest,
God's Human One had no such place
To lay his head and rest.

No time for looking back
And holding to the past
Is offered those who follow Christ
Where'er their lot is cast.

Our offerings we bring
To make our Savior known.
Elijah has his mantle cast
On us and all we own.

Our hand is on the plow,
And we must bid farewell
To lesser loyalties and claims,
Our Savior's realm to tell. Amen.

(1 Kings 19:15–21; Luke 9:51–62)

72. Whate'er We Sow

Pentecost 7—C

8.6.8.6.D.
(ELLACOMBE)

LAVON BAYLER

Whate'er we sow we also reap,
So help us, God, to plant
The seeds of hope that you desire
In ev'ry celebrant.
O keep us from all weariness,
That we may not lose heart,
But, reaching out to all in need,
Share good that you impart.

Keep us, we pray, from selfishness,
Corrupting and unfair,
Through which we sow to our own flesh,
Denying neighbors care.
We would not covet what they own,
Or cheat them of their due,
Or sell ourselves for evil gain,
But do as Christ would do.

In Jesus Christ create anew
The people you intend.
May we find glory in the cross,
Its meaning to extend
To all the people whom you love
In this and ev'ry land.
May peace and mercy crown our days
And help us understand. Amen.

(1 Kings 21:1–3, 17–21; Galatians 6:7–18)

73. Lead Us, O God

Pentecost 7—C

14.14.4.7.8.
(LOBE DEN HERREN)

LAVON BAYLER

Lead us, O God, in your righteousness;
grant us your favor.

Come with your love that is steadfast and true,
lest we waver.
Make your way straight
Before our eyes as we wait,
This time of worship to savor.

Give ear, O God, to our words
and the sound of our groaning.
Protect us daily
from those who are evil and cunning.
Keep us from lies,
That we may yet recognize
Wickedness we are condoning.

When we are called to your harvest,
equip us to serve you.
May not our wealth, but your mission
be first in our purview.
Through us increase
News of your promise of peace.
Heal us though none can deserve you.

Grant us authority over our enemies' power.
Let nothing injure your faithful
or cause them to cower.
Yet, if we must,
Prompt us to shake off the dust
Of those resisting your hour. Amen.

(Psalm 5:1–8; Luke 10:1–12, 17–20)

---

74. Go and Be Neighbors

Pentecost 8—C   *8.8.8.8.8.8.*
                                                        (ST. CATHERINE)

LAVON BAYLER

Go and be neighbors, giving aid,
Loving with heart and strength and mind,
Having compassion, unafraid
To offer self to humankind.
Do this, and you will surely live.
Forgetting self, forgive, forgive.

Pray for your neighbors, grow in love,
Bearing fruit with all of God's saints.
Seek understanding from above,
That you may serve without complaints.
May you be strengthened with all pow'r,
With joyous patience hour by hour.

Look up in faith, for God discerns
All of your thoughts where'er you go.
Share with your neighbors your concerns
That they, with you, God's love may show.
May we take up the prophet's role
'Til all shall reach God's realm, made whole. Amen.

(2 Kings 2:1, 6–14; Psalm 139:1–12; Colossians 1:1–14; Luke 10:25–37)

---

75. See How God Loved

Pentecost 9—C

7.6.7.6.D.
(MUNICH)

LAVON BAYLER

See how our God has loved us,
How blessed us on our way,
With precious thoughts unnumbered
That fill our lives each day.
Our secret, unformed substance
God fashioned as a gift
To bless the world with gladness,
Our praise, with Christ, to lift.

Those once estranged and hostile,
While doing evil deeds,
Find reconciliation
In Christ to meet their needs.
Through ages leaders suffered
In witness to your truth.
Come, God, to heal, restore us
To visions of our youth.

O grant us ears to listen
And patience while we wait.
Let not all life's distractions
Distress and inundate.

We want to choose that portion
In life which Christ called good;
May we support your prophets
As faithful people should.

How wonderful God's working
In people day by day.
Whose simple acts of kindness
Reflect our Savior's way.
We cannot count the efforts
Of those, without reward,
Who minister among us,
Proclaiming Christ as Lord. Amen.

(2 Kings 4:8–17; Psalm 139:13–18; Colossians 1:21–29; Luke 10:38–42)

---

76. Thanks Be to God

Pentecost 10—C   10.10.10.10.
                                                        (NATIONAL HYMN)

LAVON BAYLER

Thanks be to you, O God, whose strength exalts
Rulers and commoners, youth and adults.
We come, rejoicing, at the life you give,
Knowing the steadfast love in which we live.

Fullness of life in Christ will keep us strong;
Forgiven, healed, we sing our joyous song.
Powers and principalities stand mute
Before the One whose reign we here salute.

Our Father, Mother, dwelling high above
And in each person who reveals your love,
We would exalt your name, by all held dear.
Grant daily bread; bring your dominion near.

Forgive our sins and tempt us not, we pray.
Grant simple courage as we seek your way.
Whether the tasks you send be great or small,
May we respond in answer to your call. Amen.

(2 Kings 5:1–15; Psalm 21:1–7; Luke 11:1–13; Colossians 2:6–15)

77. To You, O God

Pentecost 11—C

8.8.8.8.
(HURSLEY)

LAVON BAYLER

To you, O God, we call today;
Let not your silence lead astray
Those who cry out to you for aid,
Who need their deepest fears allayed.

Protect us, God, from wickedness;
Workers of evil now address
With your firm word of discipline,
Inviting life more genuine.

Keep from real mischief those who say
They are for peace and Jesus' way,
Yet hold your works in no regard,
Making your way of concord hard.

We trust in you, O God, our strength.
Be now our shield throughout life's length.
We sing our songs of gratitude,
Blessed by the past, our faith renewed. Amen.

(Psalm 28)

78. Set Your Minds Above

Pentecost 11—C

7.7.7.7.D.
(ST. GEORGE'S WINDSOR)

LAVON BAYLER

Set your minds on things above,
Where Christ dwells with God, in love.
Seek the new and better way
Your new nature to display.
Christ, who is our life, appears,
Seeking moral pioneers.
Set your minds on things above,
Where Christ dwells with God, in love.

Put away all anger, wrath,
So to follow Jesus' path.
Let no sland'rous talk or lies
Be the way you idolize.
Evil passion put to death;
Praise our God while you have breath.
Put away all anger, wrath,
So to follow Jesus' path.

Life is more than things we own,
Or concerns of us alone.
Ample goods for many years
Cannot take away the fears
That defensive postures build,
'Mid the ones whose barns are filled.
Life is more than things we own,
Or concerns of us alone.

Covet not the things of earth,
Nor pretend a higher worth
Than the others in Christ's realm
Whom our riches overwhelm.
Think not you can take your ease,
No more seeking God to please.
Set your minds on things above,
Where Christ dwells, with God, in love. Amen.

(Luke 12:13–21; Colossians 3:1–11)

---

79. Like Clay

Pentecost 12—C

6.6.6.6.6.6.
(LAUDES DOMINI)

LAVON BAYLER

Like clay the potter molds,
By love our God enfolds
All people of the earth.
God's truth by which we see,
Creates community,
Proclaiming each one's worth.

The foolish heart denies
The God who makes us wise,

But selfish greed employs.
Forswear your evil way
To come to God's new day
With faithfulness and joy.

Take not the poor ones' bread,
But give them food instead,
That Jesus may be praised.
Sell what you do not need,
That others you may feed,
And songs to God be raised.

At times we least expect,
God judges our neglect
And bids us stretch our reach.
Let lamps be burning bright
To give God's people light
In which to serve and teach. Amen.

(Jeremiah 18:1–11; Psalm 14; Luke 12:32–40)

---

80. God of Our Parents

Pentecost 12—C

11.10.11.10.
(ANCIENT OF DAYS)

LAVON BAYLER

God of our parents, we behold your glory
In those who sojourned by your promises.
We look to Abraham and Sarah's story
To see the good that faith accomplishes.

Give us that faith that dares to love and trust you;
Grant energy to follow where you lead.
Yours is the homeland we would now adjust to,
Yours is the rule of life our spirits need.

Raise us from death to live a life victorious,
Relying not on things that we have seen.
May not our work with you e'er seem laborious,
As, seeing love denied, we intervene.

Risking our lives, and clinging not to others,
We dare to serve whate'er the time or place,

Knowing your love for all our sisters, brothers,
Summons our best to celebrate your grace. Amen.

(Hebrews 11:1–3, 8–19)

---

81. You Are with Us

Pentecost 13—C

8.7.8.7.D.
(ERIE)

LAVON BAYLER

You are with us, God, our Sovereign;
We cannot escape your pow'r.
As a dread and mighty warrior,
You confront us ev'ry hour.
We are seeking to be faithful,
Lest before your word we cower.
Save us from the hosts of evil
That would conquer and devour.

By detractors oft' surrounded,
By derision sore distressed,
We are tempted to be silent
And their whispers ne'er contest.
Yet your fire of love is burning
And demands to be expressed.
We reach out to help the helpless,
Seeing them, as Christ, our guest.

When our enemies denounce us
And attack the poor and weak,
Why, O God, do you allow them
All their boasting and critique?
We feel angry and revengeful
'Til our Savior's path we seek.
Then, with faith renewed and strengthened,
We are moved, your grace to speak.

Then by witnesses surrounded
Who have served you through the years,
We can lay aside our burdens,
Trusting to the cross our fears,
As we strive for peace and justice,
Bitter mem'ry disappears.

We can run the race before us,
Baptized by the One who hears. Amen.

(Psalm 10:12–18; Jeremiah 20:7–13; Luke 12:49–56; Hebrews 12:1–2, 12–17)

---

82. Joy Is in Our Hearts

Pentecost 14—C   8.7.11.D.
                                          (STOCKWELL NEW)

LAVON BAYLER

Joy is in our hearts while gath'ring
In your dwelling place, O God.
Singing praises, we are seeking to be shod
With the strength that you have offered
All who seek the narrow door,
To enlist in peaceful service evermore.

Souls are fainting in their longing
For the courts where you abide.
Break our yokes and bring us nearer, by your side.
Blessed are those who trust your Spirit
And abide in covenant.
Grant your glorious favor to each celebrant.

Reverent and awed we worship
God, a great consuming fire.
Lifting up our voices now in freedom's choir
We announce your faithful promise
Of a realm that yet shall be,
When we recognize your peaceful majesty. Amen.

(Psalm 84; Jeremiah 28:1–9; Luke 13:22–30; Hebrews 12:18–29)

---

83. The Word of God

Pentecost 15—C   6.6.8.6. (S.M.)
                                          (ST. ANDREW)

LAVON BAYLER

The word of God has come:
"All people shall be mine."

The righteous ones shall surely live,
And love shall be their sign.

In sharing of their bread
And clothes with those in need,
God's followers true justice seek
And turn away from greed.

They do not take a bribe
Or practice usury,
But honor truth with all their heart
And shun iniquity.

While speaking truth in love,
God's people do not seek
To gossip, or reproach a friend,
Or prey upon the weak.

Fidelity to spouse
And keeping promises
Are sacred ways to saints of God,
Christ's humble witnesses.

To poor and maimed and blind
Grant hospitality,
All you who turn from wickedness
In faithful ministry.

Remember leaders well
And imitate the just,
Forgiving those whose ways oppress,
With resurrection trust. Amen.

(Psalm 15; Ezekiel 18:1–9, 25–29; Hebrews 13:1–8; Luke 14:1, 7–14)

---

84. How Blessed Are Those

Pentecost 16—C   *8.6.8.6. (C.M.)*
                                                                (AZMON)

LAVON BAYLER

How blessed are those who hear your word
In all its chast'ning pow'r,
Who live the law that they have heard
And bring your truth to flow'r.

Your people you will not forsake,
In silence or distress,
For justice is our heritage
And faithful righteousness.

Your steadfast love, O God, shall hold
The cares of many hearts.
Your consolations cheer our souls
As troubled fear departs.

O God, our refuge ev'ry day,
The rock on which we stand,
Help us to follow in your way
And in your truth to stand. Amen.

(Psalm 94:12–22)

---

85. May We Disciples Be

Pentecost 16—C

7.7.7.7.D.
(MARTYN)

LAVON BAYLER

May we your disciples be,
Christ of God, fore'er the same.
Fill us with new certainty
As we gather in your name.
Strengthen us by grace, we pray,
As we bear abuse and shame.
Be with us in all we say,
That your peace we may proclaim.

Help us share the faith, made strong
By the love that you have shown.
May we stand against all wrong
In the truth that God makes known.
As we call our sins to view,
We repent, without delays.
May we serve as sentries true,
Warning all to change their ways.

Aid us in our quest for good,
Even though a cross should loom.
We would share our livelihood

And our rightful tasks assume.
Help us plan our future goals
And a good foundation lay
For the life your church extols,
Showing your eternal way. Amen.

(Ezekiel 33:1–11; Luke 14:25–33; Philemon 1–20; Hebrews 13:8–16, 20–21)

---

86. We Call to Mind

Pentecost 17—C   10.10.10.4.
                                                    (OVERLOOK PARK)

LAVON BAYLER

We call to mind, O God, your mighty deeds,
And meditate on wonders you have done.
Now take from us rebellion that impedes
Your work begun.

Earth trembles as your arrows split the skies
And crashing thunder sounds a judgment call.
Let not our fears, O God, immobilize,
Or harm befall.

You raise us up when we acknowledge guilt
And seek your steadfast love and healing pow'r.
May faithfulness and kindliness be built
In us this hour.

Redeemed, and led to take our place once more
Among your people, praising you today,
May we press on to know you and adore
Your holy way. Amen.

(Psalm 77:11–20; Hosea 4:1–3; 5:15—6:6)

87. Rejoice, O People

Pentecost 17—C

8.6.8.6. (C.M.)
(BEATITUDO)

LAVON BAYLER

Rejoice, O people, tell the news:
One that was lost is found.
Let us respond, true faith to choose,
And let our praise resound.

Sinners receive forgiveness here;
Mercy and grace abound.
As we repent, our God makes clear
That faith with joy is crowned.

With perfect patience God has sought
From sin to set us free,
That we may live, as Christ has taught,
In loving harmony.

Honor and glory sing we now;
God is our ruler true.
We will rejoice and faith avow,
For love will see us through. Amen.

(Luke 15:1–10; 1 Timothy 1:12–17)

---

88. O Give Thanks

Pentecost 18—C

11.12.12.10.
(NICAEA)

LAVON BAYLER

O give thanks, all people, whom God delivers.
Dwelling in God's mercy, reach out to humankind.
Live as stewards daily, with God's faithful givers,
That all the world may live as God designed.

In God's name we're gathered, facing our troubles,
Praying God's compassion will bring us safely home.
May increased devotion make us all more able
To serve with confidence where'er we roam.

We are now apostles by God's appointment,
Reaching out with longing to feel God's guiding hand.
All God's works have led us to this life's enjoyment;
May ev'ry trial help us understand.

We would feed the hungry with bread from heaven,
Sharing living water, their courage to renew.
'Though our lives be broken, may we offer leaven,
And serve with honesty in all we do. Amen.

(Psalm 107:1–9; Hosea 11:1–11; Luke 16:1–13; 1 Timothy 2:1–7)

---

89. God of Steadfast Love

Pentecost 19—C

8.7.8.7.
(GALILEE)

LAVON BAYLER

God of steadfast love and goodness,
We rejoice in all you give.
You provide our food and water,
Granting all we need to live.

In these blessings you've provided
May we learn to be content.
Keep us from temptation's power;
May our lives for you be spent.

Help us grow in godly virtues
As we aim at righteousness.
May we make a good confession
In true faith and gentleness.

Pour your spirit on your people,
That your vision we may see.
May our dreams reveal your purpose
And your mercy set us free.

We would give as you have given,
With a true and gen'rous heart.
Help us trust your faithful promise
Life abundant to impart. Amen.

(Psalm 107:1, 33–43; Joel 2:23–30; Luke 16:19–31; 1 Timothy 6:6–19)

90. We Your Servants

Pentecost 20—C

10.4.10.4.10.10.
(SANDON)

LAVON BAYLER

We, your unworthy servants, come to pray;
May faith increase.
You, who have led our parents in the past,
Grant us your peace.
Rekindle now your gift of love, that we
May live your pow'r not our timidity.

O God of mercy, keep our hearts in tune
With faithful ways.
Come to forgive the evil and deceit
Our sin betrays.
Save us from arrogance that dwells within,
And haughty looks, and words not genuine.

Grant us integrity of heart and soul
And lives, we pray.
Justice for all be ever our intent
Along life's way.
Help us to speak the truth that you reveal,
And right injustice with a mighty zeal. Amen.

(Psalm 101; Amos 5:6–7, 10–15; Luke 17:5–10; 2 Timothy 1:1–14)

91. God of Grace

Pentecost 21—C

7.7.7.7.7.7.
(TOPLADY)

LAVON BAYLER

God of grace and steadfast love,
Vindicate us from above,
For we walk in faithfulness,
Trusting that your hand will bless.
May all wrong be swept away
As you test our hearts today.

Keep us from all wickedness
And from actions that oppress.
When we find we disagree
May we make no enemy.
On this day of reckoning
Free us from our coveting.

We would serve more trustingly,
Never acting haughtily,
Seeking peace with all we meet,
As we purge our sin's deceit.
Following our Savior's lead,
May we sing your wondrous deeds.

With thanksgiving we would bless
You, our God of righteousness.
As we worship in this place
Teach us all life's wrong to face.
With a high integrity
May we Christ's disciples be. Amen.

(Psalm 26; Micah 1:2; 2:1–10)

---

92. Teacher, Have Mercy

Pentecost 21—C   *8.8.8.8. (L.M.)*
                                                        (SAXBY)

LAVON BAYLER

Teacher, have mercy for our need;
In faith and hope we look to you.
Teach us, and heal us now, we plead,
And all our energies renew.

Help us endure, with your elect
What our best efforts cannot change.
May we, your people, ne'er neglect
Missions of mercy to arrange.

Dying with you, O Christ, we'll live.
Reigning with you we shout our thanks.
For all that God is pleased to give
We offer service in the ranks.

Keep from denial all your saints;
May we be faithful to the end,
Doing our best, without complaints,
Going wherever you would send. Amen.

(Luke 17:11–19; 2 Timothy 2:8–15)

---

93. How Righteous Your Judgments

Pentecost 22—C

7.6.7.6.D.
(ANGEL'S STORY)

LAVON BAYLER

How righteous are your judgments,
O God of faithfulness;
How certain is your promise
To understand and bless.
Be near us in our troubles,
When wrong is near at hand.
May violence be thwarted
As for your truth we stand.

Fulfill the vision given
To prophets long ago,
That faith and understanding
May deep within us grow.
Inspire us through the scriptures
To follow Jesus' way,
That we may know salvation
And never turn away.

We sense your vindication
Amid our prayers and praise.
Your love and patient teaching
Support us through our days.
Empower our faithful witness;
Equip our ministry,
That we may share with others
What you have helped us see. Amen.

(Psalm 119:137–44; Habakkuk 1:1–3; 2:1–4; Luke 18:1–8; 2 Timothy 3:14—4:5)

94. O God, Our Strength

Pentecost 23—C

11.10.11.10.
(WELWYN)

LAVON BAYLER

O God, our strength, stand by us in our struggles;
Help us to deal with evil we ignore.
Amid rebellion, violence, and falsehood
Show forth your justice and our hopes restore.

We have profaned the sacred truth you gave us,
Choosing to break your law of love and grace.
Deliver all awak'ning to your mercy,
That we may keep the faith and run life's race.

We cry aloud in humble expectation,
Seeking your blessing and the heart to trust.
Enlist our speech and righteous indignation,
That we may serve our God in causes just.

Send us once more among the mean and wicked,
Not as a judge, but as a friend in need.
Bring us together, sinners seeking wholeness,
Finding in faithfulness a living creed. Amen.

(Psalm 3; Zephaniah 3:1–9; Luke 18:9–14; 2 Timothy 4:6–8, 16–18)

95. Shake Our Foundations

Pentecost 24—C

10.10.10.10.
(EVENTIDE)

LAVON BAYLER

Shake our foundations, God of all the earth,
That in our worship we may find true worth.
Melt our reliance on the things we own,
That we may share the wealth your love has shown.

Free us from fears that stifle your intent;
Save us from deeds that lead to punishment.
Turn us away from all prevailing sin,
That we may find your glorious truth within.

We would receive your presence here with joy
And, day by day, your many gifts employ.
God, make us worthy of our upward call,
That we may claim the work you offer all.

You are the hope by which alone we live,
Granting us courage and the will to give.
May we fulfill our high resolve each day,
That all we meet may know your glorious way. Amen.

(Psalm 65:1–8; Haggai 2:1–9; Luke 19:1–10; 2 Thessalonians 1:5–12)

---

96. Gracious and Loving God

Pentecost 25—C   *6.6.8.6. (S.M.)*
                                                   (TRENTHAM)

LAVON BAYLER

Gracious and Loving God,
Hear all our praise today,
That all our deeds may honor you
And grateful thanks display.

May all our fasting be
Offered to glorify,
Not our obedience, but your gifts
That bless and sanctify.

May we true mercy show
In all relationships,
Lest we judge wrongly, and oppress,
And kindliness eclipse.

May we bring hope to all
Needy, forgotten ones.
Serving the poor, may we be saved
From wrong comparisons.

Grant us the confidence
To do as you command,
Challenging nations with your truth
And judgments you have planned.

May love of neighbor reign
Whoe'er that neighbor be,

That all your comfort and your grace
May know eternally. Amen.

(Psalm 9:11–20; Zechariah 7:1–10; 2 Thessalonians 2:13—3:5)

---

97. Great Judge of All

Pentecost 26—C

7.6.8.6.D.
(ST. CHRISTOPHER)

LAVON BAYLER

Great Judge of all the nations,
Whose rule we would discern,
Reveal to us your purposes
And show us your concern.
We seek to stand 'gainst evil
And challenge those unjust,
But fear is often stronger than
Our sympathy and trust.

The wicked seem to triumph,
Denying your domain.
We feel the earth's foundations shake
As wars and tumult reign.
The good face persecution
And terrorists roam free.
Where shall the weak and needy find
True justice they can see?

We toil and labor daily
With gifts your love supplies,
While others live in idleness
That your intent denies.
Grant meaningful employment
To all your children here,
And skills to match our deep resolve
For you to volunteer.

Unite the generations,
Embracing aged and youth.
Supply us with the mind and heart
To speak and do your truth.
Grant courage that our words may be
Congruent with our deeds,

And courage to reach out in love,
Addressing human needs. Amen.

(Psalm 82; Malachi 4:1–6; Luke 21:5–19; 2 Thessalonians 3:6–13)

---

98. With Hearts That Are Full

Pentecost 27—C

10.10.11.11.
(HANOVER)

LAVON BAYLER

With hearts that are full of rev'rence and praise,
We make joyful noise, extolling your ways.
Great God of the heights and the depths, we would sing
Our loudest hosannas as off'rings we bring.

Christ Jesus is head of all in the church;
Let no earthly claims that glory besmirch.
Our Rock of Salvation, our Shepherd and Friend,
Dwell with us to bless, for on you we depend.

Forgive us when we have wandered astray
Through errors of heart that question your way.
Our Maker, whose covenant we have denied,
Be present to guide us, and reign by our side.

Now grant us endurance, patience, and joy,
As children of light in Jesus' employ.
Disciples, rememb'ring your peace through the cross,
We follow our Savior, whatever the cost. Amen.

(Psalm 95; 2 Samuel 5:1–5; John 12:9–19; Colossians 1:11–20)

Hymns for Other Special Occasions

99. How Lovely Your Place

Presentation (February 2)—A, B, C   *8.6.8.6. (C.M.)*
                                                         (DUNDEE)
LAVON BAYLER

How lovely is your dwelling place,
O God, our sun and shield.
Our souls are fainting for your courts
And for your word revealed.

In Jesus Christ, your Word-made-flesh,
Our eyes salvation see;
In one who shared our human lot
We know ourselves set free.

As you have sent your messenger
Send us along our way
To serve where others cannot go,
To say what you would say.

Now grant us all the help we need
To live, with Christ as guide.
May we, with faithfulness and trust,
In righteousness abide. Amen.

(Psalm 84; Malachi 3:1–4; Luke 2:22–40; Hebrews 2:14–18)

100. Behold Us, Dear God

Annunciation (March 25)—A, B, C   *11.11.11.11.*
                                                      (MULLER)
LAVON BAYLER

Behold us, Dear God, we are ready to serve,
Like Mary, your handmaid, to grow and observe.
Equip and empower and ever stay near,
That, knowing your favor, we never may fear.

Send Jesus among us new order to bring
In which life itself is our glad offering.

Your love is the energy, sent to inflame;
Your will is the target toward which we take aim.

Write deep in our hearts steadfast love that is law
To all who respond to your goodness in awe.
The prayers of our lips and the deeds of our days
Would further your purpose and lead to your praise.

O keep us from wearying you or our friends,
While looking for signs and envisioning trends.
Salvation and faithfulness you will provide,
And help that supports us whatever betides. Amen.

(Psalm 40:6–10; Isaiah 7:10–14; Luke 1:26–38; Hebrews 10:4–10)

---

101. We Rejoice, O God

Visitation—A, B, C

7.7.7.7.7.7.
(AJALON)

LAVON BAYLER

We rejoice, O God of power,
As you visit us this hour.
In your goodness we abide,
Understood, and fortified
By your love that purges sin
From its dwelling place within.

God of mercy, help us here
As we come in awe and fear.
Scatter all the haughty proud
Who their need have disavowed.
Feed the hungry by your grace;
Grant us in your love a place.

Give us strength, O God Most High,
You whose glory fills the sky.
We who dare to speak your name
Raise our songs, your love to claim.
Help us live in harmony
With your vast humanity.

Fill us with the Spirit's glow,
And your many gifts bestow.
May we true devotion show,

Helping one another grow,
Weeping when your people cry,
Glad when joy uplifts them high. Amen.

(1 Samuel 2:1–10; Psalm 113; Luke 1:39–57; Romans 12:9–16b)

---

102. O God, Who Loved

Holy Cross (September 14)—A, B, C   8.8.8.8. (*L.M.*)
                                            (TALLIS' CANON)

LAVON BAYLER

O God, who loved the world and sent
Your special Child to grant us life,
Free us, we pray, from sin's cruel stain
And turn us from our human strife.

Forgive the folly of our ways
That count the cross a thing of shame.
Destroy the wisdom of the wise,
Renewing us in Jesus' name.

May not impatience or despair
Turn us away from following
Through wilderness or times of pain
The Christ who conquered suffering.

Let now our lips be joined in song,
Our praises make a joyful noise.
Keep us, we pray, in steadfast love,
That all our energy employs. Amen.

(Numbers 21:4b–9; Psalm 98:1–5; John 3:13–17; 1 Corinthians 1:18–24)

---

103. Hear Us Sing

All Saints (November 1)—C   7.7.7.7.
                                        (ST BEES)

LAVON BAYLER

Hear us sing new songs of praise,
God, whose glory crowns our days.

We respond with joyous dance
To the hope your Spirit grants.

We would wise and faithful be,
Sharing in Christ's victory
Over sins that we confess
And our frequent selfishness.

As we face anxiety,
Fright'ning dreams, and treachery,
May your truth once more be shown
And your will more fully known.

We would bring salvation news
To all persons whom you choose
As inheritors of grace:
Folks from ev'ry age and place.

We would serve without complaints,
Sharing love with all the saints,
Praying that your rule may be
Realized more speedily. Amen.

(Psalm 149; Daniel 7:1–3, 15–18; Ephesians 1:11–23)

---

104. Blessed Are the Poor

All Saints (November 1)—C   6.4.6.4.10.10.
                                              (SURSUM CORDA)

LAVON BAYLER

Blessed are the poor who know
God's realm is theirs.
Blessed are the hungry ones
Who know God cares.
Blessed are the weeping ones, and those reviled,
Cast out, excluded, and by hate defiled.

Let us in Christ rejoice
When we are sad.
God comforts and consoles
And makes us glad.
When all speak well of us, we look within,
Lest we be false to God and mired in sin.

Equip us, God, to pray
For enemies.
Help us meet hate with love,
Your will to please.
When others strike at us, when they abuse,
Grant us the strength nonviolence to choose.

May we in others see
Our own desires.
May all we do be what
Your love inspires.
May we be merciful, for we have known
Your generosity by which we've grown. Amen.

(Luke 6:20–36)

---

105. We Rejoice in Goodness

Thanksgiving Day   8.7.8.7.D.
                                                    (AUSTRIAN HYMN)

LAVON BAYLER

We rejoice in all God's goodness,
Granting us this life to live,
Hearing all the prayers we utter,
Blessing all we seek to give.
When we call our cries are answered;
Signs and wonders never cease,
As affliction and oppression
Melt before the God of peace.

Make a joyful noise, all Christians,
Who have known our Savior's grace.
Put aside all anxious worry
And unworthy thoughts erase.
God, in steadfast love, has promised
All our hungers to assuage
As we do the works of Jesus,
Contemplating God's new age.

Fill our minds with truth unending;
Help us share in causes just.
Turn our thoughts to what is lovely

As, in purity, we trust.
Do your gracious work within us
As for excellence we strive.
May we sense eternal being
As you keep our faith alive.

We with gladness come before you
In thanksgiving, singing praise,
For your faithfulness and mercy
That sustain us all our days.
We belong to you, O Sovereign,
And accept the peace you grant.
May the bread of life sustain us
In fulfilling covenant. Amen.

(Deuteronomy 26:1–11; Psalm 100; John 6:25–35; Philippians 4:4–9)

---

106. God's Wonders

The Seasons   8.6.8.8.6.
(REST)

MERLE RAY BECKWITH

As now fresh dew lies on the ground
God's wonders I can see.
The lightning's flash, the thunder's sound,
The sun, the moon, and all around
Break forth and humble me.

In winter when the stormy blast
Rips through my house and land
I pray that God, as in the past,
Would, with such strength, which is steadfast,
Reach out and lend a hand.

In summer when the weather's fair
God's manifest delights
Through fields and pastures everywhere
With full abundance now declare
The wonders of God's might.

Each morning in each season grand
I marvel at the ways
Dear God brings strength throughout our land

And offers each a helping hand.
I lift my heart in praise. Amen.

---

107. We Come, O Christ

Church, Communion

LAVON BAYLER

7.6.7.6.D.
(AURELIA)

We come, O Christ our Savior,
For you have called us here
To be the church, your body,
Now reconciled, brought near.
By water you have welcomed
Each one of us to be
At one with all your people
In true community.

We hear your invitation
In breaking of the bread.
By sacramental eating
Our spirits' needs are fed.
We know ourselves forgiven,
From self and sin set free,
To be your true disciples,
Involved in ministry.

Your word now sends us forward
To meet a world in need,
To share the gifts you've given
And truly live our creed.
Empower our faithful witness
And grant us empathy
With your beloved children
Wherever they may be. Amen.

108. We Have a Dream*

In Memory of Martin Luther King Jr.

10.4.10.4.10.10.
(SANDON)

LAVON BAYLER

Thanks be to God, who lifts our vision high,
We have a dream.
Freed from the ravages of sin and shame,
We have a dream:
That all God's people need no longer cry,
As, reaching out, we live our Christian claim.

Thanks be to God, whose truth has made us free,
We have a dream.
Called as disciples, learning Jesus' way,
We have a dream:
That ours will be a fruitful ministry,
Equipped by Christ to serve as saints each day.

Thanks be to God, who calls us to be one,
We have a dream.
Leaving behind all prejudice and pride,
We have a dream:
That hand in hand we let God's will be done
Through us and all who will in Christ abide.

Thanks be to God, who bids us celebrate,
We have a dream.
Filled with the love of truth and liberty,
We have a dream:
That God will reign, destroying greed and hate,
Empow'ring faithful, joyous ministry. Amen.

*Inspired by John 8:31b–32 and themes from the first combined national meeting of United Church Educators (AUCE) and Christian Church Educators (ACCE), January 16–19, 1988.

109. Shout Your Dreams*

In Memory of Martin Luther King Jr.

6.5.6.5.D. *with Refrain*
(ST. GERTRUDE)

LAVON BAYLER

Shout your dreams to heaven;
They are echoes blest
By our God almighty,
Calling forth our best.
Cry aloud for justice
And equality;
Sing your faithful vision:
People whole and free.
Dreams don't make us equal,
Yet our God has done
What our dreams can't fashion;
God has made us one.

Summoned to one table,
We, in Christ, are led
To renounce oppression
As, by truth, we're fed.
Climbing ev'ry mountain,
Facing ev'ry foe,
We will live together
As in hope we grow.
Dreams don't make us equal,
Yet our God has done
What our dreams can't fashion;
God has made us one. Amen.

*Written for the national United Church of Christ/Disciples of Christ Christian Education Event, Atlanta, Georgia, January 16–19, 1988.

110. Welcome to the Family*

Celebration of New Members

6.5.6.5.D. with Refrain
or 11.11.11.11.11.11.
(ST. GERTRUDE)

LAVON BAYLER

Welcome to the family,
Sisters, brothers, all.
Christ will lead us onward,
Answering God's call.
Let the love of neighbor
And of enemy
Be the watchword daily
Of our unity.
Welcome to the family,
Sisters, brothers, all.
Christ will lead us onward,
Answering God's call.

One in life and mission,
One in caring grace,
May our faithful service
Jesus' footsteps trace.
We would be disciples,
Finding ways to grow,
Reaching out as partners
To both friend and foe.
Welcome to the family,
Sisters, brothers, all.
Christ will lead us onward,
Answering God's call.

Hear our prayers, Creator
In these troubled days
When your hurting children
Turn from Jesus' ways.
Love, forgive, and save us
Lest our souls be lost
In pursuit of folly,
Counting not the cost.
Welcome to the family,
Sisters, brothers, all.

Christ will lead us onward,
Answering God's call.

Save us from the evil
We do not intend.
Purify our motives
That you can depend
On authentic servants,
True in word and deed.
Widen now our circle
And expand our creed.
Welcome to the family,
Sisters, brothers, all.
Christ will lead us onward,
Answering God's call.

*Written for the reception of the Community Congregational Church of Roscoe (Illinois) into the United Church of Christ, March 1, 1987.

---

111. No One a Stranger*

Accessibility Dedication 8.7.8.7.D.
(BEECHER)

LAVON BAYLER

God, in whom no one is stranger,
We rejoice and sing your praise,
Giving thanks that you have made us
Partners in your works and ways.
You have blessed our thoughtful labors,
Linking us with all your saints,
As we seek to be inclusive,
Fighting barriers and restraints.

All we have you first have given,
All we build is by your grace.
You inspire the gifts we offer
And the projects we embrace.
Thank you for this celebration
And the love that marks this day,
Dedicated to your glory,
Giving life to what we say.

We have built on past foundations
Prophets and apostles gave.
Christ, our cornerstone, directs us,
"Welcome, all I came to save."
As your Spirit dwells within us,
We your greatness would extol.
May all glory, power, and vict'ry
Be to you who makes us whole. Amen.

(1 Chronicles 29:10–18; Ephesians 2:19–22)

*Written for the dedication of an elevator at Shabbona United Church of Christ.

---

112. Celebrate God's Family*

Annual Meeting, Installation   10.10.10.10.
                                                    (TOULON)
LAVON BAYLER

We celebrate the family of God:
People of many lands and ev'ry race,
Myriad tongues, ignited by God's grace,
Pour out their songs of praise from place to place.

We celebrate the Christ who liberates
And ev'ry hope God's covenant creates.
Now, as disciples in community,
We give ourselves that others may be free.

We celebrate the mission that we share,
Showing by word and deed our Maker's care.
May God our love-filled ministry equip:
Clergy and laity in partnership.

Now to our God we raise our hymn of thanks
For those who lead while serving in the ranks;
Direct our feet to travel where Christ trod,
As we lift up the family of God. Amen.

*Written for the Illinois Northern Association Annual Meeting, United Church of Christ, and the Installation of the Rev. Robert Meissner as Associate Conference Minister, May 2, 1987.

113. You Crown Us, God

Pentecost 10—C

LAVON BAYLER

8.6.8.6. (C.M.)
(AMAZING GRACE)

You crown us, God, with length of days
And fill those days with joy.
In serving you, in all our ways,
We would our best employ.

You speak to us through children's trust
And simple things of life.
You cut through pretense, pride, and lust,
Through anger, sin, and strife.

You hear us when we ask and seek.
We knock; you open wide.
Your healing comes to strong and weak,
As we, in you, abide.

Your steadfast love and saving grace
Are meant for all to share.
May we our Savior's life embrace,
And show Christ's love and care. Amen.

(2 Kings 5:1–15; Colossians 2:6–15; Luke 11:1–13)

114. O God, Who Blessed*

Anniversary of Marriage

LAVON BAYLER

8.6.8.8.6.
(REST)

O God, who blessed our wedding day
With love and friends and dreams,
We thank you for our work and play,
For truth and trust along the way,
And laughter that redeems.

Be with us now in moments rare
When we commune with you,
Together, side by side in prayer,

Surrounded by your love and care
And promises made new.

We honor one another here
As in your name we meet.
May Christ whose presence is so near
Help us discern your Word made clear
In ev'ry hall and street.

We seek, O God, to do your will,
To go where you would lead.
May we our partnership fulfill
In growing love no threat can still,
And deeds that match our creed. Amen.

*Written for a couples' retreat for clergy and spouses of the Northern Association, Illinois Conference, February 1988.

---

115. Stewards of God*

Stewardship and Mission

14.14.4.7.8.
(LOBE DEN HERREN)

LAVON BAYLER

Stewards of God, we assemble in glad adoration,
Bringing our thanks for the marvelous gifts of creation.
How shall our days
Echo God's love with our praise?
Risking our all for salvation.

Stewards of God, we rejoice in the church and its mission,
Teaching and building as Jesus has given us vision.
What shall we give
That we may gratefully live?
Learning to share and to listen.

Stewards of God, we will honor and love one another,
Seeing in ev-er-y person a sister or brother.
How shall we be
Members of one family?
Trusting ourselves and each other.

Stewards of God, we will serve all humanity, daring
Once more to build a society marked by its caring.
Will we address

All of the wrongs we confess?
Knowing that Christ we're declaring.

Stewards of God, we will sail on through life more united,
Willing to sacrifice, eager that evil be righted.
How shall we know
Ways God intends us to grow?
Following paths Christ has lighted. Amen.

*Written for the 1988 Annual Meeting of the Illinois Conference, United Church of Christ.

Indexes

Alphabetical Index of Hymns

Topical Index of Hymns

ADORATION AND PRAISE

ADVENT

CLOSE OF WORSHIP

May God Bless 11

COMFORT

Blessed Are the Poor 104
Come, Walk with Christ 56
Gracious and Loving God 96
O Sing Aloud 13
Tempt Us Not 34
When Jesus Was Baptized 17

COMMUNION

Fill Our Hearts 46
O Sovereign God 45
Shout Your Dreams 109
The Sun Was Sinking 52
We Behold Your Passion 42
We Come, O Christ 107

COMMUNITY

Blessed Are the Poor 104
Celebrate God's Family 112
Come, Walk with Christ 56
Give Thanks to God 3
Go and Be Neighbors 74
Like Clay 79
Make Us One 61
No One a Stranger 111
O God, Whose Love 59
We Come, O Christ 107
We Rejoice, O God 101
We Stand in Awe 20
Welcome to the Family 110
What Is Faith? 69
Your Steadfast Love 43

CONFESSION

Draw Near with Confidence 47
Receive Our Treasures 33
We Behold Your Passion 42
Who Receives from God? 39

CONSECRATION AND DEDICATION

At a Marriage Feast 19
Blessed Are the Poor 104
No One a Stranger 111
Please Teach Us 31

Stewards of God 115
We Come, O Christ 107
We Hear God Call 36

COURAGE

By Grace You Called 26
Fill Our Hearts 46
Great Judge of All 97
O Give Thanks 88
O Sing Aloud 13
Shake Our Foundations 95
Thanks Be to God 76
We Stand in Awe 20

COVENANT

Celebrate God's Family 112
Fill Our Hearts 46
Gather Your Children 35
Joy Is in Our Hearts 82
O God, Who Blessed 114
O Send Out Your Light 68
We Come to Praise 9
We Make a Joyful Noise 64
We Rejoice in Goodness 105
Welcome to the Family 110
With Hearts That Are Full 98
Your Steadfast Love 43

CROSS

By Grace You Called 26
Come, O Christ 44
Come Once Again 41
Jesus, We Follow 48
Lead Us by Love 40
May We Disciples Be 85
O God, Who Loved 102
O Sovereign God 45
We Behold Your Passion 42
What Is Faith? 69
Whate'er We Sow 72
With Hearts That Are Full 98
You Are with Us 81

DEATH

By Grace You Called 26
Come, O Christ 44
Come Once Again 41
Fill Our Hearts 46
God of Our Parents 80
Jesus, We Follow 48

FORGIVENESS

Come, O Word   8
Come, Walk with Christ   56
Faith, Hope, and Love   23
Go and Be Neighbors   74
Happy Is One   38
Holy Are You   25
Make Known Your Ways   1
My Peace Be with You   53
O God, Who Loved   102
Please Teach Us   31
Receive Our Treasures   33
Rejoice, O People   87
Thanks Be to God   76
That Sabbath Day   37
The Word of God   83
We Call to Mind   86
We Come, O Christ   107
We Have Faith   60
We Make a Joyful Noise   64
We Stand in Awe   20
We Your Servants   90
What Is Faith?   69
Who Receives from God?   39
Why Are You Cast Down?   67
With Hearts That Are Full   98
Your Ways   29

FREE (-DOM)

Celebrate God's Family   112
God of All Times   70
God of Music   51
God of Steadfast Love   89
How Lovely Your Place   99
Joy Is in Our Hearts   82
Make a Joyful Noise   64
Make Us One   61
O Sovereign God   45
Rejoice, O People   87
Show Us Your Glory   32
Sing Praises to God   54
That Sabbath Day   37
We Have a Dream   108
We Hear God Call   36
What Is Faith?   69
When God's Time   12
Your Steadfast Love   43

GOD, GLORY OF

God of Our Parents   80
Holy Are You   25

No One a Stranger   111
Now Arise and Shine   14
O God, Whose Love   59
Praise the Name   65
Show Us Your Glory   32
We Rejoice, O God   101
Weep Not, My People   66

GOD, GUIDANCE OF

Bear Fruits of Penitence   4
Blessed Are the Poor   104
Gather Your Children   35
Lead Us by Love   40
Make Us One   61
O Give Thanks   88
O Send Out Your Light   68
O Sing Aloud   13
Please Teach Us   31
Set Your Minds Above   78
Sing Praises to God   54
We Come, O Christ   107
We Have Faith   60
When Christ Was Born   16
With Hearts That Are Full   98

GOD, LOVE OF

Behold Us, Dear God   100
Blessed Are the Poor   104
Come, Holy Spirit   62
Faith, Hope, and Love   23
Fill Our Hearts   46
Go and Be Neighbors   74
God of Music   51
God of Our Parents   80
Gracious and Loving God   96
Great Judge of All   97
How Precious Your Love   18
How Righteous Your Judgments   93
How Shall We Praise You?   63
May We Disciples Be   85
O God, Who Blessed   114
O God, Who Loved   102
O God, Whose Love   59
On This Day   49
Prepare the Way   7
See How God Loved   75
Set Your Minds Above   78
Tempt Us Not   34
Thanks Be to God   76
That Sabbath Day   37
We Come to Praise   9
We Rejoice, O God   101

MINISTRY AND MISSION

NEIGHBORS

PEACE

PENITENCE

PENTECOST SEASON

We Hear God Call   36
We Trust and Praise   22
While Foxes Have Holes   71

WORSHIP

As Jesus Worshiped   21
Be Gracious, God   58
Come, O Christ   44
God of Grace   91
God of Music   51
Gracious God, We Trust   28
Holy Are You   25
Joy Is in Our Hearts   82

Lead Us by Love   40
Lead Us, O God   73
Make Us One   61
Shake Our Foundations   95
Tempt Us Not   34
We Stand in Awe   20
When God's Time   12

ZEAL

O Blessed Hope   6
Please Teach Us   31
We Your Servants   90

Index of Scripture Readings

Ezekiel

18:1–9, 25–29	Pentecost 15
33:1–11	Pentecost 16

Daniel

7:1–3, 15–18	All Saints
12:1–3	Easter Evening

Hosea

4:1–3, 5:15—6:6	Pentecost 17
11:1–1	Pentecost 18

Joel

2:1–2, 12–17a	Ash Wednesday
2:23–30	Pentecost 19

Amos

5:6–7, 10–15	Pentecost 20

Micah

1:2; 2:1–10	Pentecost 21
5:2–4	Advent 4

Habakkuk

1:1–3; 2:1–4	Pentecost 22

Zephaniah

3:1–9	Pentecost 23
3:14–20	Advent 3

Haggai

2:1–9	Pentecost 24

Zechariah

7:1–10	Pentecost 25

Malachi

3:1–4	Advent 2
	Presentation
4:1–6	Pentecost 26

Matthew

2:1–12	Epiphany
6:1–6, 16–21	Ash Wednesday

Mark

16:9–16, 19–20	Ascension Day (alt.)

Luke

1:26–38	Annunciation
1:39–55	Advent 4
1:39–57	Visitation
2:1–20	Christmas Eve/Day
2:8–20	Christmas Day 1
2:15–21	Jan. 1 (Jesus and Mary)
2:22–40	Presentation
2:41–52	Christmas 1
3:1–6	Advent 2
3:7–18	Advent 3
3:15–17, 21–22	Epiphany 1 (Baptism of Jesus)
4:1–13	Lent 1
4:14–21	Epiphany 3
4:21–30	Epiphany 4
5:1–11	Epiphany 5
6:17–26	Epiphany 6
6:20–36	All Saints
6:27–38	Epiphany 7
6:39–49	Epiphany 8
7:1–10	Pentecost 2
7:11–17	Pentecost 3
7:36—8:3	Pentecost 4
9:18–24	Pentecost 5
9:28–36	Epiphany, Last Sunday
9:51–62	Pentecost 6
10:1–12, 17–20	Pentecost 7
10:25–37	Pentecost 8
10:38–42	Pentecost 9
11:1–13	Pentecost 10
12:13–21	Pentecost 11
12:32–40	Pentecost 12
12:49–56	Pentecost 13
13:1–9	Lent 3
13:10–17	Lent 3 (alt.)
13:22–30	Pentecost 14
13:31–35	Lent 2
14:7–14	Pentecost 15
14:16–24	New Year's Day
14:25–33	Pentecost 16
15:1–3, 11–32	Lent 4
15:1–10	Pentecost 17
16:1–13	Pentecost 18
16:19–31	Pentecost 19
17:5–10	Pentecost 20
17:11–19	Pentecost 21

Index of Themes and Key Words

Pentecost 16
Distress
   Lent 6
   Pentecost Sunday
Divisions
   Pentecost 13
Doubt
   Easter 2, 7
   Pentecost 13
Earth
   Easter 7
Empathy
   Pentecost 15
Empowerment
   Visitation (May 31)
Encouragement
   Maundy Thursday
End
   Easter 2
Enemies
   All Saints (Nov. 1)
Envy
   Epiphany 7
Equality
   Pentecost 11
Equity
   Christmas Day 2
Eternity
   Lent 2
   Pentecost 19
Evil
   Advent 1
   Pentecost 9, 20
Excellence
   Thanksgiving Day
Exile
   Pentecost 14
Failure
   Lent 6
   Pentecost Sunday
Faith
   Epiphany 6, 8
   Lent 2, 6 (Passion Sunday)
   Tuesday of Holy Week
   Easter 2
   Pentecost 4, 5, 8, 12, 13, 15, 17, 18,
     20, 21, 22, 27
   Annunciation (March 25)
Faithfulness
   Advent 4
   Christmas Day 2
   Christmas 1
   Epiphany 8

Lent 6 (Palm Sunday)
   Tuesday of Holy Week
   Maundy Thursday
   Good Friday
   Easter 5
   Pentecost 2, 6, 11, 12, 13, 17, 18, 20,
     21, 27
   Annunciation (March 25)
Family
   Pentecost 26
Fasting
   Ash Wednesday
Fear(s)
   Advent 3
   Jan. 1 (Jesus and Mary)
   Epiphany 4
   Easter 2, 6
   Pentecost 24
Feeding
   Visitation (May 31)
Fire
   Epiphany 1
   Pentecost Sunday
Food
   Easter 5
Forgiveness
   Advent 2, 3
   Christmas 1
   Epiphany 5, 7, 9
   Lent 4, 6 (Palm Sunday, Passion
     Sunday)
   Tuesday of Holy Week
   Easter 2, 6, 7
   Pentecost 4, 10, 21, 27
   Presentation (Feb. 2)
   All Saints (Nov. 1)
Freedom
   Epiphany 3, 9
   Lent 3
   Easter 2
   Pentecost 6
Fruit
   Epiphany 6
   Tuesday of Holy Week
   Easter Sunday
Fulfillment
   Easter 5
Gather(ing)
   Lent 2
Generations
   Pentecost 15
Generosity
   Advent 3

Idleness
  Pentecost 26
Idolatry
  Pentecost 11
Inspiration
  Epiphany 2
  Pentecost 9
Integrity
  Epiphany 2
  Pentecost 18, 21
Invitation
  New Year's Day
Jealousy
  Lent 4
Jesus Christ
  Lent 5
  Easter 2, 7
  Pentecost 5, 7, 13, 24
  Holy Cross (Sept. 14)
Joy
  Advent 4
  Christmas Eve/Day
  Jan. 1 (Jesus and Mary)
  Epiphany 3, 6, 8
  Lent 5
  Easter Sunday
  Pentecost 6, 20, 24, 27
Judgment
  Christmas Day 2
  Ash Wednesday
  Pentecost 14, 23
Justice
  Epiphany
  Monday of Holy Week
  Pentecost 13, 15, 20, 26
Kind(ness)
  Christmas 1
  Easter 5
  Pentecost 25
Knock
  Pentecost 10
Law
  Epiphany 3
  Maundy Thursday
Leaven
  Easter Evening
Liberty, Liberation
  Epiphany 1
Life
  Epiphany 8
  Tuesday of Holy Week
  Pentecost 4, 27
  Visitation (May 31)
  Holy Cross (Sept. 14)

  All Saints (Nov. 1)
Light(s)
  Christmas Day 2
  New Year's Day
  Christmas 2
  Epiphany
  Epiphany 2
  Tuesday of Holy Week
  Easter 6
  Pentecost 8
  Presentation (Feb. 2)
Listen
  Pentecost 14
Longing
  Pentecost 4
Love
  Epiphany 4, 7, 8
  Ash Wednesday
  Lent 4
  Maundy Thursday
  Easter Evening
  Easter 2, 5, 6, 7
  Pentecost 6, 8, 10, 25
  Visitation (May 31)
  Holy Cross (Sept. 14)
  All Saints (Nov. 1)
Majesty
  Epiphany 1, 5
Maturity
  Pentecost 9
Merciful
  Pentecost 25
  Visitation (May 31)
Mercy
  Advent 2, 4
  Christmas Day
  Christmas 1
  Epiphany 7
  Ash Wednesday
  Easter 4
  Pentecost 17, 21
Message
  Lent 6 (Palm Sunday)
Ministry
  Tuesday of Holy Week
Music
  Easter Evening
Name(s)
  New Year's Day
  Epiphany 2
  Pentecost Sunday
Needs
  Easter 5
  Pentecost 26

Holy Cross (Sept. 14)
Stewardship
   Trinity Sunday
   Pentecost 11, 18
Strength
   Advent 3, 4
   New Year's Day
   Epiphany 1, 3, 5
   Tuesday of Holy Week
   Easter Sunday
   Pentecost 16, 27
   Presentation (Feb. 2)
   Visitation (May 31)
Suffering
   Lent 6 (Passion Sunday)
   Pentecost 20
Sustaining
   Pentecost 23
Table
   Maundy Thursday
Teach
   Wednesday of Holy Week
   Pentecost 22
Temptation
   Good Friday
   Presentation (Feb. 2)
Thanks(giving)
   Christmas 1
   Lent 6 (Palm Sunday)
   Maundy Thursday
   Easter 3, 4
   Pentecost 21, 25
   Thanksgiving Day
Thirst
   Easter 7
Thorns
   Epiphany 8
Time
   Epiphany 2
Tongues
   Pentecost Sunday
Touch
   Epiphany 6
Transformation
   Epiphany 2
Treasure(s)
   Ash Wednesday
   Pentecost 12
Trembling
   Epiphany 9
Trials
   Lent 6 (Passion Sunday)
Trouble(s)(d)
   Easter Evening

Easter 6
Pentecost Sunday
Trust
   Advent 3
   Epiphany 4, 5, 6, 7
   Lent 6 (Passion Sur day
   Good Friday
   Pentecost 2, 19, 2
Truth(ful)(ness)
   Advent 1
   Christmas Eve/Da
   Christmas Day 2
   Epiphany 3, 9
   Ash Wednesday
   Lent 3, 6 (Palm Sunday)
   Tuesday of Holy Week
   Maundy Thursday
   Good Friday
   Easter Evening
   Easter 6
   Pentecost 5, 8, 11, 15, 20, 22
   Thanksgiving Day
Understand(ing)
   Christmas 1
   Pentecost 27
Unity
   Epiphany 3
   Easter 7
   Pentecost 11
Values
   Pentecost 17
Vision
   Pentecost 22
Walk
   Easter Evening
Warmth
   Pentecost 18
Watchfulness
   Advent 1
   Pentecost 12
Water
   Easter 7
Way(s)
   Easter 6
Weariness
   Wednesday of Holy Week
   Pentecost 26
Wickedness
   Pentecost 21
Will of God
   Annunciation (March 25)
Wisdom
   Christmas 1
   New Year's Day

About the Author

When Lavon Bayler became the Area Conference Minister in Northern Association of the Illinois Conference in 1979 after twenty years in local church pastorates of the United Church of Christ, she resolved to spend some time each week in worship preparation, even if she didn't have a preaching invitation. The discipline of writing prayers and other worship elements on a regular basis focused late one autumn on the lenten season for the next year. Remembering how hectic life could be for a pastor with the extra services and classes before Easter, she sent a gift of worship resources related to the lectionary to all the clergy in her association. Their response was to ask for more the next year. She has been writing ever since.

When Ruth Duck was editing *Bread for the Journey* and, later, *Flames of the Spirit*, she asked for, received, and used many of Lavon's materials. As time rolled around for a sabbatical from her office in DeKalb, it was natural that Lavon chose the writing of lectionary-based resources for year A of the new ecumenical listing as her project. *Fresh Winds of the Spirit* was the result. By adopting an early morning writing schedule (before her 6 A.M. swim) and using vacation time, she was able to complete *Whispers of God* in time for year B. Now *Refreshing Rains of the Living Word*, based on year C of the ecumenical lectionary, is the third book of the series being published by The Pilgrim Press. It was begun on the long plane rides in February of 1987 with an intergenerational group of twenty-two workcampers heading for Family Village Farm in Tamil-Nadu state in southern India.

Lavon Burrichter Bayler grew up in parsonages in Ohio, Indiana, and Iowa. Her active involvement in youth work eventually led her beyond Iowa State Teachers College to Lancaster and Eden Seminaries. Her father, Emil Burrichter, uncle Otto Stockmeier, and great-uncle William C. Beckmann were all graduates of the Mission House (now part of United Theological Seminary), so she considers herself a product of all three educational streams of the former Evangelical and Reformed Church. She has since served on the National Ministerial Advisory Committee of Chicago Theological Seminary, thereby forging some Congregational connections.

Lavon Bayler has been a leader in the United Church of Christ since her participation in the Uniting General Synod in 1957. She has been active in church camping, women's concerns, youth empowerment, mission interpretation, and Christian education. Her position on the Illinois Conference staff involves her in placing clergy, planning programs, resourcing congregations, and being a pastor to pastors and their families. For hobbies she dabbles in politics, Indian finger weaving, and photography. Swimming

(2,000 miles in the past ten years) is her most consistent form of exercise. She has traveled throughout the United States and around the world, often with her husband, Bob, who is a pastor and executive with the United Church of Christ's Evangelical Health Systems in the Chicago area. Their home, in Elgin, Illinois, is still frequented by their three young-adult sons, David, Jonathan, and Timothy. The Baylers are sponsors of a "fourth son," ten-year-old Jacob Paul, at Family Village Farm.